The Battle of Democracy

The Battle of Democracy
Conflict, Consensus and the Individual

Keith Graham

Lecturer in Philosophy
University of Bristol

BARNES & NOBLE BOOKS
Totowa, New Jersey

First published in the USA 1986 by
BARNES & NOBLE BOOKS
81 Adams Drive, Totowa, New Jersey 07512

Library of Congress Cataloging-in-Publication Data

Graham, Keith
  The battle of democracy.

  Bibliography: p.
  Includes indexes.
  1. Democracy.   I. Title.
JC423.G73   1986   321.8   86-10845
ISBN 0-389-20652-0

Printed in Great Britain

To the memory of Bill Valinas

Contents

Preface

I am indebted to Doreen Harding for typing an earlier draft of this book. I am extremely grateful to G.A. Cohen for comments on selected chapters, and to Ed Brandon, Richard Lindley and Adam Morton for comments on the entire draft. Their feedback has been invaluable in removing some of the book's deficiencies. In many cases I have followed their advice, and I hope they will forgive me for the instances where I have persisted in my original views. By way of a more impersonal debt, I feel bound to add that I have learnt something from every item of literature which I cite, not least in cases where I have found myself in disagreement.

Introduction

Crudely speaking, up to the eighteenth century everyone had a clear idea what democracy was and hardly anyone was in favour of it. Now that position is reversed. Everyone is in favour of it but no one has a clear idea any longer what it is. Republicans would claim to be as democratic as Democrats. Conservative and Communist parties claim to embrace democracy. In the West we speak of western democracy, in the East they speak of people's democracies. No wonder confusion reigns on the subject.

The aim of this book is to contribute to clearing up some of the confusion. The battle of democracy is fought on two fronts: there are various practical, political struggles to establish democratic forms of life, and there are theoretical arguments about the nature of democracy and its justification. My assumption is that the political struggle is pointless, or positively dangerous, unless it is grounded in sound theory. I further assume that there really is such a thing as democratic theory, that a case can be made for democracy which relates it to other ideals and values, and that the language of democracy is not merely a convenient rhetoric for jobbing politicians. That assumption may turn out to be mistaken (and indeed I shall argue that democratic theory faces more problems than might at first be thought), but it merits investigation.

I have therefore tried to systematise and contribute to recent thinking on the topic, in a way which may help students and others to find their way through the philosophical and related literature. I have not done so by means of a simple re-hash or leaden description of what others have thought. Rather, I have developed a consecutive argument which is prompted by, and allows me to bring in at appropriate points, the arguments of

1

other theorists. (Their arguments do not receive, therefore, the kind of scholarly attention which on their own merits many of them deserve.) I have also made suggestions for further reading at the end of each chapter. Considerations of space have compelled me either to ignore or simply to make assumptions about a range of questions which in fact require further discussion. In such cases I have tried to make clear where I am making controversial assumptions and to direct the reader to sources of discussion under the suggestions for further reading.

The main body of the book is divided into Part One: Pure Theory, and Part Two: Applied Theory. In Part One I try to develop a theory of democracy relatively free of constraints imposed by particular facts about the circumstances in which we live or about human nature. In Part Two I then consider the modifications which may be thought necessary, from a variety of different perspectives, if that original theory is to have any influence in real life. The difference between the two parts is one of degree. The initial theory cannot be so pure that it rides entirely free of considerations about what human beings are like (indeed, at a general enough level I shall suggest that the strongest argument for democracy actually depends on just that kind of consideration); nor can any theory of democracy capable of doing any work simply give a description of the world which is free of all theoretical commitments. But Part One is undoubtedly more abstract than Part Two, and it makes a particular demand of the reader. It calls for a shelving of the association of democracy with such familiar institutions as candidates running for office in parliamentary elections, in favour of associating democracy with more abstract principles of liberty, equality and the like. The need to make this demand is explained in chapter 1.

I begin, in Part One, from what may be called the *liberal individualist* tradition in political theory: *liberal* by virtue of its attachment to (a particular conception of) liberty as a central political value, with an associated high regard for civil liberties; *individualist* by virtue of taking individual human beings as the atoms of its theories, in a number of ways which I attempt to spell out. For theory of this form, as well as the battle at the level of ideas and the level of practice, there is also a battle *within* democracy. Democracy is understood in terms of adversarial politics and majority rule.

Such theory is very familiar to us, and accords well with widely held conventional moral opinions. I have assumed, however, that appeal to those opinions does not constitute an argument: it smacks too much of asking for endorsement from someone you already know to be in agreement with you. Instead, I have probed the principles underlying those conventional moral views. When that is done, problems arise for the consistency of the views, problems to which there is no wholly satisfactory solution short of a change in perspective from liberal individualist theory, which I argue for in chapter 6.

Whether my arguments on that point are correct or not, it is necessary to consider the application of abstract principles of democracy to concrete circumstances. In Part Two I deal with a number of theories which involve such application. The importance of surrounding social context for the application of democratic ideas — a lesson carried over from Part One — is apparent in the deficiencies detected in elite theory and participation theory. Marxist theory and Leninist theory pay due heed to that fact, but their relation to democracy is unclear, to say the least. Whatever final view is taken of them, however, I have thought it important to acquaint the reader with theories very different from those most familiar in our own political culture. I have also thought it important to separate Marxist from Leninist theory, for reasons which will become apparent.

I do not believe that a book of this kind can be neutral and detached. It will be plain enough where my own preferences lie, and I will state them baldly now. I think the most successful conception of democracy is one which relates it to our nature as autonomous moral agents; but the problems in completing such a conception convince me that it is necessary to take a more 'collectivist' and less individualist view of human life, and to take more seriously the idea of consensus, than we normally do. When it comes to applying democratic theory, I believe that Marx's own position is more interesting and less unsavoury than is commonly supposed, and an important subsidiary aim of my argument is to rescue Marx from the tradition which has appropriated his name.

I believe my most original arguments are in chapters 5 and 6, where I explore the dilemmas which result from the importance attached to autonomy in the liberal individualist tradition; and in chapters 9 and 10, where I attempt to establish the great theoretical distance between Marx and Lenin. These are likely to be the toughest going for newcomers to these issues but also of most interest to oldcomers.

Part One:
Pure Theory

'A critic might observe that the idea of government of the people, by the people and for the people is a conjunction of a pleonasm, a contradiction and a hopeless ambiguity'.
Ernest Gellner *Contemporary Thought and Politics*

1 Conceptions of democracy

1 PHILOSOPHICAL ENQUIRY

Whatever else may be true of human nature, it is human nature to live socially. This immediately raises questions about which social forms human beings do, can and ought to adopt for living together and for taking decisions of common concern. In the contemporary world the most widely canvassed form is called democracy, and it is the purpose of this book to examine that form, to consider alternative conceptions of democracy, distinguish the component ideas holding those conceptions together and attempt an evaluation of the alternatives. The enquiry will be philosophical, and it will be as well to indicate what I take such an enquiry to comprise and why I think it is called for.

Initially, there might be some justifiable suspicion about an enquiry which proceeds indirectly in terms of conceptions, ideas and the like. If we want to discover the nature of democracy, why not proceed directly to an empirical investigation of existing democracies? This, after all, is the preferred way of working for a number of political theorists who have followed the lead set by Schumpeter 1943 in eschewing grand theory as practised by the classical political philosophers. It corresponds to the 'descriptive method' discussed by Dahl, which is to consider all the states and organisations called democratic by political scientists and investigate their common characteristics (Dahl 1956: 63).

Theories of this kind will receive more detailed consideration in Part Two. For the moment I want to show why at most they could be only part of a complete theory of democracy. Not everything about democracy could be an empirically discovered fact: at some point, philosophical assumptions have to be made or argued for. For example, suppose empirical theorists tell us, as many have, that it is an empirically discovered fact that in democracies the average voter is apathetic and incapable of correctly describing the policies of major political parties. We may then ask how they knew where to look in order to discover this fact. They must already have had some initial conception of *what was to count* as a democracy in order to fix the subject of their enquiry. That conception may gain expression in the thought that 'a democracy is a society where individuals are free to form political parties with a view to election by universal suffrage'. And then this thought itself cannot be an empirical discovery (otherwise we could again ask how anyone knew where to look in order to find *this* fact about democracy). This is a reflexion of the general fact that if I am to make an empirical claim that some subject S possesses some property P then I must have some prior means of identifying S. My prior assumptions about what is to count as an S may be unconscious, I may not immediately be able to say what they are, and they may be confused or incoherent. But I must make some such assumptions.

But does this have the absurd consequence that no empirical enquiry into *anything* could ever get going without a preceding philosophical discussion? Not really. In many cases the assumptions in question are uncontroversial and universally agreed: they could simply be listed. With democracy it is different: not only because this is a more diffuse subject but also because there are rival and incompatible ways of identifying it. Taken on a world-wide scale it is a matter of dispute whether Western democracies are *really* democracies, and similarly for so-called people's democracies. With democracy, therefore, identification of the subject is a genuine problem. The term has a certain elasticity. People may agree at a very general level over what ideas it expresses but yet disagree when it comes down to a more specific level. In the terminology adopted by some theorists, we might say that there is one overarching *concept* of democracy but several different and rival *conceptions* of it (Rawls 1972: 5; Dworkin 1978: 134-6).

Moreover, it is fairly obvious why there are rival views. The concept of democracy has a strong normative aspect: to call a system democratic is not merely to describe it, in however imprecise a way; it is generally to express a favourable attitude towards it (though, interestingly, this has not always been so). Accordingly, there is something of immense importance to be gained if one can secure identifications as a democracy for one's own preferred subject whilst retaining the favourable connotations of the term.

These considerations indicate why a philosophical enquiry into the concept of democracy is necessary. To avoid following a counsel of despair which tells us that the term has no meaning and can be used by anyone in whatever way they wish, it is necessary to make explicit a coherent set of assumptions which clarify and justify particular uses. For 'democracy' is not a proper name like 'Fred', to be bestowed by baptism on anything one likes; it is a term with a long and complicated history, which may have come to be used in a variety of ways, but not in a quite arbitrary way.

What, then, might we expect of a philosophical enquiry? First, any consistently used term will be employed according to certain principles, which the users may or may not be aware of, and in this way someone using the term will incur various commitments. The use of a given term will fit into a whole nexus of other statements in more or less complicated ways which may not be obvious to us, and the nature of these connexions — what has been called the implicit logic of the concept (Mackie 1973: 8) — will need to be unearthed.

Next, there can be other implications than logical ones following from the use of a concept. For example, there is at least some plausibility in the suggestion that a logical implication of a system's being democratic is that its inhabitants should enjoy political equality; on the other hand, there is no plausibility in the suggestion that it is a logical implication that none of its inhabitants should possess vast fortunes. Yet it might still be argued that the nature of the world we happen to live in is such that, as a matter of empirical fact, democracy is incompatible with vast differences in personal wealth. The empirical argument may or may not succeed, and it will be appropriate in a philosophical enquiry to consider arguments of that kind. There is, of course, a strong tradition in philosophy which sees the subject as being concerned *only* with *a priori* argument; my own view, however, is that the importation of factual matters into philosophical discussion is all but unavoidable, and that this ought to be recognised and a proper place found for them.

Finally, there is the normative dimension. A philosophical enquiry needs to elicit the reasons why the concept of democracy carries favourable connotations and how it connects with other values.

There are at least these three aspects of a philosophical enquiry into democracy: logical, factual and normative. It must not be expected, however, that each can be neatly separated out from the other two. The traditional positivist scheme of things, in which there is a dichotomy between logical (or conceptual) and factual (or empirical) statements, has come under close scrutiny in this century, and in fact it may be more appropriate to think in terms of a continuum. Similarly, the classical view, stemming from David Hume, that there is an unbridgeable gap between statements of fact and statements of value, has many defenders both in philosophy and in the social sciences; but it too has been questioned. A case can be made for saying that the relation between fact and value is no different in kind from that which often exists between one fact and another.

In both areas resistance to a sharp dichotomy seems to me defensible (though I do not have the space to defend it) and this will be reflected in the structure of my argument. The three aspects I have distinguished really are three aspects rather than three distinct parts. Taken together, they should provide us with conceptions of democracy and the major implications of those conceptions in a way which explains the importance attached to them. It should then be possible to compare and evaluate the rival conceptions in the relevant respects.

There is no simple recipe which can be followed to provide the method of enquiry best suited to achieving these results. It will be natural enough to begin with our linguistic intuitions about where to apply the term 'democracy' (though we should show a decent sensitivity to geographical and temporal variations when determining the scope of 'our' here). But this cannot be more than a beginning. There are options in the matter of the arrangements which the term is used to designate and the thoughts it is used to express; more generally, there are different theories lying behind different uses of the term. In order to assess the options it is necessary to evaluate the reasoning behind each of them, to know why it should be thought important to group just these features together under a linguistic label, what the point or purpose is in doing so. We need, in short, to examine not merely what we say but why we say it, not merely our linguistic intuitions but the reasons behind them, with a view to deciding whether they are good reasons or not. It is worth making this point because of the enormously strong influence of forms of philosophical enquiry which make conformity with linguistic intuition the touchstone of acceptability. I shall not repeat here the criticisms which I have made elsewhere of those forms and their continuing influence (Graham 1977 and 1985), except to stress that they preclude what ought to be left open as a possibility, namely that our intuitions about what to say may change, in a systematic and controlled way, as a result of philosophical enquiry.

That possibility is left open in the method of reflective equilibrium practised by Rawls 1972 (chapter 1), in which we attempt to generate principles which match our most settled and strongly held intuitive convictions and judgments, but the principles so generated may themselves lead to changes in judgments made at present only with hesitation. Indeed, even the judgments we take provisionally as fixed points are liable to revision. It is not clear whether that method also leaves open the stronger possibility that we might change our initial convictions entirely. We might well do so. I noted earlier that one's prior assumptions about what is to count as an instance of a given concept may be confused or incoherent. If that turns out to be so on examination of the reasoning behind the given usage, then that usage must rationally be abandoned (perhaps in favour of a new usage which reflects the construction of a new concept free of the flaws in the current one). That is a theoretical possibility which ought to remain open in any philosophical enquiry. For that reason I should wish to place far greater stress than Rawls does on the adequacy of the reasoning behind settled convictions rather than the mere existence of those convictions.

In any event it should now be clear why it is important to insist that 'democracy' does not function as a proper name. In advance of an exhaustive philosophical enquiry we do not know if the arrangements so described ought to be so described; we do not, indeed, know if *anything* should be. This cuts both ways, of course, and we have correspondingly little reason to withhold the epithet from a particular claimant at the outset. To *assume* that Western democracies (or people's democracies) or that representative (or participatory) democracies are not democratic would be pointless. But a *conclusion* to that effect might well be forced upon us.

With these points in mind we may now consider some actual definitions.

2 DEFINITIONS OF DEMOCRACY

The need for inclusiveness in the initial definition of democracy carries implications for the level of generality at which we begin. For example, it might seem most natural to offer a definition in terms of familiar political machinery, adversary politics, the party system, and so on, and to suggest that at the very least 'democratic theory is concerned with processes by which ordinary citizens exert a relatively high degree of control over leaders' (Dahl 1956: 3). But this would fail to meet the stipulation already laid down, by begging the question in favour of one particular claimant to the title of democracy at the expense of others, and it would not afford us the best route to an insight into the rationale behind the concept. There is a *basis* for the familiar usage of 'democracy' and it must be unearthed. We should bear in mind, too, that the term is employed in description of arrangements in contexts smaller than the whole of society: families, clubs, committees and university departments can all be so described. We therefore need a definition which will bring out the parallels between these and the entire social context, and that means starting at a higher level of generality.

Consider the origin of the term 'democracy'. In the Greek it denotes a form of rule by a section of the populace, the *demos* as opposed, say, to the rich or the aristocrats; and *demos* could be used to denote the citizen body, the common people or, simply, the lower orders (cf. Finley 1973: 12-13). In any event it denoted considerably less than the entire populace, excluding as it did aliens, women and slaves. This is the most striking difference between the Greek concept and our own, which stands in contrast to terms denoting sectional rule of any kind (cf. Wollheim 1962: 72). As the slogan has it, democracy is government of the people, by the people, for the people.

Now in a sense government is always *of* the people. If we add to this the thought that a benevolent despot or oligarchy might claim to govern *for* the people, then it looks as though government *by* the people is what is distinctive of democracy. We may then take *rule by the people, the whole people* as our initial and provisional definition, which captures the general concept of democracy and can be explored without any prior prejudice to rival conceptions at a more specific level. Already implicit in it are two further notions which require considerable exploration in their own right, namely freedom and equality. In so far as democracy is concerned with the issue of rule or control or decision-making it is perforce concerned with freedom or liberty; and at least to the extent that no one is excluded from a share in decision-making some rudimentary notion of equality is implicit. We shall reach these issues obliquely, however, by first raising two obvious questions about the definition. What, more precisely, are we to understand by 'the whole people'? And how is 'rule' to be construed in this context?

If we consider democracy at the societal level, nowhere, in practice, does 'the whole people' range over the entire population, but it is a matter of historical fact that in the modern period admission to the political decision-making process has gradually extended to include more and more categories. In one country after another the exclusion of women has come to be seen as indefensible and has been abandoned, property qualifications are no longer thought appropriate, and in Britain the age of majority was itself lowered from twenty-one to eighteen. On the other hand, certain other categories such as the insane, children below a given age, and criminals are very widely excluded.

Is it possible to provide a rationale for the use of the

expression 'the whole people' consistent with these general facts? Certainly not as easily as might be thought. A first attempt might be to identify the whole people with *all those affected* by the decision-making in question. But this raises problems. The currently excluded categories mentioned are certainly affected by decisions over which they have no influence, and the suggestion is therefore descriptively inadequate. Further, doubts could be raised whether the suggestion could in any case be made adequate. A given issue, let us say schooling, may affect *A, B* and *C,* whilst another, health provision, affects *B, C* and *D.* Multiply this by the number of issues which come up for decision, add in the fact that people may be affected to widely differing extents by a given decision, and the complexity of demarcating a people by reference to being affected seems wholly intractable (cf. Dahl 1970: 64-5). In any case, there will be instances where parties clearly outside a decision-making group may be just as clearly affected by the group's decisions (cf. Dahl 1979: 110). Dahl cites the example of a friend from Latin America who urged on such grounds that his people should have a say in US elections (Dahl 1970: 65-7). If the idea of democracy implies that the decision-making group is identical with the group of those affected, then he would have a point.

Notice that we are moving from the question of the descriptive adequacy of this construction of 'the whole people' to its normative adequacy. Nozick objects that it is not normatively adequate to identify 'the whole people' with those affected by a decision, on the grounds that there are many cases where someone importantly affected by a decision has no right to a say in it: the suitors for a woman's hand in marriage, the members of an orchestra whose jobs depend on Toscanini's decision whether to continue to act as conductor, the beneficiaries of some private property lent to them by me which I now intend to reclaim. In these cases, he suggests, the right to decide belongs respectively to the woman, Toscanini and me, even though others will be affected by the decision (Nozick 1974: 268-70).

Now it is certainly possible to enter some resistance to Nozick's objection. It can be pointed out that he must rely on our sharing his intuitive convictions about the cases he mentions, and that even if he secures this agreement it proves little. As I have already suggested, the mere fact of our holding certain views which coincide with the conclusions of a theory gives no support to that theory: it must also be true that there are good reasons for our holding them. At least in the Toscanini and private property case further argument would have to ensue before this was established. A similar point might be made in relation to Dahl's example: the idea, say, that peasants should influence who is returned to government in another country will strike us as strange at the very least because it is unfamiliar. But when their lives may literally depend on the outcome, it is not so obvious that it is inappropriate. This too would need further argument, and it would throw into sharp relief Dahl's point about the complexity of affected groups. Some might argue, for instance, that a Nicaraguan should be able to influence US foreign policy, though not the issue of whether the US should run a budget deficit.

An attempt could be made to cope with this complexity by introducing a corresponding complexity into the under-standing of 'rule' and a weakening of its sense, as we shall see in a moment. But even all this would still leave the very first difficulty, that children, the insane and criminals are affected by political decisions but are not party to them. And this, surely, must be the sticking point for either the descriptive or the normative adequacy of the view which simply equates the whole people with all those affected? There may be argument about where to draw the line which distinguishes children and the insane, but it is clear that some fall on the wrong side of it. To afford those who do fall on the wrong side of it the opportunity to influence political decisions would be importing more surrealism into the political scene than already exists there.

The most obvious modification is to equate the whole people with those who both are affected and possess some other characteristics which entitle them to decide issues affecting them. It would then be a matter of spelling out what those characteristics are — a certain kind of *competence* would be one candidate for inclusion — and seeing which categories in consequence gain entry into the decision-making process and which remain outside. To pursue these enquiries will take us into the whole issue of the grounds for democratic decision-making, and this will begin in the next chapter.

Meanwhile, how is 'rule' to be construed? Once again there is a considerable gap between the original Greek concept and our own. In Athens the assembly of the citizens was the paramount decision-making body, its powers were theoretically unlimited and not circumscribed by any notion of inalienable rights. It sometimes happened, for example, that the assembly passed laws abridging freedom of speech. To the modern mind the concept of rule by the people is not likely to suggest powers as wide as this. Not just *anything* which a populace might decide would necessarily be accepted as a democratic decision. But the major respect in which the modern concept of rule is different, and much weaker, is that it does not imply the same direct influence over decisions. Or more precisely, it does not carry this implication in the wider political sphere. Perhaps in more limited contexts like families or committees such direct influence is implied, but it is often thought sufficient in the wider sphere that the people should rule in the sense of selecting, in accordance with certain conditions, those who subsequently take decisions on their behalf.

Initially, then, we should recognise these two senses of 'rule' and, corresponding to them, *direct* and *representative* forms of democracy. In direct democracy the people rule by making decisions themselves, in representative democracy they elect a number of representatives to make decisions for them. The representative form may take care of Dahl's problem about the complexity of affected groups, since the influence over the decision on a particular issue has now been so weakened that overlapping interest-groups would not even be detectable in the same way. On the other hand, a number of difficulties also arise. A great deal needs to be said to clarify the notion of a representative: I might represent others by virtue of sharing politically salient characteristics with them or by prosecuting their interests, and an assembly of representatives might be differently constituted depending on which of these it was (cf. Wollheim 1960: 215). Moreover, depending on just how the notion of a representative was specified, we might seriously doubt whether the sense of 'rule' on which this form of democracy is founded is an acceptable sense at all. Is the degree of control exercised by the people over the actual outcome sufficient for it to be proper to speak of their ruling? Alternatively, if this does count as an instance of ruling, we may begin to wonder if, after all, a system where the people rule is necessarily one which we should want to applaud as realising the ideals implicit in the concept of democracy. That will depend on whether, for instance, we value democracy on grounds of equal treatment of people or of serving their interests. Once again, we are brought back to the question what *grounds* there are for favouring democracy.

We have given preliminary consideration to 'the whole people' and 'rule'. A third set of problems becomes apparent when we consider the importance of both components jointly. Under what circumstances *does* the whole people rule? Our discussion so far would suggest this is when all those affected by a decision and entitled to influence it either agree in their decision or agree in the appointment of representatives. But there is a very strong condition implicit in this, namely *unanimity*. It may be met in very local circumstances, and perhaps has been more frequently met at other times and places, but for large-scale modern society it looks a non-starter. Either, therefore, democracy itself is comparatively rare, or our original definition is unacceptable, or it does not imply unanimity.

In favour of dropping the unanimity requirement is the fact that it is likely to operate in a biased conservative way. Since decisions are normally decisions to do something, failure to achieve unanimity will result in nothing being done, thus favouring the *status quo*. And where there is a difference of opinion it would not be possible to place the same stringent unanimity requirement on the decision to do nothing too, for that would lead to the intolerable result that both particular proposals for action and the proposal for inaction would all fail to receive the required sanction. The unanimity requirement also effectively places a veto in the hands of a single dissenter and therefore falls foul of any principle of equality of influence which may be embedded in the notion of democracy (cf. Lively 1975: 17-18).

Moreover, it will seem obvious to many that the only

acceptable interpretation of rule by the whole people is 'rule by the majority'. After all, as Wolff puts it, children are taught to accept majority decisions almost before they have learnt how to count (Wolff 1976: 42). But Wolff himself is critical of majority rule, on the grounds that it involves sacrifice of the individual conscience which is the basis of moral agency; and fears about the tyranny of the majority have a long history and exponents as weighty as Madison and John Stuart Mill. There are, besides, problems about computing a majority decision from individual preferences, some relatively technical and others stemming from the anomalous result when a majority holds a view with no great conviction whilst the minority has intense passions on the issue. These difficulties have to be faced, and a tenable distinction drawn between the tyranny of the majority and legitimate majority rule.

3 CONCLUSION

We have now seen some of the complexities into which we are led — even beginning from a relatively uncontentious definition of democracy. This is partly because the terms in which it is cast lend themselves to a variety of interpretations, partly because they connect in complex ways with a network of other terms, but mainly, I suggest, for another reason, related to the points made in section 1. As we compare and assess different ways of elaborating on the concept of democracy, we have to judge how adequate they are for the purpose. And the purpose is not merely to distinguish particular kinds of procedure and arrangement, and not merely to distinguish them because we approve of them. It is to do so because they are thought to conform to specific ideals and principles which themselves gain our approval. The order of precedence is such that if a given procedure (say, basing policy on unanimity or majority preference) fails to conform to a given ideal (say, treating each participant with equal consideration), then the description of the procedure as democratic is to be withdrawn. The alternative, to insist that democracy is simply a method, an arrangement for making decisions, which cannot itself function as an ideal (Schumpeter 1943: 242) merely displaces the same issue to another place: if democracy is just a method, why does it exercise such a strong hold over us and why are people prepared to die for it? The most likely explanation is that the method is thought peculiarly appropriate for the realisation of ideals themselves thought worthwhile. In either case, a survey is then required of the ideals and principles which in this way provide the grounds of democracy. This begins in the following chapter.

FURTHER READING

The contentious nature of terms like 'democracy' was brought into focus by Gallie 1955 and is discussed more recently in Connolly 1983. The need for a specifically philosophical component in democratic theory is argued further in Graham 1985. Classical discussions of the logical/factual distinction are Quine 1953 and Kripke 1979. Alternative approaches to the fact/value distinction are represented in Hudson 1969. Dahl 1979 constitutes an extended treatment of the problem of whom to include in the decision-making body. Pateman 1983 discusses the exclusion of women; Brandon 1979 and Harris 1982 the exclusion of children. Less familiar ideas of consensus and unanimity are given sympathetic treatment in Mansbridge 1980. Technical problems of computing a majority choice are taken up in Arrow 1963 and Sen 1970, and the problems of 'intense minorities' in Dahl 1956.

2 The grounds of democracy: interests

1 INTRODUCTION

The position now is this. We are to examine the various grounds in favour of democracy, construed in a general way as some legitimate interpretation of 'rule by the people', and this examination should itself enable us to arrive at a sharper idea about *which* interpretations are most appropriate.

As a very rough and ready guide, we can classify the available grounds as follows. Democracy may be favoured for its *consequences,* which may be described in *non-moral* or *moral* terms; or it may be favoured for its *intrinsic* properties. As examples of each of these possibilities, it might be said on behalf of democracy that it enables people to pursue their interests (non-moral consequence) or to secure liberty or justice (moral consequence); or that it involves treating people with a respect to which they are entitled (intrinsic property). The classification is only rough and ready because it will depend on how 'rule by the people' is interpreted whether a given property of democracy is seen as intrinsic or as a consequence. Equally, views will differ on whether a given consequence is itself moral or non-moral in character.

To the extent that the grounds can be kept separate in this way we should expect possible conflict, in that the interpretation of 'rule by the people' which fits the requirement of maximising liberty, say, may clash with that for enabling people to pursue their interests. Where that occurs, it may be necessary to adjudicate between the grounds themselves. At the same time, it would be simplistic to suppose that an acceptable defence of democracy would rest on one such ground to the exclusion of all others.

A discussion of the grounds of democracy will provide another service: it will help with what we might call the *motivational problem*. Rooted in social life is the possibility of conflict between the individual and the collective, and as the argument of Part One progresses I shall try to show that this is a particularly serious dilemma for democratic theory. Displaying the appeal of democracy, in some of the ways outlined in chapter 1, will help to answer the related questions why anyone should favour adopting democratic procedures in the first place, and why they should continue to abide by them in circumstances where this will lead to the thwarting of their own will (and where, therefore, their first thought may be to abandon them).

2 THE INTERESTS ARGUMENT

A defence of democracy is likely to connect in some way with the thought, familiar since the Renaissance, that individual human beings as such are important. If we then try to explain what it is which gives them this importance, one form our answer may take is that each individual human being has interests which they can express and which they have a right to pursue. The virtue which may then be claimed for democratic arrangements is that they ensure that this will be done. Here we have an argument in terms of interests, popularly known as the 'shoe-pinching argument': only the individual can know where the shoe pinches. If we begin, therefore, from the assumption that any individual's interests constitute a legitimate demand, then the claimed merit of a system of rule by the people is that it extends a proper influence to the shoe-wearer. It enables individuals to express their preferences, and since this is what determines subsequent policy it maximises the satisfaction of those preferences. The alternative to this would be to exclude the interests of some individuals from having an influence on the outcome, or else to suppose that for such influence to operate it is unnecessary to consult those whose interests are in question. And neither of these, it may be felt, is supportable since they involve either not caring that some people's shoes pinch or else supposing, implausibly, that someone *other* than the wearer knows best where they do pinch.

How strong is this interests argument? Notice that it explicitly identifies what is in people's interests with the preferences they themselves express. There is a powerful tradition which gives privileged status, in this way, to people's own perceptions of where their interests lie. But that tradition is open to challenge. Formally, the idea that someone's interests can simply be 'read off' from their own expressed views is refuted by the fact that people change their minds. If I hold conflicting views at different times about where my interests lie, then at least sometimes I must be wrong. Informally, the infallibility of such judgments is refuted whenever we, as observers, see that someone will make a mess of their life, say in a choice of career or partner, in following what they judge is in their interest.

In a more theoretical vein, the identification of people's interests with their expressed preferences may be challenged in a number of ways. Most abstractly, there are grounds for claiming in a fashion reminiscent of Kant that preferences or desires are themselves a species of judgment, that they are therefore amenable to criticism in the light of what is reasonable, and that in consequence it is perfectly possible for someone to make *mistakes* in their preferences (cf. Nagel 1970: 27-32). Again, it is a commonplace that desires and preferences do not arise from pure reflexion on the part of the individual; rather, they are subject to considerable social influence. This brings with it the possibility that a social system may itself work against an individual's interests and at the same time be productive of desires and preferences which are similarly inimical to that individual's interests (cf. Lukes 1974: 34). The mere fact that this is a possibility suggests that a conceptual distance must be maintained between interests and desires. This leaves the difficult question how interests *are* to be identified. We might then identify them not with the desires an agent happens to have but those the agent *would* have *if* he or she were forming those desires rationally and/or autonomously. Alternatively, we might identify interests in an 'objective' way, by reference to what would make an individual flourish, regardless of what their own actual or hypothetical desires were (cf. Gray 1983b: 85).

Regardless of whether these ways of identifying interests will fare any better than the original way, a proponent of the interests argument might object that the difficulties raised in the last two paragraphs are directed against a stronger version of it than anyone actually needs to hold. It could be maintained that individuals have, not infallible knowledge of their interests, but probably a better knowledge than some unknown and remote person in a position of great power over them. In any case, it might reasonably be felt that only they themselves can safely be relied upon to *pursue* their interests. If that is so, then a better result might still follow, in terms of the satisfaction of interests, from democratic decision-making rather than some imposed form of decision. Alternatively, it might be held that there is merely a presumption in favour of individuals being the best judges of their interests, but one which can be defeated only by compelling evidence to the contrary (cf Dahl 1979: 126).

At this stage the issue is indeterminate. But this may in fact work against grounding acceptance of democracy in the interests argument. For suppose that compelling evidence of a particular kind were available: suppose that some undemocratic regime were able to make the trains run on time and were highly successful at providing facilities which were in an obvious way good for human beings. Should we not then have to say that this regime was in fact ministering to individuals' interests?

Now a proponent of the interests argument might refuse to allow that this *is* a possibility, and give as the reason that it could not be in anyone's interests to be treated as one is in an undemocratic regime. This response is to the point, but it fundamentally alters the nature of the grounding for democracy, and brings the present argument much closer to alternatives still to be considered. For it would no longer be a case of tracing a contingent connexion between democracy and individuals' interests described independently of commitment to particular political forms; rather, those interests are now themselves beginning to be specified in a way which favours the treatment accorded in a democratic as opposed to an undemocratic regime. We should then have to consider (as we

shall) what it is about people which might give them such an
interest.

If we confine our attention to interests which can be
specified independently of political form, however, it is clear
that our hypothetical question is a source of embarrassment
for the interests argument. Democracy as rule by the people is
interpreted and justified in that argument as a system in which
people's interests are maximised because decisions are
determined by their own preferences. In the conceivable
circumstance that some *other* type of system in fact maximises
interests, then we no longer have any reason for supporting
democracy.

At this point we have a choice. Anyone placing a very high
premium on the satisfaction of individuals' interests will not
shrink from accepting this consequence, and will argue that
democracy is not necessarily the preferable form of decision-
making in all circumstances. Others will feel that the rejection
of democracy is too high a price to pay, that there is something
deeply repugnant in subjecting people to undemocratic forms
of decision-making which cannot be offset by gains elsewhere.
For them the interests argument will carry a commitment
(albeit a hypothetical one) which they are not prepared to
accept. In that case an alternative grounding will need to be
given to justify subscription to democracy, and it will be
natural to concentrate attention on what it is about human
beings which explains this repugnance and makes democracy
an appropriate arrangement for them. In terms of the
classification set out in section 1, it will be natural to look at the
intrinsic properties of democracy, rather than seeking an
account which rests entirely on the external and contingent
benefits held to follow from that form.

3 INTERESTS AND THE FORM OF DEMOCRACY

If we leave aside these difficulties in the interests argument, the
question still remains what form of democracy it would license.
In terms of the original analogy we might ask what degree of
control the shoe-wearer is supposed to have over the shoe-
maker, and indeed whether these should be distinct roles at all.

The natural home, as it were, of the interests argument is utilitarianism — a version of it is put forward for instance by James Mill in his *Essay on Government*. There the argument is that rule of the few will produce a government in the interests of the few, a result which will be avoided if power is in the hands of the whole community, as in a democracy. If the point is that there is something disproportionate in the interests of the few prevailing, this has an egalitarian ring to it, which might be thought to be reinforced by the general egalitarian thrust present in Bentham's version of utilitarianism, according to which each is to count for one and none for more than one. Does this perhaps suggest a form of democracy in which power is diffused in a more radically egalitarian way than we are accustomed to meet with, one in which individuals exert more direct control on a more equal basis over decisions which affect their lives? James Mill does not himself draw that inference but comes down in favour of a representative system where power is distributed very unequally among citizens; but we may not be convinced by this, particularly when we recall that strand of the original argument which suggests that individuals will at least have a better idea of their own interests than some remote person in power over them. That can easily be construed as a criticism of existing representative systems, where a small number of elected politicians determine the conditions of life of large numbers of people, as well as of undemocratic systems.

However, we must remember that it would be self-defeating for the interests argument to accord any independent weight to considerations of equality. If an equal distribution of political power did in fact maximise satisfaction of individual interests that would be a reason, from the perspective of this argument, for insisting upon that distribution. But it might not. Even if each individual's interest is to be equally considered, it might be that interest-satisfaction would be maximised by some individuals' handing over political power to representatives appointed to act upon their behalf. Much will turn on such issues as how far individuals *can* be expected to have an accurate and reliable view about their own interests and their satisfaction. If we hold strong enough views on their unreliability then we can embrace representative systems involving relatively little prior responsiveness to individuals' opinions. We can say with Edmund Burke that it is the duty of a representative to follow what his own conscience tells him is the interest of his electors, rather than sacrificing this to the electors' own opinions (cf. Benn and Peters 1959: 341).

Indeed, there is a long intellectual pedigree, going back at least to Adam Smith's 'invisible hand' theory, to theories which suggest that a given result is likely to be obtained precisely by people's acting in some *other* way than with the conscious intention to realise it. In a context closely related to the present one, David Miller has recently argued that there is no *a priori* reason why legislation should not be produced which accords with electors' preferences, even though they have no direct control over it and it is the prerogative of elected leaders who merely respond to the electorate's preferences by anticipation. In the same way, he suggests, there is no *a priori* reason why a market economy in which producers act so as to maximise profits should not in fact work so as to satisfy consumers' desires (Miller 1983: 134). Whilst this is true in both cases, we should recognise that some considerable *a posteriori* argument will be required in order to establish that such a happy coincidence of outcome is achievable in this roundabout way. So too for our own case, which concerns interests rather than (necessarily) preferences and desires. That was the point of my earlier criticism: we simply do not know, in advance of a complicated weighing of evidence, whether a system in which elected leaders initiate policies with only indirect influence from the populace at large will serve the interests of the populace, just as we cannot say, without pronouncing on some complicated theories, whether people can be systematically mistaken about their true interests. But if these issues remain unsettled whilst our commitment to a particular form of decision-making is not in doubt, then we must look elsewhere for a complete account of the grounds for that commitment.

As soon as we introduce other considerations besides interests into those grounds, a further qualification must be placed on Miller's argument. Pursuing the analogy between market society and the struggle for power in parliamentary democracy, he suggests that if 'a model shows how the pursuit of private ends may lead under the appropriate conditions to social goals being achieved, then anyone who shares those goals must endorse the model — at least pending an alternative theory which shows how the goals in question may be achieved more effectively' (*ibid.*: 135). That fits the interests argument very well and demonstrates how it can end up supporting an interpretation of 'rule by the people' which exactly matches existing political institutions (always assuming that it can deliver the required *a posteriori* argument). But for anyone who departs from the pure version of the interests argument, the principle enunciated by Miller will not necessarily hold. We might, for example, wish to see the satisfaction of interests maximised but still believe that there are important constraints on how this is achieved, that there are some things you just cannot do to people for the sake of that goal. It is a common characteristic of our thinking to be concerned not just with objectives but with observing various constraints in achieving them. That explains, for example, why we face a dilemma when confronted with cases of paternalism, if this is defined as intervening in someone's life against their will but for their benefit. The benefit considered in itself is something we welcome, but the manner of its achievement causes us to hesitate over whether it is legitimately secured or not.

4 CONFLICT OF INTERESTS

For the interests argument, the ideal situation would be one where all participants to a decision had a clear and correct conception of where their interests lay and acted in concert to realise them. That would furnish a perfectly straightforward interpretation of 'rule by the whole people'. But apart from the other difficulties we have noticed, there is a further problem about coincidence and divergence of interests.

We have so far spoken as if the computation and joint realisation of people's interests would be unproblematic, but this is not so. For example, even if two people agree that it is in their respective interests that a given state of affairs should obtain, they may differ over what route furnishes the best way of achieving that state of affairs. That is the simplest case.

Where there is disagreement over *which* state of affairs should obtain, there are more difficulties. If there are any cases where people do not just happen to have differing interests but *necessarily* come into conflict, because of the relations they stand in to each other, matters are more serious still.

What are we to do in such cases? At a minimum we can review the situation, reconsider and see if resolution of the conflict is possible. We can search for unnoticed interests which individuals hold in common. We can perhaps 'trade' in such a way that I relinquish my preference for one outcome or state of affairs in exchange for your support on some other issue. Or we can make the move from thinking purely in terms of individual interests to group, and perhaps a general, interest. Each of these strategies will be attended by problems of its own; but in any case, unless they result in one hundred per cent success, a residual problem will remain. Provided the sum total of individual interests has all the figures on one side, so to speak, we can say that the people are ruling because their interest is being realised. But if some individuals' interests are being met while others are not, then the people as a whole are not ruling, because the people do not, in the sense required by this argument, constitute a whole.

At this point the natural move is to settle for majority voting. This, after all, fits in very well with the aspirations of the interests argument in so far as we have described it as being concerned to *maximise* interests. If we make certain simplifying assumptions (such as, once again, ignoring intensities of preference if interests are identified with preferences) and ignore the fact that interests can be served to a greater or lesser degree, then to meet the interests of most people is necessarily to maximise interests. So why not ensure that the people rule by having an arrangement which allows them to express views about their interests, count the results and act accordingly?

The first problem is this. Either such a summing process allows us to arrive at something which can reasonably be called the people's interest or it does not. If it does not, then we have not yet found any basis for adopting a majoritarian procedure as an expression of rule by the people. But even if it does, the relation between individual and general interest remains problematic. Where my interest and the general interest diverge or conflict — an inherent possibility in a majoritarian system — it still has to be shown why the results thrown up by such a procedure should have any impact on my convictions or my actions. If we leave the matter here, we have failed to exhibit the motivational appeal of democratic procedures so construed, a task which I suggested in section 1 ought to be discharged in a discussion of the grounds of democracy.

We might try to remedy this by adverting to the mathematics of the argument. The reason for an individual's accepting a *system* of majority decision-making, it might be said, is that on each occasion when a decision is made the interests of more individuals will be met than not (at worst, 51 per cent as against 49 per cent). Therefore, this is a system in which an individual has a better than 50/50 chance of having his or her interests met. Contrast this with the only alternative (leaving aside complete consensus) — some form of non-majority or minority rule — in which no such guarantee can be given.

One crucial unstated assumption underlies this argument: that the majority is a shifting entity, not constantly composed of the same group of individuals. For an individual who is in a permanent minority, and indeed for one who is in a minority more than on average, the mathematics of majority rule has negative appeal. In this connexion two actual cases often cited are those of blacks in the United States and Catholics in Northern Ireland, who, it is said, constitute permanent minorities with shared interests and are in just that position. If democracy itself, therefore, is not to suffer from negative appeal in these circumstances then it will have to be dissociated from majority rule (cf. Lively 1975: 26; Pennock 1979: 8-9).

Moreover, even leaving aside these difficulties, it is plain that this argument will at most help with only one half of the motivational problem mentioned in section 1. It may display the appeal of a system which most of the time serves an individual's interests; but it does nothing to explain why such an individual should accept the decision of that system on a particular occasion when to do so will run counter to his or her interests. On the contrary, for as long as we continue to think solely in terms of the individual's interests, it displays the appeal of going along with the system when its deliverances, in the form of majority verdicts, coincide with one's own wishes, but of abandoning it when this ceases to be so.

Now of course we can reply that to do this is unfairly to make exceptions in one's own favour or to treat others unequally, and it may be important to say this. But to make these points is to swing the argument into a new orbit and to forsake the attempt to ground democracy only in interests. Moreover, as I shall try to show in chapters 5 and 6, the transposition into an overtly moral context of the conflict between individual and collective does not of itself remove all difficulties. What we are encountering in the present context is one version of a more general problem which is highly resistant to a satisfactory solution when set up in the terms employed so far. One respect in which I believe the present way of looking at the problem is ultimately unhelpful is in its conception of 'the individual' with some bundle of interests which can somehow be ascertained and which the decisions of the collective may then enhance or retard. The individual is, in many different ways which need to be explored, a member of a group, and it is the first step to a more adequate presentation of the problem to recognise this.

Often the interests argument has been pursued with a background assumption about human motivation, namely that individuals always do act egoistically so as to further their own individual interests, or that it is rational for them to do so. On that assumption the very idea of participation in a political process at all becomes problematic, since the 'cost' of doing so will frequently outweigh the increased likelihood of any 'benefits' so obtained. (From a purely self-interested point of view, why should I bother to vote, or take part in political activity, if the outcome is likely to remain the same whether I do so or not?) No doubt for the purpose of a particular kind of axiomatic theorising assumptions of this kind are fruitful, but as straightforward theses about human nature they look more questionable. The conception of rationality which stigmatises altruism as irrational can be challenged and the allegedly universal self-interestedness of human behaviour is breached at the very least by actions whose aim is to benefit one's immediate family circle rather than oneself — a more significant breach of the egoistic assumption than might at first appear.

However, although bringing group as well as individual

interests into the reckoning will help with the general problem of conflict between individual and collective, it will not of itself deal with the motivational problem. For unless the group is extended to embrace the entire population, exactly similar difficulties to those already encountered will crop up again. It will be a tautology that it is in any group's interests to accept decisions which serve its interests, but not to accept decisions which go against its interests and therefore not to accept democratic decisions as such.

It should be stressed that what I have examined here is the adequacy of the interests argument for grounding an interpretation of 'rule by the people' in circumstances of conflict. I have taken some form of majority decision-making to be the most natural interpretation in such circumstances, but I have been concerned with that interpretation on its own merits only secondarily and incidentally. There is more to be said both in support of majority decision-making and against it, some of which will be said as the argument develops. But it may in any case be thought *not* to be the most natural interpretation. Dahl, for example, has argued that the distinction between democracy and dictatorship is to be sought not by reference to rule by the majority but by the 'size, number and variety of minorities whose preferences must be taken into account', so that democratic rule rests on 'the steady appeasement of relatively small groups' (Dahl 1956: 132, 146). The general issue of the merits of this 'realistic' approach to democracy will be discussed in chapter 7, but the switch from a conception of rule by the majority to rule by successive minorities will again make little difference to the present issue. Any given minority will conclude that it is not in general in its own interest that some other minority should displace it in determining what policies are pursued.

5 CONCLUSION

For most of this chapter we have explored the possibility of grounding democracy in the importance of human beings, where it is their existence as bearers of interests which provides that importance. This feature is hardly likely to be irrelevant to an understanding of democracy and why we value it. The protection of individuals' interests will figure on any list of reasons for preferring democratic to other social arrangements. But the attempt to ground a conception of democracy in these considerations alone is a limited success. It provides relatively little help in extending our understanding of the different interpretations of 'rule by the people' which might reasonably be adopted, and therefore the different forms of democratic procedure which might be actualised in our dealings in the world. More seriously, it provides only an incomplete account of the value we attach to democratic principles. At several points it has seemed likely that this can be explained only by recourse to considerations other than interests, and in particular by recourse to the moral notions we employ in our thinking about human beings.

Perhaps, then, it is necessary to look at other aspects of human beings in order to give a complete account. This we shall do in chapters 3 and 4, where we shall examine the two values most frequently associated with democracy — liberty and equality — and their connexion with what it is to be human.

FURTHER READING

Recent discussion of alternative conceptions of interests is available in Barry 1965, Lukes 1974, Benton 1982, Connolly 1983 and Gray 1983b. Invisible hand explanations and processes are sponsored in Nozick 1974. Buchanan and Tullock 1962 and Barry 1965 debate the acceptability of reaching agreement via 'trading'. The problematic nature of political participation on egoistic assumptions is explored in Downs 1957 and Barry 1970, and the adequacy of egoism as an account of human motivation is challenged in Nagel 1970.

3 The grounds of democracy: liberty

1 INTRODUCTION

Not even the most fervent supporter of democracy would claim, after any serious consideration, that democratic institutions and procedures were the most appropriate in all circumstances or that the importance attaching to them could never be outweighed by anything *more* important. The exigencies of a situation may make it more important to fill people's bellies, and historical circumstances may simply make democracy an impossible option. But de Tocqueville's prediction that democratic ideas would come to dominate modern thought in the West, in the wake of the importance attached to individual human beings as such, has not been so far wide of the mark (cf. Lukes 1973: 48). If that is so, then it is worthwhile attempting to uncover the reasoning behind this: it may not only give us a better understanding of our attachment to democracy but also help to explain those occasions when that attachment has to be tempered.

Where should we begin, if we are to describe what it is about individual human beings which makes them important? We are both active and passive creatures. We have the capacity for a range of experiences, of emotional, aesthetic, moral and other kinds; we are also capable of understanding our surroundings to some degree, of formulating intentions to change those surroundings and acting in conformity with them. It is one plausible starting point to say that an important part of being human is having the exercise of capacities like these under one's own, rather than someone else's, control. Liberty would in that way become central for human beings, and since democracy is a system of self-rule rather than rule by

33

others, its connexion with liberty would provide a reason for valuing it.

It might be argued that this attempt to connect democracy to fundamental features of being human, via the notion of liberty, would be better expressed in the language of *rights*. People, it might be said, have a basic right to liberty, and because democracy provides for liberty it is to be favoured. Thus, Hart claimed in an influential paper that 'if there are any moral rights at all, it follows that there is at least one natural right, the equal right of all men to be free' — natural rights being those possessed by all people *qua* people, rather than resulting from some particular voluntary action (Hart 1955: 53-4). There has been a considerable revival of interest in the idea of rights in political philosophy, and much has been done to cut it free from misleading metaphysical connotations. Hart, for example, explains the idea of having a right in terms of having a justification for limiting someone else's freedom, rather than in terms of possessing some peculiar kind of entity (*ibid.*: 54-60); and Dworkin explains having a right to do something in terms of its being wrong for others to interfere with one's doing that thing (Dworkin 1978: 188). These are welcome advances on more obscure ways of talking; but at the same time, these definitions of rights indicate, I believe, why it will not do to *begin* the kind of enquiry we are engaged in with that notion. To speak in terms of what there is a justification for is to raise the questions why there is a justification and what it is, and we have not reached the *basis* of an argument until they are answered.

Accordingly, I do not speak in terms of rights at this stage. Instead, I begin with the concept of liberty and consider two alternative conceptions of it. These I have called the *two spheres* view and the *integrated* view of liberty. These terms are my own, but I have constructed the views from theories available in the literature. The views are therefore abstractions which I judge worth serious consideration, but they do not match in every particular the beliefs held by any individual theorist.

I shall examine these two conceptions to see how sound they are in their own right, whether and in what form the apparently tight connexion between democracy and liberty holds, and what further implications can be extracted for democratic theory itself.

2 THE TWO SPHERES VIEW

Basic to what I shall call the two spheres view is the idea that, although there is a sphere of life where people's liberty may be curtailed in various ways, there is also a sphere where coercion and control may not legitimately enter at all. In a very general form this view is contained in John Stuart Mill's *Essay on Liberty*. I shall not be concerned so much with that general position in its own right, but rather with its development in relation to democracy and social decision-making. An appropriate starting point for such an enquiry is Isaiah Berlin's 'Two concepts of liberty' (Berlin 1969: 118-72), which initially I describe without critical comment.

The two concepts of Berlin's title are *negative* and *positive* liberty, and they are in some sense to be contrasted or counterposed. *Negative* liberty, which Berlin favours, has as its core the idea of non-interference; liberty in this sense concerns the extent to which someone 'is or should be left to do or be what he is able to do or be without interference from other persons' (*ibid.*: 121-2). As he also puts it, 'You lack political liberty or freedom only if you are prevented from attaining a goal by human beings. Mere incapacity to attain a goal is not lack of political freedom' (*ibid.*: 122). So, for example, if I am incapacitated from doing something on account of poverty, I shall describe my condition as a lack of liberty only if I subscribe to a theory which makes the cause of my poverty the conduct of other human beings. In the same vein, liberty in this negative sense is not to be confused with other values, or with the absence of other frustrations. If my liberty rests on someone else's misery and if my liberty is curtailed in order to relieve that misery, but without any increase in the other person's liberty, then an absolute loss in liberty has occurred, and we should not confuse the issue or try to disguise this by re-describing the relief of misery as increase in liberty (*ibid.*: 125). Consistently, too, with a definition equivalent to lack of interference by human beings, we should note that Berlin rejects a definition in terms of the ability to do what one wishes — that would let in the case where my wishes have themselves been tampered with or curtailed by some outside (and possibly malignant) agency, and this would surely not count as an expansion of my liberty (*ibid.*: 139-40, xxxviii).

The allegedly contrasting *positive* sense of liberty concerns the source rather than the area of control, and its core is the idea of self-mastery: 'I wish my life and decisions to depend on myself, not on external forces of whatever kind. I wish to be the instrument of my own, not of other men's, acts of will' (*ibid.*: 131). For reasons which are not at the centre of our present concerns, Berlin is deeply suspicious of the concept of positive liberty, arguing that as a matter of historical fact (though not logical necessity) the concept has lent itself to the justification of tyranny: self-mastery is construed as mastery by the 'higher' self, which comes to be identified with some 'whole' (tribe, race or state, for example) standing outside the actual individual human being (*ibid.*: 132-4). Hence his attachment to negative liberty, which provides us with a means of answering the question 'What is to be the area of authority?' rather than 'Who governs me?' If the area of authority is circumscribed then the two spheres — an inviolable one and an intervention-prone one — are preserved.

It has been difficult for subsequent theorists to escape the terms of debate laid down by Berlin even when they have wished to do so. Two notable examples are Pennock 1979 and Rawls 1972.

Pennock asserts that he has avoided making the negative/positive distinction central to his discussion (Pennock 1979: 34), but in fact he embraces a concept of liberty close to Berlin's favoured negative one. In its verbal formulation it may not seem so: 'liberty is the opportunity for spontaneous and deliberate self-direction in the formation and accomplishment of one's purposes' (*ibid.*: 28). This may seem much closer to the positive conception. But, as Pennock himself points out, everything turns on how we interpret the notion of *opportunity;* and he makes clear that his own preference is for a strict interpretation, according to which 'opportunity means the absence of external control by means of threats, physical impediments, or moral or legal obligations' (*ibid.*). I may, then, be prevented from performing certain actions by force of circumstances of some *other* kind — the nature of the social structure in which I live, perhaps — and since on Pennock's interpretation this is not in the required sense absence of opportunity it is not absence of liberty either. As with Berlin, the favoured sense of liberty is logically tied to absence of interference from other individual human beings (*ibid.*: 24-5); and there is the same insistence on keeping a distinction between disablement through lack of liberty and disablement from other causes such as poverty (*ibid.*: 25-6).

Rawls hopes to bypass the dispute whether liberty should be defined negatively or positively, since he believes that the debate is mostly concerned not with definitions at all but with the relative value of different liberties (Rawls 1972: 201). I am not convinced that these two questions are entirely separate, but in any case on the substantive question Rawls holds a view close to Berlin's. He, too, declines to count poverty or a lack of means generally among the constraints definitive of liberty: they affect the *worth* of liberty, its value to an individual, but do not determine whether that individual has liberty (*ibid.*: 204). This duplicates Berlin's distinction between liberty and the conditions of its exercise (Berlin 1969: liii), and the division is further echoed in Rawls's two principles of justice and his explicit subscription to the two spheres view.

The two principles are, roughly, that everyone is to enjoy the most extensive liberty compatible with equal liberty for others, and that material inequalities must work to everyone's advantage (Rawls 1972: 60). But the first principle takes precedence over the second, in that a departure from the specified distribution of liberty cannot be justified by reference to the material advantages it might bring (*ibid.*: 61). As Rawls emphasises, the formulation of these principles (and the conception of liberty informing them) presupposes a division of the social structure into two parts: the realm of citizenship where liberty is inviolable, and for Rawls equal, and the realm of social and economic relations, where considerable inequality may prevail (*ibid.*). We have here, then, not just a postulation of two spheres but an indication of the nature of the inviolable sphere: it concerns individuals' existence and activities as *citizens,* and is therefore an essentially political sphere.

Talk of freedom, without further qualification, may be acceptable for purposes of political sloganeering, but in the context of a philosophical discussion it is essential to recognise the incompleteness of the notion. Freedom is always freedom *from* some constraint or other and freedom *to do or be* something or other (cf. MacCallum 1967: 176). We shall then see that, although we may unthinkingly applaud the slogan that freedom is a good thing and infringement of freedom a bad thing, this is not always so. No one ought to be free from all constraints on doing whatever they like — to rape, maim and kill, for example. If we are therefore to be able to explain why freedom is desirable *where it is,* we need a theory which addresses itself to the necessary qualifications. This the two spheres view implicitly does.

Primarily the view supports the desirability of *civil* liberties, for the accompaniments of paradigmatically civic activities, such as freedom of speech, assembly and association, liberty of thought and conscience (cf. Pennock 1979: 33; Rawls 1972: 61). The chief constraint which it argues such liberties should be free from is, as we have seen, intervention by other individual human beings, and the absence of this kind of constraint is to be ensured by formal, political or legal provision. The role of the state is to keep the protected sphere protected. Because life is divided into two spheres, however, it is important to notice that not all obstacles to, say, the freedom to speak one's mind are to be legislated against. The economic and social sphere looks after itself, and that is the point of the earlier distinction between liberty and the conditions of liberty. The sphere of citizenship makes formal provision for my freedom to speak my mind, but penury in the economic and social sphere may prevent me from taking advantage of that provision in any significant way.

Why should freedom for these purposes and from these constraints be singled out in this way? There are at least three reasons which might be advanced. First, the civil liberties are so basic, they are the key to so many other liberties, that unless they are secured others will be lost (cf. Pennock 1979: 133-4). Secondly, it might be argued that generally speaking the enjoyment of those liberties does not harm others or prevent them from enjoying similar liberties, and hence these liberties can be widely and equally spread in the manner required by Rawls. This argument I return to. But thirdly and most basically, they connect in a special way with rationality. If we believe it is important that people have control of their own lives, that they formulate and realise life-plans in accordance with their own conceptions and decisions, then we must believe that they (we) are at least in principle capable of doing so sensibly and not in an irremediably stupid and self-defeating way. Whatever obstacles we may believe stand in the way in particular circumstances, or even as an abiding part of the make-up of human beings, it would be difficult to relinquish the idea of human beings trying to think their way through to reasoned decisions without relinquishing the importance attached to liberty at the same time. But then it is an essential aspect of reasoning in this way that we should be prepared to reconsider our initial judgments, be guided by the weight of argument and generally open up our views to criticism. Hence the importance of the freedom to express views, criticise those of others, associate with them, and so on.

This helps to explain why liberty should be thought to be of value, by relating it to our capacity to be rational, self-governing agents, and it helps to explain why the civil liberties should be thought to occupy a central position. It also brings us back to democracy. The grounding for a system in which the people as a whole rule is the conception of people as, precisely, autonomous or self-ruling rational agents. But of course it would be pointless making a fetish out of that system, as against others, if the people ruled, in the sense of making for themselves the decisions which governed their lives, but did so in circumstances where they did not enjoy the appropriate conditions for rational decision. Hence what this grounding supports is a form of democracy which also involves the range of liberties required for that purpose.

The introduction of civil liberties into the concept of democracy, and their connexion with the rational capacity in human nature, seems to me a point of immense importance. What we have is an embryonic model of decision-making and conducting human affairs which replaces brute force with the force of rational argument and judgment, and gains its authority from a consideration of the kind of creatures we are.

No doubt it stands in need of much development, as well as defence against criticism that it ignores other elements in our nature, and no doubt there is room for a good deal of argument about how closely different, actually existing systems approximate to the model. We shall also see in chapters 5 and 6 that this idea of the rational, autonomous agent raises its own problems. Nevertheless, the model has much to recommend it. In historical terms a relative newcomer, its fragile existence has been threatened by modish opponents of liberal democracy, and it deserves protection.

It is perhaps worth noting that although Berlin sponsors the preservation of two spheres, and negative liberty within the protected sphere, he himself sees no particular connexion between negative liberty and democracy. An individual, he argues, may have more negative liberty under an easy-going despot than in an intolerant democracy (Berlin 1969: lvii). Echoing John Stuart Mill's fears of the tyranny of the majority, he suggests that the sovereignty of the people could easily destroy that of individuals, since democracy involves no logical commitment to the inviolability of a minimal individual liberty, no logical commitment to 'some frontiers of freedom which nobody should be permitted to cross' (*ibid.*: 163-5).

Two points can be made in reply to this. First, the grounding of democracy in the rational exercise of freedom enables us to stand Berlin's argument on its head. Where democracy is identified as majority rule, as it is by Berlin, a commitment to democracy is a commitment to the sovereignty of the people *in the appropriate conditions,* and these will not include a situation where individuals' rational autonomy is not respected. Whether majority decision-making is allowed as legitimate within certain limits or not, such limits would certainly be overstepped in cases which could fairly be described as the majority's *tyrannising* individuals. That may occur in a regime which calls itself democratic, but it is not a democratic occurrence. Secondly, as Berlin recognises, his problem arises where 'democratic self-government is not the government "of each by himself" but, at best, of "each by the rest"' (*ibid.*: 163). There is at least in principle the third possibility of government of all by *themselves*. Any elaboration of that possibility would rely on making progress with the idea of government by consensus, but if that could be achieved then it would be plain that Berlin's remarks concern democracy under a particular construction, namely as majority rule, rather than democracy as such.

Some problems remain for the two spheres view. I mentioned the argument that the exercise of civil liberties does not harm others, as a possible ground for placing them in the inviolable sphere. This is an echo of J.S. Mill's more general argument in the *Essay on Liberty* that in all their 'self-regarding' behaviour, that which does not affect others, individuals are sovereign. The notorious difficulty with Mill's argument is that above a very low level of triviality there is no form of behaviour which of its nature is such that it cannot harm others. This then makes it almost impossible to specify in advance the areas where interference in individuals' lives would infringe the proposed criterion for permitted intervention. A similar problem attends the argument about civil liberties. On any reasonable construction of 'harm', the exercise of freedom of speech, for example, can cause harm to others; and in general, although we can pick out the area in which people exercise civil liberties and designate it as inviolable, there is no reason to believe that it will fall wholly within the larger area where people are engaging in conduct not harmful to others.

If that is correct, we should be left with a choice. We could either insist that the retention of the inviolable sphere is so important that, if necessary, this must be done at the expense of harm which might otherwise be avoided; or we could effectively abandon the two spheres view as expressed hitherto and concede that it is not possible to designate particular areas, such as civil liberties, as falling within the inviolable sphere. Neither of these courses is obviously in error. Taking the first of them is one way of emphasising the distance between a standpoint which judges procedures purely in terms of their outcome and a standpoint which places constraints on how a given outcome is to be achieved. Already in chapter 2, section 3 we encountered an example of the latter standpoint, in the view that maximising someone's interests may need to be tempered because some ways of treating people are objectionable, even if calculated to bring about that end. In the present context a similar position is available with regard to the avoidance of harm. It may be held that that aim is a reasonable one, but not necessarily an overriding one. Sometimes, the infliction of avoidable harm may be the price which has to be paid for protecting something else legitimately held to be of value. Once again, freedom of speech is an apposite example. Someone committed to a strong principle concerning the inviolability of this freedom must recognise that the commitment has a price, and this will include unsavoury results which would otherwise not obtain. But it is by no means a crushing objection to this part of the two spheres view simply to point out that it has a cost attached to it.

Moreover, there is one area, of particular relevance to the question of democracy, where it may be felt that a preparedness to countenance harm rather than abandon the inviolable sphere is a positive strength. This is the case of *self*-harm, connected with the paternalism alluded to briefly in chapter 2, section 3. Intervention in people's lives against their express wishes is sometimes justified on the grounds that it is for their own good. Such intervention occasions repugnance, however, and even where it is true that someone so interfered with will themselves benefit, there would be widespread assent to the rejoinder that this is an insufficient defence for forced intervention. Widespread assent on its own is no argument, but the two spheres view, in stressing our nature as rational, self-governing agents, begins to indicate where the requisite argument might be found. In normal circumstances, to subject someone to forced interference is to offer them a very profound insult, since it involves treating them as passive creatures and implicitly ignoring the fact that they have a capacity for reaching their own decisions about what states to be in.

There is, of course, a problem about what constitutes 'normal circumstances'. For although there is a general repugnance for paternalism, it is difficult to sustain the view that *all* paternalistic intervention is unjustified. We have spoken of our *capacity* to act as rational, self-governing agents, but a moment's reflection is enough to make it plain that this is not how we always do act. Opinions will vary on the range of cases where the general embargo on paternalism should lapse, from the case where someone is in a temporary state of depression and wishes to commit suicide, to one where they wish to start taking heroin, to the hypothetical case of someone who wishes to sign a contract selling themselves into slavery. The argument available for making such exceptions has interesting implications for democratic theory. It is plausible to say that the exercise of autonomy cannot simply be identified with acting in accordance with one's wish at a particular moment, and must at least be the expression of considered judgment. Intervention in some or all of the cases mentioned may then be justified precisely by reference to the restoration or development of autonomy, in this richer sense, which may follow.

This line of argument reinforces the idea that the repugnance towards paternalism has another source than any question of consequential harm, and that justifications for occasional breach of a general embargo on paternalistic intervention may similarly rest on the overall importance attached to respecting autonomy, rather than on any consequences quite separate from this. But the argument has obvious dangers of its own, very similar to those which Berlin discerned in the concept of positive liberty. The natural form for it to take, in one of the exceptional cases where it is felt that paternalism is justified, is that although one is imposing a state of affairs contrary to an individual's wishes, he or she *would* not object to that state of affairs *if* they were acting and choosing rationally, and that the imposition of that state of affairs will significantly increase the likelihood of their being able to act rationally in the future. This is a reasonable form for the argument to take, and it makes plain that concern for rational autonomy is not being displaced by something else. But there is clearly scope for abuse in the *application* of such an argument, by virtue of the fact that it necessarily involves discounting the individual's present choices and speculating on the truth of contrary-to-fact conditional claims. As we shall see in Part Two, awkward questions can be raised, such as *whose* judgments of this kind are to be trusted most, and these need to be dealt with, to allay the fear that in practice this defence of paternalistic intervention may be used as a pretext for rather more thoroughgoing interference in people's lives, for their own good, than a genuine subscription to autonomy would allow.

The second way of responding to the objection that insisting on an inviolable sphere allows harm to result was, I suggested, effectively to abandon the two spheres view, to give up the insistence that areas could be marked out as sacrosanct in advance, without answering the detailed empirical question whether allowing, say, freedom of speech in *this* context will result in harm or not. But there are variants of this second response which do not entail such a clear capitulation. So far we have assumed a stark choice between allowing preservation of autonomy to prevail over infliction of harm and vice versa. But there are other alternatives. We could hold, for example, that autonomy is sufficiently important that, of itself, the mere fact that its preservation may produce a certain amount of harm is not a good enough reason for curtailing it, but yet that if the harm is very great or very widespread then under those conditions curtailment *would* be justified. In other words, we cease to regard autonomy as *absolutely* sacrosanct but insist that specially important considerations must be called upon in order to defeat its claims.

It is difficult to comment on the likely success of this response without developing further the conception of autonomy under discussion; but when that is done, it begins to look less clear that it is in fact a suitable grounding for the two spheres view after all. That, at least, is the argument to examine in the next section.

3 THE INTEGRATED VIEW

It is striking that adherents to what I called the two spheres view should have recourse to ideas of autonomy in explaining their conception of liberty. 'At issue when freedom is being discussed', says Pennock, 'is individual autonomy, self-rule' (Pennock 1979: 33). Berlin argues that 'if the essence of men is that they are autonomous beings . . . then nothing is worse than to treat them as if they were not autonomous, but natural objects' (Berlin 1969: 136). He further suggests that 'to manipulate men, to propel them towards goals which you —

the social reformer — see, but they may not, is to deny their human essence, to treat them as objects without wills of their own, and therefore to degrade them' (*ibid.*: 137). These thoughts are remarkably close to the idea of positive liberty described at the beginning of the previous section. The *integrated* view of liberty suggests that in fact the negative/positive dichotomy is a false one, since liberty as freedom from interference and liberty as self-rule cannot be kept apart in the required way. Generally, a much richer conception of liberty needs to be developed, which extends far beyond mere legal provision for the absence of humanly imposed obstacles and includes the idea of the provision of all means required for liberty to be enjoyed in a given context — wealth, opportunity, knowledge or whatever it might be. As with the two spheres view, the name and precise characterisation of the integrated view are my responsibility, but elements of the view which I elaborate can be discerned in Macpherson 1973: 95-116; Keat 1982: 66-70; Norman 1982: 92-6; and Skillen 1982: 153-9.

One likely reaction to this suggestion for a richer conception of liberty is to object that it confuses substantive and definitional questions. This, as I noted earlier, is the line taken by Rawls in an attempt to sidestep the positive/negative debate (Rawls 1972: 201-2). Pennock argues similarly that people may dispute about how exactly to extend the agreed core meaning of liberty, when some take the view that a proposed extension would simply be better considered under some other heading than liberty (Pennock 1979: 132 n.5). But the integrated view need not be regarded simply as a rival conception of liberty. The point is recognised that we have options over which phenomena we group together and apply a label to, that the cake can be cut in different ways; but it is not arbitrary which option is chosen. We have purposes and interests in constructing different conceptions, and the grouping together of given phenomena should be governed by the nature of those purposes and interests. The integrated view can then be sponsored as a preferred alternative on the grounds that the two spheres view is deficient *in the light of the purpose which its own proponents wish their proposed conception to serve.* The criticism is not external, but grows from assumptions made in the two spheres view itself. Both theories, therefore, begin from the same place, the need for a conception of liberty which reflects the importance of human autonomy, but it can be claimed that the integrated view reaches the right destination. I shall begin by constructing the argument against the two spheres view and seeing how this leads on to the proposed alternative.

We saw earlier that liberty is always, at least implicitly, liberty *from* something or other and liberty *to* do or be something or other. The two spheres view of the former is the object of criticism by the integrated view, but the latter need not be. The range of civil liberties, as we saw, is given special importance by the two spheres view and this is underpinned by relating them to our nature as autonomous agents. To the extent that the relation is a strong one this will be acceptable on the integrated view; but it will be held that the range of constraints on liberty, what we are free *from,* is too narrowly drawn in the two spheres view. Why should this be so?

In some moods, adherents of the two spheres view confine the notion of constraints to deliberate human intervention (cf. Berlin 1969: 122; Pennock 1979: 24-5). But this, surely, *is* too narrow? Whether I lock you in a room deliberately or accidentally I have equally deprived you of the freedom to leave it. Pennock resists this way of talking, chiefly on bad grounds connected with ordinary language philosophy (cf. Graham 1985: 23-7). On the other hand, Berlin, inconsistently with his initial position, concedes the point that absence of freedom may be due to the intended *or unintended* operation of human agencies Berlin 1969: xl). And it is in any event this, the action of individual human beings, which figures as the paradigm constraint.

But we must recall the paradigm of autonomous decision-making which lies behind this formulation of the concept, and ask whether it is not arbitrary to confine constraints in this way. We have the picture of individuals conceiving plans, goals and objectives and acting to realise them in accordance with their own formulated intentions. But that process can be interrupted or curtailed or altogether pre-empted by factors which are in the first instance quite distinct from individual action by other human beings. A lack of material means, or other wider social or institutional arrangements, may prevent me from acting in accordance with a chosen plan just as much as what some immediately specifiable person does to me. Of course, it may be that these wider arrangements are always in the last analysis a complicated matter of individuals behaving in certain ways, that force of circumstance is always reducible to the actions of forcing human beings (cf. Cohen 1983: 4-7). But that, if anything, strengthens the argument against the two spheres view. If the point in forming its conception of liberty is to reflect the idea of my making my own autonomous decisions and acting according to my chosen rational plan, then there is as much reason to include these other factors in the definitional constraints on liberty as there is to include interference by specific human beings.

Berlin had argued, justifiably, against a definition of liberty as the ability to do what one wishes, on the grounds that in that case liberty would be enhanced simply by contracting or eliminating one's wishes. But parallel considerations indicate what is wrong with a definition of liberty as being left alone to do what one is able to. The scope of what one is able to do may be, for reasons not directly to do with interference by others, very impoverished indeed. In that case, it will be a mockery of freedom to say that you are at liberty because no one prevents you from doing those few things within your repertoire. Or to put the point less dramatically and more definitely in the terms of the present argument, the concept of autonomy will extend into the area of an agent's abilities, and their curtailment by factors other than the agent's own rational decisions will itself count as an absence of freedom. In short, if the point of the concept of liberty is to reflect the capacity of autonomous agents to achieve rationally conceived goals, then it will not do to define liberty as being left alone.

How, then, *are* we to define liberty? The integrated view will define it as the absence of constraints, of whatever kind, on rational action, and it will recognise that associated with this ideal it will be necessary to speak of degrees of liberty, since constraints can be of varying degrees of severity as well as being of different kinds. In this way it will become possible to speak of legal, economic, moral liberty, and so on, without supposing that the range of constraints implicit under each of these heads is the range which is exclusively definitive of liberty as such.

This view integrates in a number of different ways. Most clearly and obviously, it integrates the different types of obstacle which may stand in an agent's way: lack of money, oppressive laws, the threat of an assassin's bullet, or the nature of the social system, may each count as an obstacle to my embarking on some course of action. Though it is possible to discriminate between these various factors, they are assimilated to the extent that it is held that any one of them can result in my being unable to do something; and the idea that an agent is unable to do something carries one straightforward sense, whatever may be the difference or multiplicity of reasons which explain *why* the agent is unable to (cf. Graham 1977: 250-62). Accordingly, the presence of any such obstacle will be sufficient, on this conception of freedom, to render me unfree.

Next, in one way the view integrates the civil liberties with other liberties. As I have said, it can continue to regard the liberties of speech, assembly, association, conscience and the like as special because specially connected with rational agency; but unlike the two spheres view it will not regard those liberties as having been secured merely by the existence of legal provision for them. It can continue to regard legal provision as something of great importance: it is, after all, a very public and effective deterrent, generally speaking, against other individuals who might deprive me of such liberties, and their interference is one potential source of unfreedom. But it is not the only one. If, say, my economic circumstances prevent me from acting in accordance with my conscience then that is just as much a deprivation of freedom and a denial of rational autonomy.

Consider the implications of this. The projects which a rational agent might conceive will all, with the exception of suicide, involve material prerequisites the absence of which will constitute an obstacle to the fulfilment of the project in question. This follows from the fact that staying alive is a precondition of fulfilling any more specific project, and for a material creature a number of material needs must be intermittently satisfied to ensure survival. In consequence, access to the material means of life is a standing necessary condition for a rational agent to have any significant degree of freedom to bring chosen projects to fruition. But, generally speaking, the provision of these means of life is a relatively complicated business in our society, calling on the effort and co-operation of large numbers of people. It follows that the potential interferences with my rational plans are very wide and very diverse in nature. In consequence the two spheres themselves become integrated. The division of life into the civic and the social/economic sphere is perfectly possible, but it now loses its rationale in the context of forming a conception of liberty. For the very notion of autonomy which lay at the base of the two spheres view in fact, on further examination, points to the interpenetration of the two areas.

How acceptable is the integrated view? One fear it is likely to provoke is that it integrates so much that it becomes completely all-absorbing. If not only personal interference and material conditions but *any* obstacle is to count as diminishing my freedom to some extent, then it begins to look as though I shall never be entirely free to do anything. Even the law of gravity will curtail my freedom to do things I might otherwise be able to do.

But this may actually be a virtue of the integrated view. It forces us to keep in mind the incompleteness, previously remarked on, of the concept of freedom. There are many things the freedom to do which it is not worth discussing since they are things no rational agent would aspire to (defiance of the law of gravity, for example), and there are many obstacles to liberty which are not worth discussing because they are in a strong sense irremovable. But in the breadth of its considerations the integrated view calls attention to the distinction between *lack* of freedom and *deprivation* of freedom by immediately identifiable human agency: having my capacity to act in a certain way curtailed by deliberate human intervention is one guise that curtailment may take, but not the only one. Consequently, it is only in some cases of unfreedom that it is appropriate to designate specific human agencies as responsible, and raise the issue of blame; in other cases we shall have to look elsewhere, and raise other kinds of question, if we are concerned to remove constraints on action.

A more serious difficulty is whether the view can make sufficiently precise sense of the notion of a *constraint* on rational action. It is an essential feature of rationality to be open to persuasion, and somehow the idea of legitimate persuasion has to be kept distinct from various coercive forms of intervention. At the practical level there will certainly be difficulties in identifying a given influence as being of one kind or the other, especially when there is a background of unequal power relations: X made a suggestion to Y which it would be rational to adopt, but did Y in fact adopt it because it would be rational, or because X is the boss/teacher/spouse? Alternatively, consider the case where individuals internalise rules which originated outside themselves but now influence them to act in a certain way. Does this count as a constraint on rational action or not? The theoretical problem is to deal with such questions in a way which does not rely on any circular move, such as defining constraints as influences which are, simply, non-rational. That would be true but entirely uninformative for the purposes of *identifying* an influence as a constraint.

A similar problem arises in a case involving more people. It seems acceptable not only to attempt genuinely rational persuasion by way of influencing someone but also simply to avoid their company if one feels that one's rational persuasion has not been heeded. That hardly looks like an illegitimate influence. Yet suppose that a large number of people embark on the same course of action *vis-à-vis* the individual. Then it looks far less obvious that no coercive constraint is involved: one can imagine considerable damage resulting from such avoidance, for example. Why should mere numbers make any difference to the case? It may be that they do not. It may be, for example, that something changes when what we are confronted with is a corporate action rather than simply a number of individuals acting in a given way. The ramifications of such a possibility will occupy us in chapter 6.

Generally speaking, it looks as though the attempt to give a fuller characterisation of liberty on the integrated view will bring back into the centre of the picture a number of questions to do with relations between the individual and the collective, and it is not clear whether the integrated view as I have described it would be an adequate theoretical standpoint from which to cope with them. It shares with the two spheres view an orientation which focuses almost exclusively on individuals rather than collectives, though it differs from it in giving greater emphasis to the interrelation *between* individuals. I shall argue later that more than this needs to be done by way of recognising the reality of collectives as well as individuals, and the existence of corporate actions will be pertinent in that regard.

4 CONCLUSION

Both views of liberty which we have examined enable us to make progress with the question of the grounds of democracy. By drawing out some of the implications of what it is to be a human being they are able to display the considerations in virtue of which repugnance attaches to the idea of human beings being ruled over, instead of ruling themselves. Since both ground liberty in the concept of autonomy they stand in the tradition stemming from Rousseau and Kant, according to which freedom consists in obedience to rules one has framed for oneself. We have principally been concerned to examine the idea of freedom itself rather than coming to any conclusion about the appropriate *extent* of freedom, though the incompleteness of the notion which we have noticed makes it clear that the question cannot be avoided. In the next chapter we shall look at claims for equality, which might be invoked to answer such a question. But we have already also seen some of the complications in the idea of liberty which will bedevil any theory as to its appropriate distribution: the impinging of one human will on another, which raises questions of the form of social organisation in the first place, and the ubiquitous possibility of conflict raise difficulties here. Indeed, as I shall argue in chapter 5, there are interpretations of the doctrine of autonomy which threaten to undermine, rather than support, the argument for democracy.

Perhaps the most significant part of the present discussion, however, is the point made in the integrated view that many different kinds of condition may affect our degree of liberty. If this is accepted, as I believe it should be, then it not only works against the two spheres view of liberty: it also works against what one might call a two spheres view of democracy. This would be the view that questions of democracy are to be confined to, so to speak, the official political sphere, the province of government, and that all else is a separate matter. If the grounds for supporting democratic arrangements are to secure a high degree of liberty to pursue rationally chosen aims, and if constraints on such freedom arise not merely in the overtly political sphere but from elsewhere — from other institutions such as large corporations or trade unions, for example — then there is the same argument for democratisation in these other areas.

FURTHER READING

The most influential text in bringing discussion of rights back into political philosophy is Dworkin 1978. Classical considerations of the principles enunciated by Mill in the *Essay on Liberty* are Hart 1963 and Devlin 1965. The issues are more recently discussed in Ten 1980 and Gray 1983a. Dworkin 1971 and Hodson 1977 address the problem of paternalism. The special nature of freedom of speech as a civil liberty receives attention in Scanlon 1972 and Skillen 1982.

4 The grounds of democracy: equality

1 INTRODUCTION

In the previous chapter we saw liberty as a component in a conception of democracy which explains the value of democratic decision-making by relating it to the nature of human beings. If human beings are, actually or potentially, rational autonomous agents, then liberty is of crucial importance in enabling them to act according to their nature. We also saw sufficient of the complexities in the idea of liberty to recognise that the question of its legitimate extent remains. Easy slogans, such as that liberty is always to be secured, or even that it is to be maximised, raise more questions than they settle. We saw the need to recognise that the liberty to embark on such-and-such a course in such-and-such circumstances may be outweighed by some other moral value, such as the harm resulting from that exercise of liberty, or the infringement of someone else's liberty. In consequence, the maximisation of liberty, if it is to be morally defensible, will itself be subject to certain limits.

Equality enters in very naturally at this point, as a factor to determine what the appropriate limits should be. Thus, in one influential theory of justice, Rawls's, his first principle of justice, which provides for liberty, takes precedence over the second principle, which allows material inequalities only where these work to everyone's advantage. And the extent of that liberty is the greatest which is compatible with the same for everyone: 'Each person is to have an equal right to the most extensive total system of equal basic liberties compatible with a similar system of liberty for all' (Rawls 1972: 302). The idea is attractive that since liberty is so important to a person, and since it is so important to *all* persons simply by virtue of their being persons, it should be fostered for all equally.

That is one point of entry for the idea of equality — specifically in connexion with liberty. But equality also has independent weight in democratic theory, and it is standard to include both liberty and equality in definitions of democracy. Indeed, the most familiar democratic voting procedure itself embodies one kind of equality. Each member of the body of decision-makers has one vote, and in that sense influence over decisions taken is equally distributed.

The focus for discussion in this chapter is specifically *political* equality. In political philosophy there are many difficult questions concerning equality in general, and the advisability or otherwise of equal distribution of various kinds of goods. These questions I do not address, except in so far as it is necessary to do so because of their connexion with political equality. That connexion is, as we shall see, a significant one; but the wider questions require, in their own right, far more consideration than I can give them here. There will in any case be a presumption in favour of specifically political equality in any conception of democracy, and it is the argument surrounding that commitment which I wish to explore. Among the issues to be considered are the conditions for initial political equality amongst the participants in a democratic decision-making procedure; the extent to which such equality can be sustained at subsequent stages in the procedure; how far we can make sense of the idea of full political equality; how far it is desirable; and (as in the case of liberty in the previous chapter) what the grounds are on which political equality is valued, to the extent that it is.

2 FORMAL AND SUBSTANTIVE EQUALITY

At first sight, it may be felt that the voting procedure mentioned in the previous section is itself an adequate embodiment of political equality as contained in the notion of democracy. If decisions are taken by reference to votes, and if each person has one vote, then that appears to accord equal influence over the outcome. Certainly it is true that this procedure possesses certain formal features of an appropriate kind: it is indifferent to the identity of proposers or supporters of any particular measure which might be proposed, and neutral as regards the nature of the proposals themselves. A moment's reflection, however, will reveal that contingent circumstances may conspire to thwart this projected equality. Thus, in existing systems where voters are electing representatives, examples of gross inequality between the power of different votes occur, either because of disparities in constituency size or because of the anomalies produced in a first-past-the-post system. There was, for instance, an occasion when one Californian State Senator represented six million electors and another one fourteen thousand electors (Potter 1981: 114); in February 1974 constituencies in England varied from 96,380 to 25,007 electors (Hansard Society Commission 1976: 7); and in the United Kingdom between 1945 and 1976 nine out of ten of the elected governments acquired more than 50 per cent of the seats, but none acquired 50 per cent of the votes cast (*ibid.*: 9). When the United States Supreme Court asserted that it had jurisdiction in the matter of huge disparities in the value of citizens' votes it did so, significantly, by referring to the Fourteenth Amendment, which guarantees equal protection of the laws.

Now it may be felt that these are merely matters of practical detail, which can be dealt with as such, in the interests of preserving equality of influence at the point of voting. Equalisation of electoral districts is something which can be taken seriously for that reason, and has been taken seriously in the United States. (We should note, however, that further practical difficulties may attend equalisation if it dictates the splitting up of 'natural' constituencies, or if vested political interests benefit from existing inequalities.) In the same spirit, if considerations of political equality require that the composition of an assembly of representatives should more closely mirror the composition of the popular vote, then it is possible to employ systems of proportional representation which facilitate this.

We should note that further problems may arise with this latter attempt to preserve equal influence. It is often maintained, against proportional representation, that its employment results in an absence of stability and strong, effective government. If that charge can be sustained (it is not completely clear that it can), then we may be confronted with a state of affairs where the promotion of political equality comes into conflict with the promotion of some other goal held to be of value, and judgments as to their relative importance may have to be made. There is also another intriguing possibility from the point of view of our own present discussion. Proportional representation is meant to correct the disproportionately weak influence of a minority. But where a minority party holds the balance between two closely matched major parties and is in a position to dictate terms to them, then the influence of the minority may become disproportionately strong rather than disproportionately weak. It is possible, therefore, that provision which is intended in general to ensure equality of influence may in particular circumstances result in a state of affairs inimical to equality itself.

Rather than pursue these points, however, I wish to turn to a more deeply-rooted problem concerning the role of a voting system — *any* voting system — in serving the end of political equality. Voting initiates the official decision-making procedure, as it were; in that sense it stands at the beginning of a process. But it may, and frequently does, stand at the *end* of a series of social processes which are themselves entirely permeated by substantial, material inequality, with consequences for the degree of political equality at the voting stage. For example, even though the value of my vote may be the same as the next person's, if that next person happened to be William Randolph Hearst or Rupert Murdoch, Ronald Reagan, Mikhail Gorbachov or Margaret Thatcher, then the influence I have over what millions of other electors end up voting for is nothing like equal to theirs, nor is my chance of being a candidate myself. Opportunities for influence or activity of this kind are very unequally distributed and vary with such factors as the amount of wealth at my disposal, the degree to which my own views reflect those of one of the powerful political parties in my society, or, if I am less fortunately placed, the degree to which they conform to the views of the only legally permitted party. Against the backcloth of inequalities of this order, the technical equality when we all come to vote can easily pale into insignificance.

Clearly there is an echo here of one of the central issues of the previous chapter. Just as a particular range of constraints on liberty is given special attention in the two spheres view, so it is possible to associate political equality with formal or legal provision of equal influence at the point of voting. And similar questions can be raised why, if political equality is thought important in the first place, it should be confined to a particular stage in the decision-making process, and why a more thoroughgoing provision should not in any case be made for its achievement at that particular stage. The question does not imply an extremist rejection of the importance of suffrage and the institutions surrounding it, but rather the suggestion that what underwrites the importance of these features of a democratic polity also requires much more. Dahl, for example, a theorist not noted for extremism, makes the point that power is greatly enhanced by many influences, including wealth and control over resources, and in the light of this observes that the social processes leading up to the process of voting 'may properly be spoken of as highly inegalitarian and undemocratic, although less so than in a dictatorship' (Dahl 1956: 66).

We should take seriously the mention of *many* influences on unequal power prior to the vote: sensible suggestions for the removal of such influences will vary according to what kind of influence is in question, and some, we may feel, are not illegitimate anyway. The influence of wealth, however, is a very clear and central case, and has been recognised as such at least since Rousseau, who suggested in *The Social Contract* that democracy required a large measure of equality in rank and fortune, without which equality of rights and authority could not long subsist. He would, perhaps, have been unsurprised by the contemporary example in which eleven out of fifteen senatorial candidates in the seven largest US states in 1970 were millionaires (Potter 1981: 127).

But if the fact of a causal connexion between wealth and unequal political power is obvious enough, it is not so obvious what remedies someone should adopt if they believe that political equality is too important to be disturbed by such an arbitrary contingency. The simplest proposal would be to attempt to secure political equality by requiring equality in wealth. But as a solution this would itself be productive of further problems. Many believe, for example, that the appropriate and reasonable basis for wealth distribution is something *other* than equality: need, achievement, merit or effort might all be offered as plausible bases. For anyone who carried such a commitment there would be the difficult choice of somehow making the principle of unequal wealth distribution and the principle of political equality compatible, or of abandoning their commitment to one or the other.

The first choice could be supported by the argument that it is not disparities in wealth as such which lead to political inequality but *gross* disparities, or the form of disparity which we see around us, so that mere inequalities designed to meet disparate needs, say, would not necessarily produce the same result. This could be supplemented by the idea that, where there are disparities in wealth which threaten to interfere with equal political effectiveness, neutralisation or compensation for the effects of wealth may be a more successful strategy than any attempted equalisation. In this spirit, the practice of requiring signatures in support of candidature would be preferred to the demand of a financial deposit, limits may be set on expenditure in connexion with election campaigns, and provision can be made for funds to be made available for campaign purposes.

Perhaps it would be possible in these and similar ways to ensure not merely a formal equality at the stage of voting but a more full-blooded equality, at least so far as the effects of wealth were concerned. But even if this were achieved, other factors would interfere with the goal of equal influence. It is likely, for example, that the outcome of particular decisions will be affected by force of personality, or by someone's superior cunning or rhetorical skills. A concern with equality not just in formal provision but also in substantive conditions dictates that these factors too be brought under control in some way, if that is feasible. What that may cause us to do is take more seriously the need for *education* for participation in democratic processes. Articulateness is obviously of central importance, and where people are put at a disadvantage at the very outset of the political process in that regard, then it is sensible to consider programmes to aid the less articulate, just as it will be sensible to consider educational measures which improve the extent to which political audiences decide questions on the balance of the argument, rather than for extraneous reasons.

So far we have considered the suggestion that the provision of a voting system which treats everyone equally at the point of voting may fall short of the requirements of political equality. It will depend on particular concrete circumstances what else must be done to ensure substantive, material equality in the political influence which everyone has at that point. Ensuring such material equality would be difficult enough in any case, but now we must countenance the possibility that in making all these adjustments we should simply be aiming for an unreal goal.

In a political context, voting for individuals is inseparable from a consideration of issues and policies. (We might vote for an individual on the grounds that he or she would be an effective political agent, able to achieve their aims, but this would be an irrational thing for us to do unless we thought, independently, that those aims were desirable, or wise, or in our interests, or in some way had something to be said in their favour.) But is equality a real possibility when it comes to consideration of different policies and proposals? John Rees argues that it is not. There are, he suggests, informal yet formidable pressures which restrict what is put on the agenda for serious political discussion (Rees 1971: 56). In Britain at the time when he was writing, for instance, he gives as non-starters in the prevailing political climate proposals for government control of the press, the abolition of divorce, a return to former severity in criminal punishment, massive reduction in the welfare services, restoration of royal power in government, and the legal enforcement of a strict sabbatarianism (*ibid.*: 57). If that is correct, then it seems pointless to make a great issue of materially equal initial conditions — equal access to the mass media, for example — when equal consideration is ruled out for other reasons. As Rees puts it, respect or derision will be accorded to the opinions which people express, and that is one reason why 'there is no equality of opportunity or equality of access for all opinions. And it is difficult to foresee a time when things will be otherwise' (*ibid.*: 57). Hence, although Rees believes that a liberal democrat should welcome, if it were practicable, the establishment of several television networks where different political opinions could compete on equal terms, he is unenthusiastic about the likelihood of a mass audience treating all such views impartially (*ibid.*: 54).

Now there are changes over time in the matter of what gets on to the political agenda for serious consideration, and some would wish to argue that several of the proposals ruled out by Rees in 1971 did in fact receive serious consideration in Britain, in the later 1970s, by successive Labour and Conservative governments. But Rees himself insists that we do not have to resign ourselves fatalistically to current beliefs about what is or is not on the political agenda, and his point is not defeated by changes in that agenda. For it will still remain true that at any given *point* in time the exponents of many views will fail to receive equal consideration, even if the identity of such exponents will change over a *period* of time. Hence the objection remains that the objective of initial equal consideration is unattainable.

This objection is plausible but should nevertheless be rejected. It rests on a misunderstanding of the requirements of substantive political equality at the stage of initial consideration of proposals. It is of the nature of a political proposal that it recommends the pursuit of some policy or other, and the same is true, in effect, of political candidates. The point of political proposals is, and their consideration leads to, action. The choice of a political policy necessarily leads to the exclusion of others and therefore unequal treatment of them, and it would be demanding the impossible — the logically impossible — that this be otherwise. But that, surely, is not what the requirement of political equality amounts to? What is demanded is an equal opportunity to present proposals (or oneself as a candidate), with the issue to be decided and the outcome determined *on its merits* rather than by extraneous considerations. In other words, whatever the advantages or drawbacks of speaking in general of an equal opportunity to become unequal, that is precisely what is in question here. The case where an option is excluded from consideration (or wide consideration) because its advocates do not have the resources to present it is quite different from the case where the option is so presented and is then laughed out of existence because it is idiotic. A supporter of political equality will deplore the first but not the second. In short, the result of compensating for the whole range of factors which militate against initial equality would be that, of course, there would still be a distinction between the reactions of respect and derision; but it would be interesting to observe how close the distribution of those reactions was to their present distribution.

3 LIMITS OF POLITICAL EQUALITY

It is necessary to find a place for political equality of some form in a developed conception of democracy. So far, I have argued that the identification of political equality with the formal provision of a voting procedure will not suffice (and we should recall that even on the issue of 'one person, one vote' it was possible for John Stuart Mill to argue that those who were more intelligent or better educated should have greater voting power than others). If voting is thought important by virtue of extending an equal influence to all, then this provides a reason for ensuring that other material arrangements serve the same end.

I have made this observation in connexion with the initial stages of the political process, but it will have as much validity in connexion with any later stages. Wherever political equality is important, there will be reason to create conditions conducive to its realisation. However, it is a separate question, and one we must consider now, what the extent or limits of political equality must be, beyond this initial stage, to satisfy the requirements of democracy. Here opinions vary considerably among theorists over what is possible or desirable, and how far any existing political systems match up to what is required.

Implicitly, the argument of the previous section constitutes a criticism of any existing arrangements where formal equality at the initial stage is nullified by the effects of, amongst others, social and economic inequality. But when it comes to the question of the appropriate limits of political equality, there is a particular onus on critics of existing arrangements. Criticism presupposes some workable conception of what it is that existing arrangements fail to secure. As Rees puts it, critics may be expected to outline some state of affairs which exhibits the proper and legitimate extent of political equality, or to provide some yardstick for making relative judgments about existing regimes and the varying degrees to which they fail or succeed in that respect (Rees 1971: 49-50). In the light of our own earlier discussion in chapter 1, section 1, I should argue that just pointing to particular states of affairs, whether existing or merely possible, will be of limited value. Of greater help will be an account of the rationale or principles behind setting the limits to political equality in a particular case.

In searching for such principles we might start from the one embodied in the slogan 'like cases alike': democratic practice demands that people be treated equally in the same circumstances, and it takes some reason, not merely an arbitrary difference, to justify departure from equal treatment. It is sometimes objected that this is an extremely feeble principle as it stands, on the grounds that there always are differences between cases, and unless it is further specified what differences are relevant to the issue the principle will license the most monstrously unequal treatment. Now it is certainly true that the distinction between an arbitrary difference and a difference which provides a reason will need to be spelt out, but the principle is not entirely vacuous, even as it stands. It is closely associated with the ideal of citizenship or membership of the community as conferring equal status, and it creates a certain onus in social dealings on those who wish to justify inequality. It can also combine with the formal/substantive argument of the previous section. If it is thought right and important that a given person should have the opportunity to propagate a set of political views, let us say, then a reason rather than merely an arbitrary difference must be found if it is not to be thought equally right and important that a second person should have the same opportunity. And a difference in antecedent financial circumstances can plausibly be regarded as a paradigm instance of an arbitrary difference rather than a reason.

This is to emphasise such strength as there is in the principle 'like cases alike'. On the other hand, its relative weakness can be brought out if we consider a recent formulation by Robert Dahl of a principle, closely related to it, which he thinks should govern the matter of inclusion in a democratic community. He suggests that no distribution of socially allocated entities (including actions and objects) is defensible 'if it violates the principle that the good or interest of each member is entitled to equal consideration' (Dahl 1979: 125). The point is, of course, that equal consideration is not the same as equal outcome or distribution, and the principle is therefore compatible with a resulting state of affairs where there is widespread inequality of distribution. Whether such inequality does in fact result will depend on whether there are good reasons for distinguishing between cases, or in other words on whether and where cases are *un*like. The issue turns, therefore, on a question which the 'like cases alike' principle does not itself answer, namely what counts as a good reason for treating cases differently.

In the theory of democracy, we are concerned with the distribution of power and with the departures from equality in its distribution. The commonsense view would be that, beyond the initial stages already discussed, severe limits must be placed on equal distribution, that wide divergence from it is not only permitted but unavoidable. The good reasons which would be cited for this have to do, simply, with the nature of modern society. Leaving aside any particular contestable empirical theories (to be examined in Part Two), it is just an undeniable fact that the society we live in is extremely large and extremely complex. One aspect of the problems which this creates is graphically brought home in an example of Dahl's, where he points out that if the chief executive officer of a city the size of New York gave over ten hours per day, every day of the year, to meeting citizens, allowing ten minutes per citizen, he would be able to meet three-tenths of 1 per cent of the population in a year; if, instead, the citizens attended in groups of 100, each for ten minutes, this would still rise to only 30 per cent of the population (Dahl 1970: 144). If we add to this the point that public officials have to take decisions on a whole range of issues, which require expertise in such diverse fields as science, technology, economics, medicine, and so on, then any glib thoughts about an equal distribution of power throughout the population at all stages ought to be held in check. Indeed, one of the most celebrated critics of the elitist conclusions to which these thoughts have sometimes led, has to confess that the exigencies of modern life are such that key political decisions in a democracy, as in totalitarian societies, must be made 'by a handful of men', and that participation in their making 'must remain extremely limited' (Bachrach 1967: 1, 95). All he insists is that 'each individual's judgment on the general direction and character of political policies is given equal weight with all others' (*ibid.*: 3).

At this point, therefore, it is natural to call on the theoretical resources provided by the distinction between direct and representative democracy, referred to briefly in chapter 1, section 2. Where it is not possible for each member of a community to exert influence throughout the decision-making process, let them all elect a small proportion of that body to take such decisions, as it were, under licence. Given the right conditions, such as that potential electees are supported on the basis of some general programme to which they commit themselves and that there are periodic re-elections, then the required influence on the general direction of policy is likely to be secured. The threat of subsequent dismissal will hold electees to the general lines of policy originally embraced. The link with equality is maintained, moreover, if all electors themselves continue to have an equal initial influence in the elections.

This system certainly secures only indirect influence over decisions. No doubt it is vastly preferable to no influence at all, but unless I can find a potential representative who shares all of my views on general lines of policy, then my influence — as compared with his or hers — has already become attenuated at the pre-election stage. This can, perhaps, be met to some extent by the provision of organisations where the general programmes are composed and to which I, as an elector, have access; and again this will be vastly preferable to a state of affairs where there are legal and other obstacles to forming such organisations. But, unless retribution for failure to comply with such programmes is swift and relatively frequent, then the influence I wield via the threat not to re-elect on a subsequent occasion will also be weak, as compared with the influence of an elected decision-maker.

A conception of democracy which is based on representation of the kind sketched, therefore, places very severe limits on political equality. That does not necessarily vitiate it, either as a conception of democracy or absolutely. For one thing, it makes a difference to the case if a populace itself opts for such a system: that will permit the *ad hominem* argument that *they,* at least, are in no position to complain of their unequal position. But we need to tread very carefully in deciding what implications for the limits of political equality follow from uncontroversial facts about the nature of modern society. We must certainly allow that the nature and volume of political decision-making is such that it would be quite impossible for everyone to be fully and equally involved at every stage. This fact on its own, however, should not panic us into concluding that the distribution of political power must necessarily be as unequal as that implied in the sketched representative system.

Consider what one might call the *committee analogy.* It is a familiar experience in many different kinds of body that at times decisions must be taken and tasks executed which it is not practical for the body as a whole to engage in. It is an equally familiar solution for the body to set up a committee or sub-committee, charged with doing what the whole body itself cannot do. This arrangement does not of itself entail that there are widely differing degrees of influence as between members of the whole body and members of the committee. That *may* result — if, for example, the whole body gives the committee *carte blanche* to take whatever decisions and actions the committee itself sees fit. But instead the body may issue some general instruction to its committee concerning how it is to discharge its duties, or provide it with a set of options to work from; it may reserve to itself the final approval of any actions which the committee decides to take; it may periodically review the decisions of its committee and retain powers to reverse or nullify them; and it may operate sanctions of varying degrees of severity, including removal, where it disagrees with its committee. This is enough to show that there is an entire range of theoretical alternatives between a body's total involvement at every stage of a decision-making process and the kind of representation described. It also shows that the degree of independence from the whole body can vary considerably, with corresponding variety in degrees of political inequality as between members of the whole body and members of the committee.

But do we really have an analogy here? That is, do these general facts about the relations which can obtain between a body and its committee have any relevance for the case of modern society? Do not the size and diffuseness of modern conditions of life precisely rule out many of the options which are available in a much more limited and specific context?

It is not possible to give a complete answer to these questions at this stage. That will depend on issues to be confronted in Part Two: what can be established with reasonable certainty about the psychology of members of modern political society, and the implications this has for their involvement in decision-making; what features of modern society must be taken as unalterable, standing conditions, rather than features of a particular stage in human history which may be superseded. It is preferable to explore the idea of political equality implicit in the concept of democracy on its own terms, before deciding how far and in what way that idea can best be exemplified in concrete circumstances.

But a sufficiently persistent critic might object that we do not need further evidence on these particular matters, before being able to conclude that very severe limits must be placed on political equality. That conclusion, it might be said, we already know to follow from the size and diffuseness of modern society and the concomitant need for division of labour and expertise. These, surely, are known and unalterable facts about our life?

Let us grant that division of labour and expertise are known and unalterable facts. This does not render the committee analogy entirely inapplicable, or lead straight to the political conclusion about the severe limit on equality of influence. Of course, it will then be true that a modern populace will have to defer to different kinds of experts when it is a matter of ascertaining the facts concerning which they have expertise. But in the political context it is necessary to distinguish between ends and means, or between acquaintance with data and decisions on the basis of the known data. For example, specialists can provide invaluable information on the risks involved in developing nuclear power, or on the possible use of scarce medical resources. But it is no part of their specific expertise to pronounce on whether it is worth taking a risk with nuclear power or on how to decide the allocation of the resources. At that point the benefit of their expertise for the purpose of making decisions has already been received; but it is only at that point that political decision-making proper begins.

The obvious move for our critic to make now is to argue that there is also distinctively political expertise, on a par with expertise in physics or medicine, and that we should defer to those who possess it when it is a matter of deciding which policies to pursue in the light of the facts. But this is a dangerous line for anyone who professes to be a democrat. As I shall attempt to show in the next chapter, it is deeply offensive to the liberal conception of moral agency, and that conception underpins much of the argumentation of the preceding chapters which has gone towards building up a rationale for the attractiveness of the concept of self-rule. To admit the idea of specifically political expertise in this way threatens to undermine the idea of democracy altogether.

Our critic might now say that it is so much the worse for the idea of democracy if it involves failure to recognise the facts. But by this stage it should be obvious that it has ceased to be plain and uncontroversial what the facts are. That there is such a thing as the kind of political expertise under discussion here — an expertise in working out what goals we should be pursuing, not just an expertise in telling us the best route to goals already specified — is not something we are forced to admit from a consideration merely of the nature of modern life. If that is so, then it remains worthwhile to develop ideas like those implicit in the committee analogy, as a means to increasing our understanding of the principles of democracy, and alternative conceptions of them, at a fairly abstract level.

The introduction of the committee analogy serves a further purpose. It reminds us that democracy is a property not just of society at large, but also of clubs, families, committees themselves and other similar bodies. We need, therefore, to develop a conception of democracy for these contexts too, where it is not at all obvious that direct influence needs to be departed from in such a way as to produce gross disparities in degrees of influence. Indeed, this may be the right direction from which to approach a conception appropriate for the larger context, even if it is allowed that there are many important differences between the two types of context. Plato wanted to get clear on justice in the individual by seeing it writ large in the state; perhaps we can get clearer on equality and democracy by first seeing them writ small.

This may also provide a means of supplying the yardstick of political equality sought by Rees. Anyone who wishes to subscribe to a high degree of political equality but feels that this is lacking in the wider society may be able to illustrate whatever principles they enunciate by reference to the smaller contexts where this can be achieved without interference from other factors. This is particularly apposite in the case of any organisation which is itself committed to a high degree of political equality, such as a political party. It might, for example, emphasise the importance of substantive equality by seeking locally to neutralise the distorting effects of wealth (it might refuse to accept money with any strings attached regarding its use, and make its own publicity facilities available equally to all members) and it would have the opportunity to sustain direct influence through later stages of any decision-making than those afforded in a large-scale representative system. In these ways, the principles espoused could actually be *exemplified* in a limited context.

If the arguments of this section are correct, the known and unalterable facts about the nature of modern life may well dictate that there has to be *some* limitation on equality of political influence, but they do not show what that limitation must be. In particular, they do not of themselves justify the structural and very considerable inequality implicit in the model of representative democracy as outlined. The option remains open, therefore, of tracing the limits on political equality which *normative* considerations would dictate, and only subsequently considering any further modification made necessary by pragmatic factors. In order to do this, we must broach a further question which we have not yet addressed. We must ask what is the source of approval of political equality in the first place.

4 THE GROUNDS OF POLITICAL EQUALITY

We recognised in the previous section that equal consideration is not the same as equal outcome or distribution. That is a point we shall return to, but first we must ask what is the source for a subscription to equal consideration in the first place. What is it about human beings that elicits approval of an even-handed approach in dealing with them? Notoriously, we are unequally endowed in attributes such as strength, wisdom, beauty and the like. Is there any significant respect in which we *are* equal, which might provide the required basis?

In an influential article Bernard Williams suggested as a starting point the fact of our common humanity (Williams 1962: 112). It is not a truism to state that all people are human if we then go on to specify the significant properties this includes, which are liable to be forgotten in actual social interaction. For Williams, these properties include the capacity to feel particular kinds of pain, the capacity to feel affection, and their various ramifications.

What follows from the fact that all people share this 'common humanity'? It is a familiar claim that this endows them with a certain dignity and entitles them to a certain kind of respect from others. But the terms employed in this familiar claim suffer from a kind of nebulousness. One advantage of Williams's discussion is that he translates this relatively vague idea into more accessible and concrete terms. He does so by linking the idea of *self*-respect to that of identifying with what one is doing, being able to realise purposes of one's own, and the idea of respect for others to that of seeing them as persons who *have* a number of social roles, labels and so on, rather than relating only to the roles themselves, of making a sympathetic attempt to identify with people *as* human beings (*ibid.*: 114-16).

Generally speaking, it is properties closely connected with the existence of human beings as *moral* beings which theorists single out as the appropriate grounds for respect. There are differences of emphasis and nuance, but that is the common thread. Thus, for Rawls the basis of equality is 'moral personality', which is identified as the capacity for having a rational plan of life and a conception of justice (Rawls 1972:

505); for Pennock, human beings alone possess certain qualities which enable them to be moral beings, they alone can 'develop rules of right conduct, and regulate their own behaviour to conform to them', and this is the basis for human dignity and at least a presumptive claim to equal treatment (Pennock 1979: 147); for Lukes, the capacity for autonomous choice and action, for engagement in valued activities requiring a private space and for self-development, provides the grounds on which respect is accorded to people (Lukes 1973: 133) and 'the principle that they should be respected as persons implies that they should be *equally* so respected' (*ibid.*: 126).

But now the question can be raised why these facts about the moral nature of human beings should be thought suitable for grounding claims about equality. After all, people possess moral qualities to different degrees — X may have greater integrity or firmness of moral purpose, for example, than Y — and on that basis I might accord them greater or lesser, rather than equal, respect. In short, the features being focused on here are features in which all people may be *alike;* but that is a qualitative claim, and it is compatible with it that, quantitatively, people should not be *equal* at all.

This observation seems to me to be correct: we have not here found any features in which all people are equal. But it does not follow that we have found no basis for equal treatment of them. It is possible to argue as Rawls does, for example, that although people may possess these capacities in varying degrees, they are very basic ones which virtually everyone possesses to *some* degree. But then provided that some fairly minimal threshold is reached this can itself provide the grounds for according them equal justice, equal liberty, or whatever (Rawls 1972: 506). More specifically in line with the political equality which is implicit in the concept of democracy, we might note Dworkin's gloss on Rawls's point, to the effect that individuals have a right to equal concern and respect in the design and administration of the political institutions governing them (Dworkin 1978: 180), and Lukes's stronger formulation, that citizens are denied respect to the extent that they do not have opportunities to participate in decisions which have a major effect on them (Lukes 1973: 135).

Suppose the case for equal respect can be made out along the lines discussed. We are then in a position to return to the earlier claim that equality in respect and consideration does not necessitate equality in outcome. Dworkin, for instance, argues that once a principle of equal concern and respect has been conceded, further argument must ensue about what particular political arrangements satisfy that principle — a system of equal opportunity for achieving differential status based on merit, a system of absolute equality in income and status, or whatever. And the view he expresses elsewhere in his argument is that, whereas the principle of equal concern and respect is fundamental, the right to an equal *outcome* in the distribution of some good obtains only where this is for some special reason derivable from the more fundamental right to equal consideration and respect (Dworkin 1978: 273).

Now when it comes to the distribution of political power then I believe that the idea of equal respect, and the grounds we have examined for that idea, point to a much stronger conclusion than this. Notice, first, that these grounds involve attention to both the passive and the active aspect of human beings. To talk of how people should be *treated* and of the need to give consideration is to treat them as recipients; to advert to their *moral* nature, their capacities for reasoning and action is to treat them, obviously, as agents. Now passive equality, equality of consideration, even in its strong form as equality of outcome, does not necessarily connect with democracy at all. An enlightened despot could be impressed with the facts about human beings we have surveyed, and arrange political institutions to conform to the requirements they imply. We must therefore recall that democratic theory is concerned with a particular distribution of power, one where the people *rule,* not just where they receive a certain kind of treatment. This is to invoke the active side of human nature, and it is this very basic idea in the concept of democracy which gives the cutting edge to the suggestion that an undesirable kind of inequality is occurring, from the point of view of democratic theory, if people are excluded from shaping the institutions which in turn shape their life.

If respect is due to people *as* moral agents, formulating conceptions of right behaviour and conforming to them, then it is due to them *in those activities*. And if we take the Rawlsian line that the possession of these features to some minimum standard calls for equal treatment, then it gives as much reason to insist on equal active participation, an equal amount of power in arranging the world. This is ignored if we talk at this point (as theorists frequently do) in terms of what a principle of equality requires by way of a government's treatment of its citizens. For to divide the population up at this stage into governors and recipients is to make a move which, on the grounds for equality which have been described, has no justification. It is to fail to give human beings equal power, though they have the acceptable minimum capacities.

Lest the point is misunderstood, it is perhaps important to stress that this move has no justification so far *on the grounds of equality*. It may have a justification from elsewhere. Thus we may follow Rawls in thinking that the tired metaphorical ship of state still has a few knots left to travel and argue that, just as the passengers of a ship are willing to let the captain steer because he is more knowledgeable than they, so if 'some men can be identified as having superior wisdom and judgment, others are willing to trust them and concede to their opinion a greater weight' (Rawls 1972: 233). More generally, we may feel that the decision of moral agents to create a situation in which they themselves became subject to inequality of power is something which would itself have to be respected. There are, in fact, more complications in that argument than at first appear, as I shall suggest in the next chapter. But for the moment my point is simply that the grounds cited for valuing political equality — the moral nature of human beings — do not of themselves carry any implication of the desirability of limiting equality of power. Whether the exigencies of life or considerations from elsewhere do so is another matter.

5 CONCLUSION

There are parallels between our discussion of equality and the earlier discussion of liberty. In the case of both of these values it is possible to construct a relatively restricted conception and to argue that liberty or equality so construed is secured by formal or legal enablement; and this is consistent with failure to foster the value when construed in some broader way, because of the intervention of different disabling factors, such as social and economic circumstances. In both cases I have suggested that a restricted conception of liberty or equality is not simply to be rejected, nor is legal enablement to be held in contempt as compared with complete absence of regard for it. But in both cases I have also suggested that a regard for the value, and the considerations which provide the grounds for that regard, indicates the appropriateness of a far more thoroughgoing commitment to its realisation. From the separate discussion of equality, therefore, we can draw reinforcement of a claim made earlier: as we begin to build up a conception of democracy which displays clearly the grounds for valuing a system where the people rule, so it becomes increasingly difficult to regard the conception as one relating merely to an explicit area of decision-making. Precisely because so many other aspects of social arrangements have an effect on the decision-making sphere it becomes necessary to consider how the conception can be enriched to reflect the features of a democratic *society*.

It may seem that we have got off to a poor start in that enterprise, especially in the later part of the present chapter, if the enriched conception has features so far removed from actuality. But that would be a premature reaction. We shall have to give more consideration in its own right to the question of the relation between theory and reality, but already at this stage we can give reason for not accepting the constraint implicit in this reaction. The conception of a community where power is equally distributed can serve as a standard against which to measure existing arrangements, rather than simply measuring one existing arrangement against another, even if it is not strictly realisable itself. That is one role, and an important one, which a conception in a pure theory of democracy can serve.

There is a further connexion between equality and liberty. In both cases we have traced the importance attached to them to facts about human nature, and the facts in question are not two distinct sets. The nature of human beings as reasoning agents is central to both. The claim is often made in relation to contemporary society that extensions of equality can be achieved only at the cost of restricting liberty, and vice versa. The common root for the importance attaching to the two values gives us some reason for doubting whether there is such a general head-on clash as is suggested here. That said, we shall in the next chapter have to confront a particular problem about the combination of liberty and equality in the context of the power to make social decisions. This will take us to the very heart of the liberal conception of democracy.

FURTHER READING

An excellent recent discussion of equality in the general distribution of goods, rather than political equality, is Dworkin 1981. See also Nagel 1979. Anti-egalitarian sentiments are available in Lucas 1965 and 1977. Alternative systems of proportional representation and their merits are assessed in Hansard Society Commission 1976, and a more partisan view is taken in Lakeman 1982. Pitkin 1967 discusses many varieties of representation, and Dunn 1979 grapples with the problems thrown up by division of labour and expertise. Norman 1982 challenges the conventional wisdom that liberty and equality are competing values.

5 Conflict and the individual

1 INTRODUCTION

So far we have traced the strongest case in favour of democracy to views about the nature of human beings: their status as autonomous, rational agents and their importance as individuals. There comes a point, however, at which an argument based on the nature of people as autonomous, rational agents seems to turn from a support of democracy into its opposite. The threat which is then posed to the acceptability of democracy is one which I believe cannot be fully met within the terms of reference of the liberal individualist views which the argument so far has presupposed. In the present chapter I shall set up the problem which individual autonomy poses for democracy; consider what may be thought to be fairly obvious solutions to it and attempt to show why they are unsatisfactory; and then suggest what I believe is at least a partially satisfactory solution.

The central problem in question is not a new one. Essentially it is one to which Rousseau thought the social contract provided a solution, namely to find a form of association which protects all individuals but yet in which they are still answerable only to themselves. In other words, is it possible to cope with the conflict of individual wills by setting up an authoritative body which still leaves each individual's autonomy intact? Whether the social contract, either in Rousseau's or in more recent versions, does provide a solution is something we shall have to consider. In fact, as we shall see, the problem has been posed in more recent times in forms which suggest that *nothing* could be a solution to it.

75

2 THE PROBLEM

Endemic in social existence is the possibility of conflict
between individuals, both at the level of judgments and at the
level of implementation of judgments in action. By extension,
the possibility is also endemic of a clash between the individual
and some collective entity responsible for making and
implementing decisions which impinge on that individual. This
will be just as true where the individual is a member of the
collective entity in question, and that is what provides the focus
for the problem to be investigated.

The strongest way of expressing the difficulty (a way which I
believe is far *too* strong) would be to assert that it involves a
paradox — 'a paradox in the very heart of democratic theory'
(Wollheim 1962: 79). This is held to come about in the
following way. Imagine an individual participating in a
democratic system, on an occasion when two mutually
exclusive options A and B have to be selected from. The
individual's own considered judgment is that

(1) A ought to be enacted.

Being committed, however, to the democratic procedure, the
individual also believes that

(2) The democratic choice ought to be enacted.

As it happens, on this occasion

(3) The democratic choice is B.

By a simple substitution in (2), it therefore seems to follow that
in this individual's view

(4) B ought to be enacted.

But if A and B are mutually exclusive, then

(5) B is not-A,

from which it follows by a further substitution, this time in (4),
that the individual is also committed to the view that

(6) Not-A ought to be enacted.

By virtue of the dual commitment to (1) and (6) the individual
apparently holds inconsistent, contradictory beliefs, and that
is the paradox.

The possibility here is a perfectly general one — it does not depend on the content of the policies A and B, nor on the mechanisms for arriving at the democratic choice. If there is a problem here at all, therefore, it will be a problem in both the social context and smaller contexts such as clubs and committees. It looks as though my commitment to a particular policy and my commitment to the principle of democracy compete, as it were, for my attention: to embrace both is to run the risk of ending up in contradiction. The only way to avoid this seems to be to make sure that I am always on the winning side — there is no problem in coming by two different routes to the conclusion that A ought to be enacted. But this, of course, is hardly a generalisable solution. *Someone* has to be on the losing side except in circumstances of unanimity, and so there will always be a problem for someone.

With a paradox like Zeno's, purporting to show that motion is impossible, it is clear that the argument will not affect our conduct; even if we cannot show what is wrong with the argument we are psychologically incapable of believing its conclusion. A belief in democracy, however, might be more easily dislodged than a belief in the possibility of motion, and that is why it is important actually to show what is wrong with an argument like this, rather than simply rejecting its conclusion. This will involve more than an impatient rejoinder that in practice a democrat will allow one commitment to override the other, for where contradictory beliefs have a bearing on action that *must* happen. But it does not of itself deal with the stigma of being caught in a contradiction in the first place.

I have argued elsewhere that the strict charge of contradiction can be rebutted (Graham 1976: 234-8), and I shall not repeat those arguments here. That charge concerns the logical relations of a set of propositions, and it is therefore open to utilise relatively technical logical considerations in its rebuttal. On that basis I have offered a number of alternative solutions which help to *explain* the commonsense reaction that we can simply allow one of these beliefs to take precedence over another. Even if we take that as established, however, a broader problem remains. Whether the two commitments are formally contradictory or not, they clearly pull in opposite directions, and that pull will have been experienced by many of us in circumstances where we are required to abide by (perhaps in local contexts even to implement) some decision which in our personal judgment is a mistaken one. We still need theoretical resources to enable us to deal with that dilemma, to show us when we should be pulled in one direction and when in the other, and *why*.

In this broader form the problem is well recognised by theorists. On the one hand, there is the obligation to abide by democratic decisions, which derives from the moral advantages of a democratic system, and the fact that an individual is a party to these decisions rather than their simply being imposed; on the other hand, there is the duty to one's own conscience, one's own bona fide and sincerely held views about how matters ought to be. The commonsense view, once again, would presumably be that the advantages of a democratic system are so great that one ought, up to a point, to accept democratic decisions even when one disagrees with them, but that nevertheless there may be issues of very strong principle where one must insist on retaining the right not to accept them. In that spirit, Dworkin points out that a very wide spectrum of opinion recognises a general duty to obey the laws which, nevertheless, must be tempered by the fact that one has a right to follow one's conscience, which may on occasion tell one that a law is immoral (Dworkin 1978: 186-7). If I have a right to follow my conscience, he argues, how can the state be justified in punishing me for doing so? Theories of conscientious objection and civil disobedience may then be developed, which attempt to delimit and justify the instances where refusal to comply with a law may be in order. Dworkin's own answer is that such a refusal is justified where a government has itself infringed an individual's rights (*ibid.*).

However, the problem has been posed in a different and more challenging form by R.P. Wolff (1976). Whereas, generally speaking, attempts are made to find an accommodation which allows a place for both the demands of conscience and the demands of collective decisions, Wolff insists that the demands of conscience are so important that nothing may be allowed to displace them. He confesses that he has 'simply taken for granted an entire ethical theory' in reaching this conclusion (*ibid.*: viii). His premises are recognisably Kant-inspired if not Kantian, and are fairly close to the assumptions about human beings which have figured in the previous two chapters.

People are able to embark on various courses of action on the basis of making reasoned choices, and this imposes on them a certain responsibility. If we possess free will and reason, then we have an obligation to take responsibility for our actions, and that means 'making the final decisions about what one should do' (*ibid.*: 15). But to claim that right for oneself is necessarily to deny that an external authority can rightfully have such power, and consequently to deny any duty to obey the laws simply because they are the laws. According to Wolff, if I place myself in someone else's hands and allow them to determine the principles by which my behaviour is guided then 'I repudiate the freedom and reason which give me dignity' (*ibid.*: 72). Hence, just as the idea of each person being his or her own priest is inimical to religious authority, so the idea of each person being his or her own moral authority threatens the acceptance of some *other* moral authority. We perhaps begin to understand why Heine said that if Kant had not beheaded the God of the theologians, Robespierre might not have beheaded the King.

Wolff, then, belongs in the same tradition as Henry David Thoreau, who asserted that 'The only obligation which I have a right to assume is to do at any time what I think right' (Bedau 1969: 28). I may frequently think it right to abide by a decision democratically arrived at, but it is my prerogative to decide whether I abide by it or not. We should note, too, that for Wolff this will apply universally, and not just where I think some very grave principle is at stake which will be upset by abiding by the democratic decision. In matters both great and small, it is finally for my conscience to decide how I shall act. Wolff, we might say, embraces the *principle of autonomy:* given the kind of moral creatures we are, capable of forming our own conceptions of what is right and of acting in accordance with them, we have a duty always to follow the deliverances of our own conscience, rather than allowing some other agency to determine how we shall act.

Now the conception of moral agency assumed in Wolff's

argument is not universal or inescapable, but it is not eccentric either. Whereas in other times and places moral agency may have been located in some particular social role, the idea is perfectly familiar to us that any ordinary rational creature qualifies for that status, and that the essence of virtue is for such a creature to act according to its own view of what is right and wrong. This is, as Macintyre has observed, a peculiarly *democratised* conception of moral agency (Macintyre 1981: 30). It is ironical, therefore, if that conception comes to undermine democracy itself.

Yet that is certainly what Wolff claims. Initially, he allowed that the conception was compatible with one theoretical form of democracy, namely unanimous direct democracy where 'every person votes on every issue — governed by a rule of unanimity' (Wolff 1976: 23). That, however, is effectively the case where everyone is on the winning side, and therefore hardly a testing situation for the strains between individual autonomy and collective authority; and in any case Wolff subsequently withdrew his concession that this provided a theoretical solution to the problem (*ibid.*: 88).

The more familiar representative system is dismissed on the grounds that there is no real sense in which I enact the laws which it promulgates. They are made by people who are not obliged to vote as I would and may have no effective way of discovering my preferences (*ibid.*: 29). Taking the view that my autonomy is clearly compromised in these circumstances, Wolff quotes with approval Rousseau's remark that the people of England are free only during the election of members of parliament, after which they are again in chains (*ibid.*: 34). A similar judgment is made on the acceptance of a state's decisions when they are based on majority rule. If I retain for myself on each occasion the decision whether to abide by them, then I am thereby denying the authority of the state; if, on the other hand, I always submit to them and accept the authority of such a state, then I have forfeited my autonomy (*ibid.*: 40).

Although Wolff believes that it must somehow be possible for rational creatures to create a form of association which does not deprive anyone of their moral autonomy he is able in the end only to produce an extremely sketchy account of an anarchist society (*ibid.*: 78-82), which need not concern us at this stage.

3 SOME SOLUTIONS

Is there any way of meeting this problem which does not involve abandoning the premium placed on autonomy, a premium which there are independent grounds for keeping?

We might begin by tempering our enthusiasm for autonomy in the most obvious way. We might say that it is important for individuals to frame their own ideas of right and wrong, to respond to their own moral imperatives, *other things being equal* (cf. Pennock 1979: 87). When are other things not equal? That may seem obvious too. Rawls, for instance, argues that the idea of equal liberty of conscience is one of the fixed points in our conception of justice, but that nevertheless everyone agrees that this liberty is limited by the common interest in public order and security (Rawls 1972: 206, 212). More generally, we might say that the pursuit of autonomy is permissible up to the point where it begins to involve damage or harm to others, and it is perfectly in order for collective decisions to limit autonomy at that point. It is, after all, the classical position outlined by J.S. Mill in the *Essay on Liberty* that self-protection is the only legitimate reason for interfering in someone else's chosen form of behaviour. Surely, then, we can argue that this is the point at which enthusiasm for autonomy should be qualified?

It might then further be argued that an active decision to abide by the decisions of a system which operates according to the sorts of principle criticised by Wolff does not of itself amount to any loss of autonomy. I can simply recognise that there are vicious and disruptive people around, against whom I and other people need protection if our own autonomy is to be worth anything. Accordingly, we may agree to set up a supreme coercive power to protect us against this eventuality, and we may in our wisdom decide that such power will reside henceforth in the majority decisions of all of us, or the decisions of representatives elected periodically by all of us. It might further be argued that even after a legitimate coercive power has been created in this way, we can still keep a separation between its legitimacy and my obligation to conform to its requirements: in general I recognise its legitimacy because of the tremendous moral benefits which it confers, but I can still reserve to myself the decision whether, on a particular occasion, to accept its edict (cf. Reiman 1972: 54).

There are clear similarities between the suggestions being developed here and social contract theory (both in its classical form in Hobbes, Locke and Rousseau and in its revived Rawlsian form), and it may be said that Wolff himself has provided the model for such suggestions in his own argument about unanimous direct democracy. Though he may not accept that decisions issuing in that form are creative of political authority, he does hold that if everyone, including me, votes for a particular arbitration procedure for settling disputes, then I become bound by the decisions of that procedure whether I like it or not, since they issue from my will (Wolff 1976: 24-5). Why not the same, therefore, for a unanimous decision to abide by some other decision procedures? In any event, whether social contract theories are relied on or not, it may be felt that Wolff has drawn too starkly the choice of following my conscience or submitting to some other authority: I can allow a limited and qualified acceptance of decisions issuing from some other body; and my own autonomous decisions to follow those decisions, where I do, can be based partly on a consideration of the good effects which follow precisely from having a system involving obedience of that kind.

Are these suggestions convincing? It is difficult to deny the starting point, that the unrestricted behaviour of some people would have grave consequences for the autonomy of others. It is a long way from here, however, to the conclusion that acceptance of the forms of decision-making which Wolff criticises does not compromise one's autonomy. All that we should be entitled to infer so far is that, if my bringing to fruition plans which I sincerely believe are right is obstructed by the fact that other people are wicked, or misguided, or simply pursuing goals which bring them into conflict with me, then I must make my own autonomous decision about how best to respond to that difficulty.

At this juncture the traditional liberal view, that autonomous decisions are to be tolerated up to the point where they threaten harm, is of limited usefulness. The equally traditional objection to that view has been that it is deficient until a clear and acceptable account is given of what constitutes harm in the relevant sense. This is not a merely academic point about the absence of a definition. People might very well agree on the verbal formula, that autonomy may be restricted when allowing it free rein would involve harm to others, and yet disagree widely about what interventions in someone's behaviour would be sanctioned by following the formula. Take an example from the political realm. Suppose that a government deliberately disseminated false information to the populace about the nature of an armed conflict which its forces were involved in. There might well be very deep disagreement over whether such an act of deception in such circumstances constituted harm in the relevant sense or not. (If we amend the original formula to say that autonomy may be restricted when its exercise would produce a *balance* of harm over good — as perhaps we should — then this problem is merely intensified.)

This explains why the traditional liberal picture is at once seductive and disturbing. It rests on the idea that a separation is possible between public, other-related activities, where autonomy must conform to agreed requirements of social life, and private behaviour, where autonomy is supreme. But it is utterly unclear what characteristics a piece of behaviour must possess for it to qualify for one of these spheres rather than the other, and this is at least partly because it is utterly unclear in concrete terms what the requirements of social life actually are.

There is an important corollary. It is a matter of controversy whether a piece of behaviour infringes 'public order' or the requirements of social life, and therefore whether, on the view being considered, curtailment of autonomy becomes justified. Where the question is being considered for the purpose of decision and action, then as well as a theoretically adequate answer to it, we cannot evade the question *who is to decide* whether a piece of behaviour merits such a description. If the agent or agency whose action is at issue determines that question then there is indeed no forfeiture of autonomy, but equally there is no genuine circumscription of the agent's own decisions. On the other hand, if the question whether harm accrues in a particular case is turned over to some other body, then an area has indeed been marked out where the writ of the autonomous individual agent does not run. But by the same token anyone who has as strong a commitment to autonomy as Wolff's ought to find this unacceptable in the extent to which it involves giving hostages to fortune — or rather to whatever body is allowed to determine the issue, whether a majority or a collection of representatives.

A similar dilemma confronts the attempt to evade problems about the tyranny of the majority by claiming that certain decisions it might wish to take are precluded, because they would constitute infringements of individual rights. Rights do not stalk the streets with their name stamped on their forehead, nor, on the views of modern rights theorists, are they peculiar metaphysical entities whose existence might have to be established in some peculiar metaphysical way. Accordingly, human beings have to determine when a right exists and when a decision would constitute an infringement of it. If a majority decides this question then there is, after all, no prior consideration other than the majority's decision which places a constraint on majority decisions. On the other hand, if the majority does not decide, the matter still has to be placed in the hands of *some* group, and then it would be the decisions of that group, rather than the majority, which determined the issue. There might be nothing wrong with this, but additional argument would have to be put forward to justify allowing the decisions of that group to take precedence, and this would still be a different argument from the one which held majority decisions only to be limited by some neutral, impersonal entity.

Effectively, the suggestions we have considered attempt to meet the problem by postulating a limited acceptance of decisions emanating from a source other than one's own conscience, combined with a high degree of retained autonomy. The tensions in that position are evident. If I say, for example, that I will abide by decisions from that source (be it the majority, a group of representatives, or whatever) except when I believe that they are morally wrong, that may seem like a generous compromise. But of course it is not. I am not quite saying that I shall accept that other source's decisions only when they coincide with mine (it might take a decision towards which I felt moral indifference), but the scope I concede to them is still very limited, and it is, as a matter of fact, a far smaller concession than actual states demand of their subjects (cf. Graham 1982b: 125-6). Similarly, it might be, by miraculous coincidence, that my own views on how I ought to behave and what states of affairs ought to prevail in my environment always agreed with those of the other decision-making body; but that simply leaves unanswered the question which direction I would move in if the two views fell apart.

It is not clear, either, that the considerations from social contract theory provide a real accommodation with the original demands of autonomy. This turns partly on whether those demands are met if I make one decision to abandon my autonomy in future over an indeterminably wide area — as I do if, in general, I contract to abide by the decisions of a majority or of a group of representatives in advance of knowing what those bodies will themselves decide. Certainly this does not meet Wolff's requirement that I reserve to myself *in each instance* the final decision whether to co-operate (cf. Wolff 1976: 40), and in that respect it differs from his model of unanimous direct democracy, where I agree to abide by the application of definite principles in determining some issue and continue to think those principles fair (*ibid.*: 24-5). There is a case for saying, therefore, that an undertaking of the kind supposedly given in the social contract constitutes an irresponsible abandonment of autonomy, a fact which will not be altered even if it is an undertaking unanimously offered.

Moreover, even if this point is not conceded, the posited act of consent carries further difficulties. Of itself it does not provide an argument specifically in favour of *democratic* decision-making. If it is voluntarily given consent which is crucial, then presumably a unanimous undertaking to abide by decisions arrived at in some non-democratic way would become binding. In addition, if voluntary consent is crucial we have no leverage in the case of the individual who withholds such consent. When the motivational question arises — why accept the democratic process either in general or in a particular instance? — then we have nothing to persuade the conscientious autonomous individual if we have placed our faith in consent and the individual conscientiously refuses to give it.

If, on the contrary, we believe that the irresponsibility lies in a position which refuses to recognise any legitimate constraint except that of an individual's conscience, we may be drawn after all to a rejection of the principle of individual autonomy. That would be premature, however. There is still further scope for exploration of that position, with a view to wringing different concessions from it in the matter of compatibility between autonomy and acceptance of collective decisions.

4 A RECONSIDERATION

Take any object of moral regard and concern, such as happiness or justice or autonomy, and call it a *value*. Any such value can be viewed in at least one of two ways, as a *goal* or as a *side-constraint* (cf. Nozick 1974: 28-9).

We hold a value as a *goal* if we view it as something to be fostered, protected or maximised. If we attach importance of that kind to a particular value then it may be necessary on occasion to deprive someone of it in the interests of a greater fostering of it overall. Nozick uses an example familiar from discussions of utilitarianism. Suppose a mob is rampaging through a town, in outrage at the commission of some crime, bent on destruction and killing. If I hold the non-violation of rights as a goal to be maximised, then this may commit me to the view that some innocent person should be framed and punished, thereby having their rights violated, if this is the only course which will reduce the overall level of rights violation.

In our own case we might cite circumstances where the autonomous act of a given individual will severely curtail the autonomy of many more people. In the same way, we might argue for the curtailment of that individual's autonomy in the interests of a lesser curtailment overall. That, indeed, is a position which I want to argue is finally a defensible one to take with regard to autonomy, even if one begins from the same premises as Wolff. But we are not entitled to that conclusion yet. We have first to notice that the attitude displayed here towards an object of moral regard is not the only possible one.

The value which is so regarded may function as a *side-constraint*. For example, I may take the view that whatever else I do in the pursuit of some goal I may not violate someone's rights, or curtail their autonomy. I shall regard certain values as side-constraints if I hold that the requirements of morality are not exhausted in a consideration of the *consequences* of what I do and that there are certain things which are not eligible as options, whatever the consequences. I may feel, for example, that the use of hideously sadistic torture is not justified even in the service of preventing a greater incidence of hideously sadistic torture; or — a case discussed by Bernard Williams — I may take the view that it would be wrong for me to take an innocent life even if I know that the result of my not doing so will be the taking of more innocent lives (Williams 1973: 98-118). Here the available routes to a given goal are restricted by other considerations. I may take the view that there are certain courses of action which I simply cannot contemplate if I am to retain my integrity as a moral agent.

Now the contrast between goal and side-constraint is probably overdrawn as presented here. It may be that often we hold values in not quite either of the ways outlined. Certainly it is doubtful whether anyone, including Nozick, should or would wish in the end to regard the non-violation of rights as a side-constraint on action. Nevertheless, it is useful to begin by asking how a regard for autonomy might fit into this schema. Suppose that we embrace a principle of autonomy of the kind described in section 2 above, and for the sorts of reason also described there. Does this commit us to regarding the preservation of autonomy as a goal or a side-constraint?

Nozick suggests that side-constraints reflect a concern with people as ends in themselves (Nozick 1974: 30-1). This, together with the sorts of reason which were put forward for regarding the individual's conscience as paramount, may encourage the conclusion that preservation of autonomy must function as a side-constraint. That is precisely the conclusion which I wish to deny. It may be that the preservation of autonomy cannot be straightforwardly regarded simply as a goal, but it is at any rate wrong to regard it as a side-constraint. When we see why, we also see the limitations on the worryingly strong conclusions which Wolff wished to draw.

Let us begin by re-stating the obvious. Except in circumstances of consensus, where people either all agree to do the same thing or so arrange matters that the fulfilment of one person's autonomous decision never leads to the thwarting of another's, violation of some individual's autonomy must occur. If human beings were isolated individuals whose paths never crossed this would not be so. But human life is not like that. Characteristically, human beings impinge on one another via the projects they conceive and their attempts to realise those projects in action. The last point is crucial: it would be a mockery to claim that autonomy had been preserved in circumstances where people were free to form their own views about what states of affairs should prevail but where they were prevented by force from taking steps in their action to bring those states of affairs about. Autonomy consists not just in making up one's own mind but in acting upon it.

Accordingly, a concern for autonomy itself dictates a concern for consensus wherever possible. An autonomous agent should listen to other views and be prepared to review his or her own position before reaching a final decision, in the hope that a conflict necessarily leading to curtailment of some agent's autonomy can be avoided. Such a conflict, looking at it from the detached point of view, is the most undesirable outcome. It therefore begins to look as though avoiding the curtailment of autonomy is to be treated as a goal.

But, it may be objected, why adopt this detached point of view? Is not the whole point of the autonomy principle that, since I am responsible for what I do, I must take my own decisions and live with them? I will recognise that other agents will take a similar view of their own decisions and actions, if they regard autonomy as seriously as I do; but that is for them to worry about, not me. In the last analysis, all I can be expected to care about is the preservation of my own autonomy. That, therefore, will function as a side-constraint on what I do or, by extension, allow to be done.

This response, I suggest, betrays a misunderstanding of the importance of autonomy and the implications which follow for social decision-making. The issue of responsibility will receive further comment in the next chapter; what we should focus on now are the *grounds* for regarding autonomy as important.

Why is it important that I should reserve the right to make up my own mind in each instance how to conduct myself? It is not because I am me but because of the kind of creature I am. In

Wolff's Kantian terminology, it is because I am a creature possessing free will and reason that I have an obligation to take responsibility and think out how I am to act. But now on equally Kantian grounds I must be prepared to *universalise* this claim. If it is in virtue of these general features that my autonomy becomes important, then consistency demands that I attach the same importance to the autonomy of any other creature possessing those same features. If my possessing free will and reason provides the reason why my autonomy is important, then your possessing those features provides a reason why your autonomy is important — and not just important to *you,* but important *sans phrase* (cf. Graham 1982b: 130-2).

Moreover, I not only have the same reason for *regarding* your autonomy as important, if you possess the same characteristics as the ones that give the grounds why my autonomy is important. I have the same reason for *acting* to preserve autonomy in both cases. Recall that one reason why it was important that I should preserve my own autonomy was that I am responsible for what I do. But the interconnexions between people are such that we need to recognise the qualifications which must be placed on that idea. I may also be partially responsible for what someone else does: not just because I may influence their behaviour, either by rational or by non-rational means of persuasion, but also because what I myself do will make a difference to the range of alternatives which lie open to them. It is plain, therefore, that it is within my power to affect in a substantial way another agent's autonomy, for good or for ill. The general requirement that a regard for autonomy should manifest itself in appropriate action really does have bite, then, in the case of serious regard for the autonomy of another person.

We can in this way, I believe, establish the shape, as it were, which a serious regard for autonomy must take if it is built on the premises originally outlined. That regard must extend beyond the boundaries of any given individual's own skin and must be manifested in action.

Many other difficult questions about the nature of this commitment will, of course, remain. For example, the questions what is to count as an autonomous decision and what is the most appropriate way of preserving autonomy do not admit of simple answers. My immediate judgment on how to behave may not constitute an exercise of autonomy: it must at least be the result of an attempt to think matters out for myself. Even then, as we saw earlier, it may not constitute an exercise of autonomy of the kind required of me as a rational creature if its intended effect is to remove the possibility of future exercises of autonomy over a wide area. It looks, therefore, as though it is autonomy over time which it is important to preserve.

This brings with it further complications, including the possibility that forfeiture of my autonomy with respect to a particular decision now may greatly increase the probability of my making, or being able to make, many more autonomous decisions in the *future*. (That may serve as a reason for putting myself in the hands of a teacher who I believe will teach me something useful.) It would be difficult for an exponent of autonomy to resist these complications in the interest of valuing only autonomy at each moment in time: that would presumably cut out any kind of promise-keeping or undertaking for the future, since at the appointed time, if I regarded my promise or undertaking as binding, I would have lost my discretion in the matter.

Even without attempting to deal with these further complications, however, I hope enough has been said to establish the claim that we should regard the preservation of autonomy as something far more like a goal than a side-constraint on action. We should look to minimise the curtailment of autonomy but we cannot (literally cannot) hope to place the curtailment of autonomy on particular occasions beyond the bounds of consideration. Where individuals' final judgments conflict over whether to realise a given state of affairs or not, then someone's autonomy must be curtailed, and it is simply a question of whose. Or rather, just as there can be reasons for curtailing autonomy now in the interests of a lesser curtailment later, so there can be reasons for curtailing one person's autonomy in the interest of another's.

The threat presented in the earlier sections of this chapter was that, if we began from apparently unexceptionable premises about the inviolability of individual conscience and the importance of autonomy, we should end up with the unwelcome conclusion that obedience to any form of political authority, including democratic authority, was not possible. It is a significant result if we can show, by adverting to considerations entirely internal to the principle of autonomy itself, that a regard for autonomy does not make all social decision-making impossible in the way it first threatened to. In particular, it is important if we have shown that the principle does not permit autonomous agents to make exceptions in their own favour, as it were — to be concerned only to preserve their own autonomy, when that in fact is materially equivalent to ensuring that other agents are not able to preserve theirs.

The most significant result, however, is this. Looking at the problem purely in terms of the requirements of autonomy, where wills conflict the objective must obviously be to preserve autonomy to the highest degree possible, in recognition that total preservation is *not* possible. But in so far as we look at the issue purely in these terms, we shall regard it as irrelevant to raise the question what the nature of the proposals is over which individuals' judgments are in conflict; and in so far as our respect for their autonomy rests on the general features of free will and reason which they possess, we should certainly regard it as improper to raise any question of the *identity* of the proponents of different options. But this suggests an obvious formula for minimum curtailment of autonomy. At least if we leave aside the complication of preserving autonomy over time, the more autonomous decisions there are in favour of a given option, the more autonomy will be curtailed if that option is rejected. By extension, if most individuals' autonomous decisions are in favour of a given option, then autonomy will be maximised on that occasion if that option is followed. In short, the requirements of autonomy themselves, as we have now expounded them, seem to provide an argument in favour of accepting majority decisions. (We could then reintroduce the complication of the preservation of autonomy over time by leaving in the hands of individuals themselves the decision whether a curtailment of autonomy on the given occasion could be defended in the interest of autonomy-over-time. This would reinforce the argument for majority decisions at another level.)

5 CONCLUSION

In effect, in this chapter we have explored the consequences of adopting a particular standpoint on the question of individual conscience. We have not questioned the grounds on which that standpoint was adopted in the first place, since it seemed to grow very naturally from the discussion of earlier chapters. The consequences do not, I hope, look as dire as they did at the outset, in that we have reduced the plausibility of the claim that an appropriate regard for conscience precluded acceptance of democratic decisions in any form. It is worth stressing that if the original claim had been valid it would have shown much more than this: it would have shown that acceptance of the authority of *any* external body, whether democratic or otherwise, was precluded. However, we have now seen sufficient of the complications in the standpoint to conclude that it must allow a place for the curtailment of autonomy, and therefore a place for discussion of the best arrangements to deal with that whilst sustaining autonomy as far as possible.

I have suggested that majority rule is one obvious candidate for that role. If that is correct, then the principle of individual autonomy and conscience certainly does not undermine democratic forms in the thoroughgoing way we may have feared. On the other hand, even now that we have seen the limitations on any very simple version of such a principle, it may still undermine forms of democracy where decision-making becomes the prerogative of a small group, with relatively little direct control by the populace at large. To be sure, now that we have seen the complications involved in protecting autonomy we may conclude that some forms of representation are also compatible with its protection. What will be crucial, however, is that the entrusting of decisions to any agency other than the individual should be recoverable at will *by* the individual; and that is not a feature of the representative systems in the midst of which we live. In that case it looks as though, from the standpoint examined in this chapter, a commonly accepted form of democracy is incompatible with a set of values which are not only themselves commonly accepted, but are generally thought to provide support for that form. For liberal, representative democracy, it is often thought, is the best arrangement for protecting the individual and his or her conscience.

The issue needs further investigation. We have to scrutinise the premisses of the standpoint which we have allowed without question in this chapter, and in particular the assumptions which themselves lie behind a belief in the paramountcy of individual conscience. In doing so we shall reach the limits of the kind of liberal individualist theory so far discussed in Part One. Wolff castigated one of his critics who had said that political systems begin from the assumption that some areas of behaviour are too crucial to the well-being of the community to be left to the consciences of its members. It was mystification, Wolff objected, to posit 'the state' as a solution to that problem, for the state is 'either a real group of persons or it is fiction' (Wolff 1976: 99). This is in some ways a salutary reminder that we cannot put matters for human decision somehow beyond human beings, and that the state, an essentially coercive instrument, works through the agency of human beings. But, as we shall see, there is more than one way of looking at the issues here, and at the whole issue of moral agency.

FURTHER READING

The Kantian origins of the premium placed on individual conscience are further discussed in Wolff 1973. For the nature and role of conscientious objection and civil disobedience, see Rawls 1972: 363-91 and, more generally, Bedau 1969. Rawls 1972 also furnishes the most celebrated contemporary use of social contract theory. Pateman 1979 examines other contemporary discussions. Anscombe 1958, Bennett 1966, Nagel 1972 and Graham 1975 all contribute to the issue of whether there are any types of action which are prohibited under all circumstances, and therefore to the debate about side-constraints. Lindley 1986 constitutes an extremely useful general discussion of the value of autonomy and Graham 1982b provides a more detailed argument for the need to recognise the importance of autonomy in general rather than simply for oneself. A more abstract argument for this 'transference of reasons' between people is contained in Nagel 1970.

6   Collectives and consensus

1 INTRODUCTION

Our entire discussion began from the fact that individuals must live together in some social form. We have sought an elaboration and justification of a democratic form of social life, and considered that an argument which proceeded from premisses about the nature of individuals themselves would provide the most plausible grounds for that elaboration and justification.

Along the way, however, we have encountered problems. If individual human beings are held to be important in themselves, then it is a natural wish not to allow their social dealings completely to engross their personal existence, but to keep a clear distinction between public and private spheres. At a number of points that aspiration has looked in danger. In connexion with liberty, the idea of an area where interference was ruled out *ab initio* looked precarious. In connexion with equality, a parallel attempt to confine attention to inequalities within the public decision-making area also seemed implausible. More generally, the notion that the individual can pursue his or her own path for the observance of the demands of social morality, while it may be a tenable one, requires considerable elaboration so as to cope with the contentious question what the demands of specifically social morality actually are. Finally, the strains were evident in the issue of accommodating the individual's autonomy within a social framework for social decisions: if consent was crucial to legitimate demands on the individual, then it seemed that demands could not be pressed if that consent was not forthcoming.

Yet, it may be felt, we cannot depart from the intrinsic importance of the individual within a theory of democracy, and we cannot depart from the starting point that individuals have to live together in some fashion *whatever* standpoint we adopt. Of course, in a sense this is true. There are physically distinguishable parcels of flesh and blood walking around and interacting with one another. But there are very different ways of conceiving of those facts, very different theoretical frameworks within which to make sense of them. The difficulties we have experienced so far indicate a need to renegotiate our theory of the relations between individual and community.

In the present chapter I shall attempt to show that the theoretical framework which has been presupposed in much of our discussion is inadequate. I shall distinguish different kinds of individualism and probe their limitations. In their place I shall suggest the need to construct a theory which recognises the existence of various types of collective or corporate entity, and consider what difference this makes to the idea of consensus in decision-making, which has appeared intermittently in our discussion so far.

2 VARIETIES OF INDIVIDUALISM

It is worth pointing out that in one respect the bulk of the argument hitherto has been less individualistic than it might have been. In chapter 2, section 1 I referred to the motivational problem of providing argument why anyone should favour adopting democratic procedures in the first place, and why they should continue to abide by them in circumstances where to do so would lead to the thwarting of their own will. In subsequent discussion I have assumed that such argument can be provided, and the appeal of democracy adequately displayed, if democratic procedures are described in a way which links them with certain moral requirements concerning the treatment of human beings. I have assumed that it is not necessary to link the description of democracy with the egoistic concerns of a particular agent before democracy can have any rational appeal for that agent. In other words, I have assumed that to describe democracy as, let us say, involving a respect for human freedom is already to provide anyone with a reason for favouring it.

Both in life and in theorising relevant to democracy, the contrary assumption is often made. It is often assumed, that is, that any practice, action, or whatever, which does not somehow serve the self-interest of an agent is necessarily to be seen as a burden, not something which could be rationally chosen. If we start as far back as that in our assumptions, in what we might call *egoistic individualism,* then we have a prior problem why moral considerations should weigh with an agent at all. A particularised and sharpened version of that problem which then arises in democratic theory is why anyone should bother to participate in a democratic process, to vote, for example, when a decision is taken, if their doing so is a 'cost' to them and is in any case unlikely to affect the outcome.

Whether problems of this kind present a strong threat to the project of displaying the motivational appeal of democracy depends on the plausibility of egoistic individualism. I do not have any arguments which show that it is a completely untenable doctrine, but I suggest two reasons for doubting its plausibility. First, it is a difficult position to sustain in trying to make sense of one's normal range of attitudes towards human interaction. For example, I should normally regard someone's treading on my toes as not merely something which is not in my interests, but also something I am entitled to resent or get indignant about. But it is difficult to make further sense of these responses without admitting a certain generality into the picture, of a kind which applies across the distinction between people. Why does it *matter* that people should not tread on my toes? It is difficult to avoid the assertion that this is because that is no way to treat a *person,* rather than because the toes happen to be mine. But then to introduce the consideration that I am a person is to introduce a generally re-applicable description, and in this way giving the grounds for my attitudes actually begins to undermine my egoism. This does not, obviously, show that egoistic individualism is false: it may be that the whole range of attitudes like indignation and resentment are themselves suspect and should be discarded. It does make plain, however, that the doctrine comes with a price tag attached, in terms of the commitment which it enjoins to relinquishing other attitudes. And we might well feel that the price demanded is too high.

Secondly, egoistic individualism, as an account of either actual or defensible human behaviour, implies a degree of isolation of one human being from another which is unrealistic. People frequently care for their immediate family circle in a way which it is simply perverse to represent as disguised individual self-interest, and with a pattern of consistency different from isolated acts of altruism towards strangers. This may seem only a small change from the original egoistic picture since it has replaced individual with very small group interest. But the change is of far more importance than it appears: once the egoistic assumption has been breached, the question arises what groups it is rational to identify with and why — a question we shall take up subsequently.

These points have a bearing on the other types of individualism underlying the arguments of previous chapters, but those types must be distinguished before that becomes plain. For example, as a means of characterising individualism as a whole we might notice Pennock's formulation, that the individual, 'regardless of how he came to be what he is, forms the ultimate unit of society . . .' (Pennock 1973: 83). There are different types of ultimacy, however: the individual might be ultimate for explanatory or for moral purposes, for example.

The context makes plain that Pennock has the latter in mind, and *moral individualism* is the next variety to be distinguished in the theories I have discussed and others like them. The individual is seen as the primary object of moral regard and deserving of protected status. That view is exemplified in the thought entertained by Rawls, 'Each person possesses an inviolability founded on justice that even the welfare of society as a whole cannot override' (Rawls 1972: 3). It is sometimes expressed in the language of rights, as in Dworkin's claim that individual rights are 'political trumps held by individuals' (Dworkin 1978: xi) and Nozick's assertion (the very first sentence of his book), 'Individuals have rights, and there are things no person or group may do to them (without violating their rights)' (Nozick 1974: ix). The parenthesis makes clear that this protected status is not necessarily absolutely inviolate, a point echoed in Dworkin's insistence that we need not claim that a state is *never* justified in overriding a right (Dworkin 1978: 191). All the same, strong reasons will need to be given for breaching that protected status, because of its source in the nature of individuals as formulaters of life-plans and autonomous decision-makers.

Associated with the moral thesis that individuals merit special regard and protection, but distinguishable from it, is what I shall call *psychological individualism*. This is the idea, implicit in the theories we have discussed more often than it is stated explicitly, that the individual is the *originator* of the moral decisions, goals, projects and aspirations which he or she embraces. The picture is the Cartesian one of building out from the individual to the social context rather than vice versa. Projects are undertaken and then the question arises what the social world must be like in order to allow their realisation. There is relatively little emphasis on the extent to which an individual's choices are themselves framed and influenced by the surrounding social context, relatively little emphasis on the degree to which rationality itself is a social affair, consisting not just in plucking projects out of the air and making them one's own but also in argument and discussion, a preparedness to consider other points of view and to modify one's own position in the light of reasoned criticism. There is, too, relatively little emphasis on joint decisions to undertake shared projects.

In other words, there is an underestimation of the extent to which the individual self which is to be the object of special moral regard is a *social* self. The point was summarised, but also crucially overstated, by Mannheim many years ago. We belong to a group, he suggested, not merely because we are born into one and give it our allegiance, but primarily because we see the world in the way in which the group does (Mannheim 1936: 19). The overstatement lies in the failure to recognise that, though people may be moulded by social circumstances, it is also possible for them to transcend them, at least to some extent. That is a point made by Lukes, who insists on the importance of recognising the social formation of individuals but also notes that they are able on occasion to transcend socially-given involvements, and that respect for them requires us to treat them as 'actually or potentially autonomous centres of choice' (Lukes 1973: 149).

This may encourage a belief that the weaknesses in psychological individualism need not reflect on moral individualism: whatever the story about how the individual came to be the way he or she is, and their connexions with others, that is the way they are now, and a certain kind of respect is therefore due, it might be felt. However, to take this line is to misconstrue the link between psychological and moral individualism. The latter is not held gratuitously or as a piece of dogma; and although it would be a massive oversimplification to imagine that the argument runs 'psychological individualism is true, therefore moral individualism is true', nevertheless the psychological doctrine must be taken to inform and give support to the moral one. If it is deficient, therefore, the moral doctrine is to that extent cast adrift.

Moreover, if we reflect on the difficulties in the moral position which we have encountered along the way, many of them are traceable precisely to the psychological background presupposed. The picture of individuals atomistically going about their rational business inadequately represents the degree of interaction between them, and so leaves us ill-equipped to deal with the problem of projects which clash and the resultant harm to individuals. The degree of interdependency is likewise inadequately represented, encouraging a conception of freedom equivalent to being left alone when in fact being left alone may be just what diminishes an individual's freedom.

Requirements of generality and consistency likewise prove to be a problem for the atomistically-conceived individual. As I argued in chapter 5, section 4, I cannot hold my own autonomy to be important, on the grounds that I am a creature possessing freedom and reason, without extending that importance to other creatures possessing the same characteristics. That, I suggested, enabled us to make a formal breach in the position which refuses to acknowledge any possibility of legitimate corporate decisions which override the autonomous individual's own view.

However, though it was possible to introduce considerations in favour of majority rule in this way, that solution is still not entirely satisfactory. It leaves us with a dilemma which I have elsewhere characterised as the dilemma of the liberal wet or the dictator (Graham 1984: 56-7). We should not be at all impressed by a dictator who professed to set great store by autonomy, and told us that she would respect her subjects' wish to reach their own conclusions about how they ought to conduct themselves, if she added that, of course, as she was a dictator she would continue to ensure that they did not translate those conclusions into action but did as *she* thought they ought to. We should rightly conclude that such respect for autonomy was a sham. On the other hand, take the case of a philosopher I knew who embraced the principle of autonomy as his primary ethical belief, expressed in the form that people ought to do as they think they ought to do. On an occasion when a South African cricket team arrived in England, he explicitly embraced all of the following beliefs: (1) that the South Africans should play, (2) that members of a protest movement which had been formed should prevent them from playing and (3) that the police should prevent the protesters from preventing the cricketers from playing.

Now there is no actual inconsistency here, but there is something uncomfortable in holding a principle which yields these conclusions, for the question it leaves is 'What concrete state of affairs does this person think ought actually to obtain?' To this it might be replied that all the principle yields is a set of beliefs that the various agents ought to *try* to do what they think they ought to do (a point put to me by G.A. Cohen and Richard Lindley); in which case our philosopher can add that the concrete state of affairs which he thinks ought to obtain is whatever would result from *his* doing what he thinks *he* ought to do. The problem, however, is this: why should we allow that his behaving in that way reflects any more serious concern for another's autonomy than that shown by the dictator? We are still, it seems, haunted by the shadow of the challenge posed at the beginning of the previous chapter, that in conditions of conflict a respect for autonomy results in paralysis, but that action according to one's own convictions betokens a flouting of someone else's autonomy. Even a

resolute attempt to act in such a way that violation of others'
autonomy is kept to a minimum does not escape that dilemma.
Whatever morality we adopt, we have to face the question
'Who decides?' If *I* decide what actions violate others'
autonomy then I am depriving them of that decision and to that
extent already curtailing their autonomy.

There is one further point about how the weakness of
psychological individualism reflects on moral individualism.
We should recall Wolff's suggestion that the importance of
autonomy lies in the fact that 'men are responsible for their
actions' and that that is why they should *take* responsibility for
them (Wolff 1976: 12). This amounts to the idea that moral
responsibility must follow causal responsibility. That is, it is
reasonable for me to feel proud or ashamed, and for others to
praise or condemn me, only in relation to what I myself have
brought about. Now that is at least a plausible idea to hold. But
our recognition of the inadequacy of psychological
individualism ought also to put us on our guard against any
simplistic interpretation of the idea that I am solely causally
responsible for what I do. In so far as that idea leaves out of
account the enormous social influences and pressures which go
into the process of an individual's decision-making, they give a
false picture of the causal locus of an individual's decisions and
actions. In that sense, as I also noted in chapter 5, section 4, the
causal responsibility for what I do is partly in others' hands,
and it is an oversimplification of causal networks to leave this
out of account.

This point can be resisted, at a price. It may be insisted that,
whatever the preceding events in the causal chain, the
immediate cause of an individual's behaviour is that
individual's own decision. Accordingly, when all allowance
has been made for social pressures, the framing of options
before they reach the individual's consciousness, and so on,
there is always still the matter of the individual's conscientious
decision. Moral individualism can then be sustained, it may be
concluded, even in the light of the inadequacies of
psychological individualism.

We might then wonder why so much importance should be
attached to what is in effect the precipitating cause in the chain,
rather than underlying causes, but let that go. It is more

important to notice that in the background at this stage of the discussion is another variety of individualism, what I shall call *ontological individualism*. This is the view that the only agents which the moral world contains are individuals, so that the only proper objects of moral appraisal are the *individual's* actions, attitudes, or whatever. Individualism of that form is embodied in Wolff's complaint that the state is just a group of persons, that it is not an institution if that means something other than a group of persons occupying certain roles, and that a mistake is involved in giving the state an ontological status different from that of individual persons (Wolff 1976: 97-8). It is also embodied in Nozick's argument that we cannot justify imposing burdens on some people so that others may benefit for the sake of some overall social good, for, he says, 'there is no *social entity* with a good that undergoes some sacrifice for its own good. There are only individual people . . .' (Nozick 1974: 32-3; author's italics). I shall now try to cast doubt on this form of individualism.

3 THE REALITY OF COLLECTIVES

The opposite of ontological individualism I shall call *ontological collectivism*. This is the view that, in addition to individuals, there are also corporate entities or collectives which act in a manner that makes them, too, appropriate objects of moral appraisal. My claim is not, of course, that there is a different kind of entity stalking the world which individualists have somehow failed to notice. It is rather that there are theoretical reasons for *conceiving* of social actions in a particular way which is incompatible with ontological individualism.

There are many different corporate entities, no doubt differing in their nature and internal structure. I want to hold that some of those entities are irreducibly collective in this sense: although they consist of nothing over and above individuals in certain relations, it is not *as* individuals but only as members of the collective in question that those individuals have any role in the process which constitutes that collective's deliberating and acting. Take as an example the case of a jury.

Jane Smith holds and expresses views as to whether the prisoner is guilty. But this has no significance except in so far as she does so in the appropriate circumstances *as* a member of the jury. We can describe her various activities in purely individual terms, and the actions of the jury are themselves reducible without remainder into similar activities undertaken by other such individuals. But it is only by a backward loop which brings in again the collective term 'jury' that the peculiar relevance of those activities is revealed. In a similar way, the entire membership of a committee may be in the same place and express opinions on some issue, perhaps even unanimously, but if they are not meeting *as* a committee then the committee itself has not done anything.

It is characteristic of collectives of this kind that, though the acts of the collective may be analysable into the acts of the individuals who go to compose it, what the collective does is not the very same thing as what an individual does when acting as a member of the collective. Thus, *finding the defendant guilty* or *returning a senator or a member of parliament* is what a jury or an electorate does, but not something the individual who is a constituent of the collective does. That must be described as *casting a vote* or in some other way which makes plain that it is contributory to the action of the collective but is not itself the same action. In a similar way, a climate of opinion may produce a particular kind of insecurity in the members, say, of an ethnic minority, in the way that actions of individuals as such could not do.

What follows if ontological collectivism is true? We have, in the course of preceding chapters, discussed individualist theories which up to a point help to explain and justify the attachment we feel to democratic procedures; but beyond a certain point those theories begin to break down and cause problems. One tempting diagnosis of this would be to suggest that moral individualism is the foundation on which those theories of democracy are built, and then to take refuge in the commonly held opinion that no properly rational debate is possible in disputes over ultimate moral premisses. This would short-circuit all the difficulties we have encountered, to be sure, but only at the cost of rendering impossible the project of actually thinking out what our commitments on the question of democracy ought to be.

Even leaving aside, however, the general issue whether it is possible to engage in rational debate about moral premises, there are reasons nearer to hand for rejecting this diagnosis. As I have already indicated, moral individualism is not held as a gratuitous dogma — attempts are made to argue in its favour — and I should suggest that it is actually the stance adopted on the ontological issue now under discussion which brings us to the bedrock assumptions. Those assumptions are not in themselves moral. They are, rather, assumptions about what sorts of entity need to be postulated as social agents if we are to describe and respond to various social phenomena in the ways we wish to. In other words, given that it would be an agreed starting point that, for example, electorates return candidates to positions of power, committees and other bodies hold things to be the case and resolve to act in certain ways, and the like, there is the further question what theoretical assumptions must be taken to lie behind these agreed facts. The possible answers to that question — ontological individualism and ontological collectivism — are not themselves moral claims at all.

There is, of course, a close connexion with moral questions, since often the claims we wish to make about a given social agent are themselves moral. For example, it may be held not just that a particular kind of collective entity does carry out a certain kind of action but that it has a *right* to, and the right of an electorate to decide an issue would be very much to the point in the context of our present discussion. The most important repercussion in morality from the ontological issue, however, is over the matter of *responsibility,* to which I now return.

In the previous section I called attention to the dependency of moral individualism upon theses about responsibility, a dependency which might enable moral individualism to survive, in some form, the demolition of psychological individualism. Moral responsibility, it seemed plausible to say, followed causal responsibility. And then, whatever the truth about the importance of the social processes which go to form the individual, we were still left with the undeniable fact that they lead up to a point where it is the individual him or herself who must make a decision and act in a particular way. Hence, the moral importance of the individual could be sustained, and a case made for protecting the individual and his or her conscientious decisions from invasion by others.

In that earlier context we were concerned with purely individual action: it is not clear that the same claims about causal responsibility can be preserved when we come to the question of collective actions which ontological collectivism brings into focus. In the earlier case we had the temporally separate point of the agent's decision and its role as a precipitating cause. But in the collective context, although a temporal point for the individual's decision and action will still be locatable, their role will be the very different one of being a contributory factor to what the collective itself does. Accordingly, responsibility in this case is dispersed in a quite different way: there is no one place which is the source of agency in the case of collectives, not even at the point of precipitation. (At least not normally. I may be in the position, as a member of a collective, of having a casting vote at the point where the other votes are known to be evenly balanced. What I do can then be seen as the precipitating cause of the collective's action. But that is not the typical case.)

Consider what now follows if we continue to subscribe to the idea that moral responsibility must follow causal responsibility. An agent can only be held to account, criticised, praised, blamed for what that agent does or brings about. Suppose then that X, Y and Z are members of a university senate which resolves to close one of the departments. I can certainly hold X, Y and Z individually to account for being members of the senate in the first place and for taking part in that sort of decision-making process. I can blame them individually for voting in favour of closure if that is what they did, and I can blame them for not resigning over the matter. But I may well feel that the most important action in the matter, which is not covered by any of these descriptions, is the act of closure itself — and I cannot say of any individual that he or she performed that action. If I wish to adopt an attitude of appraisal to that action, therefore, I must recognise that its causal origin is in the collective itself, and accordingly that any attitude I may take up must also be taken up towards that entity.

This then has implications for the unresolved problems of

autonomy. The argument which generated those problems but also resisted any obvious dismissal was that since I, as a moral agent, am responsible for what I do, I must retain for myself the final decision how to behave. But we can now place an important qualification on this, and say that it is true with respect to my behaviour *as an individual moral agent*. It is not so obviously true with respect to my behaviour *as a component of a collective*. It is not true, it is at best a misleading exaggeration, to say that *I* am causally responsible for what the *collective* does. I am at most *partially* responsible for what it does. But then the causal grounds which support the claim that I ought to retain the prerogative of deciding how *I* behave are not available to support the claim that I ought to retain the prerogative of deciding how the *collective* behaves. The blanket reason which the principle of autonomy seemed to provide for resisting the implementation of social decisions has been removed. It turns out that the principle was based on a faulty ontology. Or, to put it less abstractly, it was based on a faulty view of how an agent involved in making a social decision should see that process and his or her own role in it. We have therefore found a point at which we can resist the unqualified argument which gives rise to the problems. Moreover, this is not *ad hoc* resistance, arising from the embarrassment of the fortuitous fact of individual autonomous wills coming into collision with one another. It is a resistance based on the nature of collective decision-making itself.

The conclusion reached so far is essentially negative. It is that our attempts in the previous chapter to clear up the problems set by the principle of autonomy were insufficiently radical. They did not challenge the terms in which those problems were set up. This still leaves the question what difference the theoretical points about ontology are supposed to make to an individual moral agent within a collective. Conscientious resistance to collective decisions may still be justified, and if so we need to know when and why. All I have attempted to show is the defectiveness of the set of arguments purporting to establish that such resistance on the part of a conscientious moral agent is *always* justified. I shall now attempt to extend my own argument in a more positive direction, and indicate the relevance of these theoretical points for pure democratic theory.

4 THE POSSIBILITY OF CONSENSUS

I remarked earlier that the possibility of conflict is endemic in social existence and social decision-making. It does not, of course, follow that it is inevitable. In many limited contexts where people have to make decisions, they are able to do so in unity and harmony. This gives us a model of consensus which it is legitimate to aspire to and which a proper understanding of decision-making within a collective, as described in the previous section, may help to foster. Where consensus exists, one of the most disagreeable and morally offensive features of human interaction — coercion — can be avoided. That is what motivates the thought which must have occurred to everyone at some time, 'If only all people could agree!' The dubious aspect of extreme forms of individualism lies in the tendency to add in parentheses '(with me)'.

In fairness, however, we should note that the possibility of a kind of proto-consensus may be raised even by individualist theories, and in a way which is not necessarily morally suspect. As I noted in chapter 2, section 4, there are those theories which stress the rationality of bargaining and agreeing 'trade-offs' in circumstances where individuals disagree. In that spirit, it can be argued that where individuals recognise a conflict of preferences they can still rationally seek to achieve unanimity. I can opt to give way over issues where I hold a preference but with no great degree of intensity, in exchange for others giving way in the reverse direction over an issue where I do feel strongly.

Now it is true that a strategy of this kind is sometimes regarded as morally suspect. It may be objected, for example, that it encourages a disposition to trade in one's moral convictions. In that case, although it may facilitate a move towards consensus, this will occur in a form which does not preserve autonomy but, on the contrary, compromises it (cf. Nelson 1980: 64-5). This need not be so, however. The trade-off approach may, rather, simply act as a deterrent to regarding one's moral convictions as settled for all time. It will be the mark of a rational agent to be prepared to revise them, and especially in the light of what others' moral convictions are. If my persisting in holding some conviction will create problems for someone who holds a different conviction with great passion, that may change the case and give me a reason for no longer persisting in my view.

All the same, there is a fairly severe limit to the help available, from a purely individualist standpoint, when we wish to replace conflict with consensus. The most we can say is that I may be prepared to change my moral views if they get in the way of other people's. A preparedness *always* to do so would spell the death of all moral reformers, and would leave me at the mercy of those who held moral opinions with greater intensity, though not necessarily with greater justification, than I. The problems we wrestled with in chapter 5 concerned precisely what the commitments of a sincere moral individual should be when all attempts at accommodation with other individuals had been exhausted in good faith. It is therefore time to ask how the perspective changes when we recognise that individuals are not *just* individuals.

We should note, first, that some ways of recognising that we are not just individuals nevertheless fall short of embracing the ontological collectivism of the previous section. For example, we often think of ourselves not just under the description 'individual' but under some more particular description: 'parent', 'construction worker', and so on. To think of oneself in this way is to classify and therefore to employ general terms which are at least in principle applicable to others, and so at least potentially to place oneself in a group. Suppose, then, that we explicitly define a *group* as any collection of individuals sharing some significant common property, and an *interest group* as any collection of individuals sharing some significant common interest (waiving in each case the question how to determine significance). Then it is plain that neither kind of group need constitute a collective of the kind described in the previous section. Its members may not engage in any corporate action of the required type, and indeed may not consciously think of themselves as members of a group or an interest group at all. It may equally be doubted whether a collective is necessarily always a group. The members of a collective will, it is true, have in common the property of all being members of that collective, but since that is tautologically true it might be held not to be a significant common property of the right kind. There is no doubt, either, that collectives can exist whose members do not constitute an interest group. I may be an unwilling conscript in a collective containing others whose interests stand in opposition to my own.

Speaking generally, we can say that any individual will belong to many groups of both kinds, as well as many collectives. It will be a matter of contention to plot the exact kinds of politically significant descriptions in categorising the groups I belong to (a prominent feature of political debate in recent years, with the rise of the women's movement and the gay rights movement, among others). There will also be the question of the interrelations between the different interest groups to which I belong. I will have different interests as a householder, construction worker, tax-payer, cyclist and so on, and an extremely important political question will be which interest group I take as indicating my primary political allegiance in cases where those interests conflict. For as long as I think of myself purely as a member of different groups and interest groups, however, there is nothing in my calculations which should necessarily loosen the grip of my own personal convictions when it is a matter of how I should act.

But how exactly does this change when I bring membership of collectives into my thinking? After all, similar and additional complications to those concerning groups will arise here. I may belong to collectives which overlap, as in the case of an electorate and a political party, and this may raise problems for me about the correct order of allegiance. A collective may not have a corporate interest as such: a court, for example, is a collective, but we could ascribe an interest to it only in a strained way — by saying, perhaps, that it had an interest in seeing that justice was done or in executing its function properly. Equally, I may or may not have any option in belonging to a given collective. So if I find my personal convictions at odds with the views of the collective, why should there be any greater pressure here for me to depart from my own decisions than there is elsewhere?

The question is a fair one. Collectives are real, and the nature of human life is such that, though there may be a limited option over which ones to belong to, there is probably no option over whether to belong to any at all. But none of this will settle the question what difference these facts should make to my deliberation and action. We have established that my identity is not exhausted in my individuality, that part of what I am is a constituent in different collectives, that what I am doing can sometimes be adequately described only in terms which reveal its contribution to a collective action. Equally, we have seen that the causal nature of collectives is such that the strongest reason for resisting decisions opposed to my own is void in that context. Nevertheless, there may be other reasons for insisting on following my own conscience even in the context of a collective.

For this to be otherwise, we need a clear understanding of the circumstances where my identity is bound up with that of a collective not only in the sense just described, but where it is rational for me to identify with it in the sense of regarding its decisions as my own, and to feel as little justified in resisting them as I should in resisting a decision of my own merely because I could see some reason against it. These will, obviously, be fairly special circumstances, and they will not obtain wherever I happen to belong to some collective or other. At the level of pure theory, however, I believe we can give a specification of one case where they do obtain. That is the case where a number of individuals, with good reason, voluntarily and explicitly form themselves into a collective with specific and definite purposes in mind. It is worth dwelling on a very simple model of this kind, in order to understand its implications.

Where I am a member of this kind of collective, not only is it true that in that context I exist solely as a constituent in the collective, but it is entirely appropriate for me to think in those terms. Of course it would still be possible for the collective to pursue a course which as an individual I found abhorrent (since after all I still *am* also an individual) and that is a conflict which I should have to deal with. And precisely because it is the collective which resolves and acts in certain ways, it may be necessary for me to consider resignation from it in such circumstances, if I no longer feel it proper to identify with it. Whether I take that step will turn on how I evaluate the strength of my views as an individual against the interest of the collective. But that is already a considerable shift from the form in which the problems of social decision-making presented themselves at the beginning of chapter 5.

What is the precise nature of an individual's contribution to the decision-making of a collective in this sort of case? There is a partial analogy here with the 'performative' use of language. In that use, if the circumstances are right and appropriate procedures are gone through, the utterance of certain words may constitute not merely a description of an action but the performance of the action itself (cf. Austin 1962: 6-7). For instance, my uttering the words 'I promise . . .' may constitute an act of promising, a substantive event in the world which alters social relations and from which various consequences flow. In the appropriate circumstances, my saying 'I promise . . .' *makes it true* that I promise (cf. Graham 1977: 76). When a proposition is before the collective that it *holds* such-and-such or *resolves to do* so-and-so, then the contributions and activities of an individual can be seen not just as expressions of opinion, exhortations, arguments and so on, but also as an attempt to bring it about or make it true that the collective does hold or resolve in that way. In the end, though, it is the collective as such which either does or does not hold or resolve. The analogy with performatives lies in the fact that, typically, it is the collective's *saying so* which determines that it does hold or resolve, and, as with performatives, substantive social consequences follow from this becoming true. Where it is not obvious that the collective has decided in a particular way then the procedure of voting will be the clearest means of determining that. If all its constituents support a particular decision then that is what constitutes the collective's having decided in that way.

What if not all the constituents do support it? It is certainly possible for a collective to make a decision not shared by all its component parts. The provision for majority decisions is one means of securing this, and there is no longer the same absolute prohibition on majority decisions as there was on the grounds of their involving the individual in compromising his or her moral principles. If I am on the losing side in a vote taken in the circumstances being discussed, then I have failed to bring it about that the collective decides in a particular way. I can still go on holding the views I did, but that gives no licence to obstruct what the collective then proceeds to do on the basis of the decision it has taken if majority rule is accepted. In a collective of the kind described, therefore, a unanimous decision to abide subsequently by majority decisions would not carry the same stigma as it did where the whole problem was set up with autonomous individual agents as the only entities involved. The reason which stood behind the need to reserve one's autonomy *in each instance* — complete causal responsibility for the outcome — has dissolved.

However, it is more important to emphasise how many stages are possible before resorting to the second-best of majority rule. Where consensus is not achieved in initial unanimity it will often be possible to postpone a collective decision in the interests of further discussion with a view to achieving consensus. If reconsideration still does not result in consensus, dissenters from the majority view can be asked whether they are prepared to *allow* that view to prevail, notwithstanding their own convictions. Where they are thinking and behaving as constituents in a voluntarily formed collective with a definite set of aims which they set store by, the knowledge that they may obstruct the achievement of consensus will have particularly strong independent value and will weigh heavily with them. In these special circumstances, far from being a compromising of one's convictions, a willingness to give way has much morally to recommend it. A great deal is possible, therefore, before the drastic step of withdrawing from the collective which was mentioned earlier.

Of course, we have been discussing the case where an individual's reasons for identifying with the collective are clearest and where the possibilities for consensus are most favourable. It is highly problematic whether or how far the argument could be extended beyond this. To decide that, we should need to incorporate theories about the nature and status of different kinds of collective, and their proximity and similarity to the favoured model. But even on the worst outcome of further consideration, we still have the model itself to serve as a principle or touchstone in other areas.

However, doubts may remain about the satisfactoriness of the model in *any* circumstances. It may be felt, for instance, that talk of consensus merely encourages aspiration to a drab uniformity, that it fails to take account of the evident diversity of people, and fails to appreciate that this diversity is a desirable state of affairs which should not be eclipsed. Moreover, though the idea of a collective consensus may appear elevated, the dangers of corporate selfishness are as great as those of individual selfishness. As J.R. Lucas reminds us, the first person plural is still the first person, and it threatens to exclude third-personal outsiders (Lucas 1977: 265).

The point about the eclipse of diversity, if it works at all, works only against a version of the consensus view which spreads to cover the whole of human life: general diversity is not threatened by pressure to achieve consensus in a specific area. But even in that larger arena the consensus view does not threaten diversity as such, whether in lifestyle, views, or whatever. It simply prescribes a particular approach where individuals already impinge on one another's existence to the extent of jointly performing corporate actions. Here, diversity must harden into disagreement unless consensus is reached, and disagreement will be manifested in coercion. A view which lays stress on the power of discussion, debate and reconsideration in avoiding the need for coercion is not to be dismissed lightly. This is especially true when it does so by making a breach in the literally self-ish approach to decision-making. The first person plural is still plural. The question with what size and nature of collectives I can sensibly and successfully identify is a difficult one to answer, but it is already an important step to establish the *principle* of that kind of identification.

5 CONCLUSION

The arguments about the reality of collectives and the implications for social decision-making serve as a corrective to the individualist arguments of earlier chapters. But it must be stressed that those earlier considerations are to be modified rather than simply abandoned. After all, the earlier characterisations of people as individuals capable of forming rational judgments, of transcending their social situation and so on, are still correct, and the consequences which flow from them are still important. Respect for individuals, in different forms and in different contexts, is not to be wiped out, any more than individuals themselves are. The argument has been not that individuals are less than individuals but that they are also something more than that.

In consequence, the project of grounding an account and defence of democracy in the importance of individual human beings as such has not been abandoned either. Rather, we have provided a theoretical framework which helps to explain why each individual's judgments and actions need not, indeed *cannot,* be taken as paramount in all circumstances. Individuals are not exhausted in their individuality, and this leads rationally and defensibly to a modification both in the attitude to take up to them and in the way we ourselves should think in the context of the collectives we compose.

There is a certain irony in the fact that the model of unanimous direct democracy, where all individual judgments are accommodated, should have been proposed from an individualist position. For that position rests on an ontology which is least likely to serve the end aspired to. When I cease to approach social decision-making in terms of 'What is *my* judgment in the matter?' and begin to recognise the reality of the collective, then I shall cease to feel myself under an external constraint, under threat from an entity only accidentally and contingently related to me, in asking 'What is the consensus? How do *we* judge in the matter?'

On the other hand, what the new theoretical framework has in common with the old is that it has failed to throw up any consideration which points in any obvious way in favour of representative systems of decision-making. In emphasising the individual's existence as a constituent in the entity which makes decisions, it argues for a participatory involvement rather than the relinquishing of this to other individuals. There may be other arguments in favour of representative systems — the exigencies of practical life may seem to make them inescapable — but so far nothing in a normative grounding for democracy has pointed in that direction.

FURTHER READING

The relation between public and private spheres is examined in Strawson 1961 and Benn and Gaus 1983; the relation between egoism and morality in Williams 1972. See also chapter 2: further reading. Lukes 1973 is an informative and wide-ranging survey of different varieties of individualism. The impact of individualism specifically on understanding in the social sciences is the topic of a number of papers in Ryan 1973. For the issue of responsibility, see Honderich 1973 and Watson 1982; and for 'trade-off' theories, see, again, chapter 2: further reading.

Interlude

Interlude

The materials assembled in the course of Part One have gone some way towards achieving the objectives laid down at the beginning. Having examined the web of theories underlying the idea of democracy, we can conclude that we are not dealing here with a term of pure rhetoric, but with a concept which can be elaborated on in a number of ways, some at least of which withstand the test of critical scrutiny. We have seen some of the reasoning which can be used as a plausible support for the basic idea of the people as a whole ruling themselves, and, at a fairly abstract level, how that idea is to be expanded.

Briefly, I favoured a defence of democracy which concentrated on its intrinsic appropriateness for treating people in certain ways, given their nature, rather than on its extrinsic consequences. Within that type of defence, I concluded that a realisation of the key values of liberty and equality which democratic practices are supposed to embody required a permeation of those practices through social life, rather than their confinement to an official 'decision-making' sphere. Latterly, I have sought to give some grounding for the notion of the people as a whole ruling by pointing to contexts where people do form a whole, and this has gone some way to extricating democratic theory from the difficulties which it faces when the importance of the individual is pressed in an unqualified way.

Apart from the fact that all of these arguments stand in need of further elaboration, there are two general points to make about them, which may have occurred to the reader long before now. The first is that, throughout, we have been concerned with a conception of human beings as they can be and sometimes are, rather than as they must be or always are.

Certainly anyone who has been caught up in a street fight, and perhaps anyone who has been involved in anything as mundane as a domestic row, will realise that the picture of human beings as selecting goals in a dignified and rational way, which they then choose appropriate means for realising, is of less than universal application. If the normatively grounded theories which we have developed are to have any application, therefore, they need to be woven into the texture of a more realistic account of the imperfect mess of humanity, which constitutes the only raw material available.

The second point concerns collectives and the associated sense of community. I have pointed to the different, overlapping and conflicting collectives which individuals may belong to, and have suggested that being part of collectives is a central fact of human life. This may be conceded whilst at the same time it is insisted that precisely what is lacking in the modern world is membership of any overall collective and consequently any sense of overall community (a prominent theme in Macintyre 1981). Accordingly, though a model of democracy which depends upon collectives and community may have limited application in limited contexts, it may be thought entirely inappropriate for the wider social structure, for which we also wish to find an applicable theory of democracy. It may have been applicable in the original home of democracy, ancient Greece, but it is not apposite for us, a critic might say.

These two responses are the responses of untutored common sense, and themselves stand in need of embedding in a theoretical context. The aim of Part Two is to survey some of the major options available for constructing a theory of democracy which takes due note of empirical reality. I shall therefore attempt to assess the plausibility of those theories, consider what their consequences are, and measure how well they accord with the normative requirements implicit in the arguments of Part One.

A word may be necessary in explanation of the options selected for discussion in Part Two. I begin with *elite theory,* which may perhaps be seen as a robust and realistic corrective to the theorising in the later stages of Part One and the direction in which it seems to be pointing. Elite theory has its practical feet planted firmly in the soil of existing institutions and forms of life. It therefore provides the best starting point for considering the implications of the two responses mentioned a moment ago.

Participation theory is next discussed. It involves a similar attention to the existing facts of political and social life, but its orientation is very different, and in some ways it can be seen as a reaction to elite theory. The data of concrete experience are assembled in the service of a theory for change, a theory which amounts to the advocacy of the need for new forms of life as embodiments of democratic principle.

Elite theory and participation theory take us into the realms of applied theory by virtue of their much greater concern to describe and explain concrete arrangements than the type of argument discussed and employed in Part One. Nevertheless, though they carry political connotations (of a conservative and reforming nature, respectively), they are both recognisably academic types of theory in the first instance, in their presentation, mode of argumentation, and so on.

Not so the final two subjects of discussion in Part Two, *Marxist theory* and *Leninist theory*. Marx and Lenin were, in their different historical contexts, political activists; and although the published writings of each are voluminous, they are not, for the most part, academic treatises. All the same, to the extent that they contain explicit or implicit theoretical claims it is possible to subject them to academic examination. We can ask how far they are conceptually cogent, plausible and normatively acceptable, in the same way as for other writings, even if their authors would not thank us for that kind of attention.

I believe that it is not merely possible but desirable to subject these theories to such critical examination in the context of this book. For of course, as well as being different in form from other theories discussed here, they are strikingly different in content. They provide the strongest opposition to the liberal individualist tradition defined in the Introduction and discussed in the main body of the book. Whether properly understood or not, they have been historically influential. Their relation to democratic theory is, to say the least, problematic, and the disentangling of that relation is consequently of some importance.

As will emerge, however, I have a further reason for paying attention to Marxist and Leninist theories in this context, and for treating them separately. I believe that Marx's relation to democracy has been on the whole poorly understood, and that one of the reasons for this is that his theories have generally been viewed through the filter provided by Lenin. I therefore attempt to differentiate between these theories in a fairly thoroughgoing way, and assess their (very different) contributions to democratic theory.

Part Two: Applied Theory

'The first step in the revolution by the working class is to raise the proletariat to the position of ruling class, to win the battle of democracy.'
Karl Marx and Friedrich Engels *The Communist Manifesto*.

7 Elite theory

1 INTRODUCTION

We live in a society with centres of population containing millions of human beings. For most of them, the limit of involvement in official politics is to vote periodically for someone else to take decisions on their behalf, and for many there is not even this minimal degree of involvement. Those elected to take decisions almost invariably belong to large political parties which possess considerable funds and are likely to hire the services of an advertising agency to sell them successfully to the electorate. (Such niceties are unnecessary in parts of the world where political opinion is ruthlessly contained within one monopolistic political party.) Within the small group of elected decision-makers, an even smaller group will have control over such decisions as whether to embark on courses of action which may, quite literally, lead to the extermination of the human race.

This state of affairs, though it is utterly removed from anything which could reasonably be regarded as an embodiment of the notions evolved in Part One, is generally called democracy. We have here, therefore, a matter calling for explanation. Are the theories developed in Part One simply irrelevant to the real world? Or are we wrong to describe systems of the kind just specified as democratic?

In this chapter we shall examine theories of a type which has emerged in this century in answer to these questions. The theories have their origin in texts by different authors, and there are important differences among them. I have not sought to concentrate on these differences, however, or to give a systematic account of any one author. My concern is, rather, to focus on a particular core which they have in common. This is a recognition of the reality of a state of affairs where elites compete periodically for endorsement by the wider population, with that wider population playing little or no part in substantive decision-making. I shall consider and evaluate the arguments surrounding this realist description of existing systems and the conclusions drawn from it, as well as the question exactly how to construe the status of theories of this kind. Often they carry the assumption that this not only is the existing state of affairs but that it must be, and that is one point at which these theories require scrutiny. There is also the distinct and trickier question whether they carry the further assumption that this is how things ought to be, whether there is in this sense a normative dimension to these theories.

I shall speak in this context of elite theory. The terms 'empirical theory' or 'empirical democratic theory' are sometimes used instead, in reference to the body of theory in question. This is an indication of the detailed attention to empirical features of existing systems which is a central characteristic of these theories. I regard these alternative terms as misleading, however, precisely because of the issue of the status of the theories in question. To employ them is to suggest that those theories might be *purely* empirical, carrying no excess conceptual or normative baggage. The term 'elite theory' at least avoids that complication, and it will be clear that the theories under discussion do all postulate elites of one kind or another as a central feature of democracy. This term itself is not perfect, in fact. As we shall see in chapter 10, the Leninist argument, which is in other respects very different, also postulates an elite as a central part of its theory. Still, the term does indicate a feature shared by the theories described in this chapter, even if it is not possessed solely by them.

2   THE THEORY STATED

An absolutely central early influence in elite theory is Schumpeter's *Capitalism, Socialism and Democracy* (Schumpeter 1943). There can be little doubt that Schumpeter would dismiss the arguments of Part One of this book as irrelevant to applied theorising about the real world. Arguing against what he calls the classical doctrine of democracy, he objects that there can be no common good which people can be got to agree on, since they face 'irreducible differences of ultimate values which compromise could only maim and degrade' (*ibid*.: 251). Moreover, he would not be interested in a more adequate theory of the same type as those discussed in Part One. Democracy, he insists, cannot function as an ideal or an end in itself, since it is simply a method, a particular institutional arrangement for arriving at political decisions (*ibid*.: 242). Hence, his own definition of democracy is 'that institutional arrangement for arriving at political decisions in which individuals acquire power to decide by means of a competitive struggle for the people's vote' (*ibid*.: 269). This definition places an elite very firmly at the heart of democracy by virtue of its division between individuals and the people, and its allocation of the power to decide to the former rather than the latter.

Robert Dahl, whose influence ranks with that of Schumpeter, argues via a rather different route to a similar conclusion in his *A Preface to Democratic Theory* (Dahl 1956). Beginning from a conception of democracy in some respects similar to those discussed in Part One (it includes considerable stress on political equality, for example), Dahl argues that it makes a crucial difference once we raise the question what conditions must be met for approaching a democracy in the real world (*ibid*.: 64). No human organisation of more than a few people, he suggests, is ever likely to meet the appropriate conditions, amongst other reasons because of greatly varying levels of interest in decision-making and ability to influence it (*ibid*.: 71-4). His conclusion is that the majority rarely rules, but that democracy is to be characterised by the rule of minorities (*ibid*.: 131-). There may be a plurality of such minorities, and their membership may change, but that is what must be put at the heart of a theory of democracy applicable to the real world.

Apparent as an influence in these and other elite theories is the work of Michels, who much earlier this century had propounded the famous 'iron law of oligarchy', according to which it was an inescapable fact of human experience that a dominant minority class must exist in society, with the equally inescapable consequence that the majority cannot rule (Michels 1915). Schumpeter regards leadership as 'the dominant mechanism of practically any collective action which is more than a reflex' (Schumpeter 1943: 270), and a recent commentator has described Michels's critique of democracy as 'sound and unanswerable' (Corcoran 1983: 18).

The twentieth century is indeed fertile ground for the propagation of views of this kind. Those aspects of life in modern society which we might gather together under the slogan 'size, time and complexity' conspire to increase their plausibility. The volume of decisions which modern governments have to make, their complex and often technical nature, mean that the average person — of whom there are millions — simply does not have the time, the knowledge or the interest to make any significant contribution to those decisions. Schumpeter, unkindly but perhaps not inaccurately, invites us to consider the different degrees of effort and intelligent thought which people bring to politics, on the one hand, and some leisure activity like bridge, on the other (Schumpeter 1943: 261). A line has to be drawn somewhere, however, and the curtailment of political activity by the ordinary person need not always be seen in a disreputable light. Dahl reminds us that there will be a multiplicity of bodies which govern matters that affect us in some way or other. There must be a limit to the extent to which we can contribute to their decisions, if we are ever to have any time left over to do anything else which we find of value (Dahl 1970: 42-6).

Further explanation is forthcoming for the lack of serious involvement in social decision-making. Schumpeter argues that in affairs falling within one's personal experience it is possible to form definite preferences and to manifest a high degree of rationality. The connexion between one's own decisions and the results is perceptible and immediate. But as we move away from that situation, he suggests, there is a loss of a sense of reality and a reduced sense of responsibility. This is at its most acute when we reach the national and international levels, where a citizen may have grumbles and wishes, but nothing which could be called a will, since at that stage the citizen is a member of an unworkable committee, the committee of the whole nation (Schumpeter 1943: 256-61). In a similar vein, Dahl argues that as the size of a meeting increases, so rhetoric and crowd manipulation begin to take over (Dahl 1970: 70).

So far, this all looks very bleak news for the elevated picture of a body of free and equal autonomous agents earnestly striving to reach a consensus. The theoretical problems raised in Part One about justifying majority rule begin to look like an unattainable luxury, in the face of a social reality where in no meaningful sense can it be said that the majority does rule. However, we need to temper the starkness of the contrast between the total involvement of the whole populace throughout the decision-making procedure, typical of the abstract theories of our earlier discussion, and their relegation to the periphery in elite theory. For one thing, the possibilities change when groups, parties and representatives are introduced into the process. An individual can join forces with others, even if they disagree on a range of issues, if they take the view that their pursuit of certain common aims is sufficiently important to them to sink their differences. In this way, what is lost in terms of individual discretion and influence may be outweighed by the superior effectiveness of group action. In the absence of all the time-consuming acquisition of knowledge, and so on, which is not practical, the individual may also evaluate the records of different potential representatives who may aspire to act on his or her behalf, and in this way have an indirect measure of control over decision-making.

In fact, the wider population may exert some influence or control in an indefinite number of ways, and to varying extents, over those who rule in the strict sense of actually making political decisions. Schumpeter points out that even a dictator has to enlist the co-operation of some people, neutralise the effects of others, and so on (Schumpeter 1943: 245). The issue is not therefore a straightforward one of either ruling in the strict sense or being in subjugation. No more is the role of a member of a ruling elite to be seen as consisting in either a complete freedom from all constraints to act as he or she chooses or as being subject to a specific mandate from the rest of the population. In both cases, matters of degree and exact relations within the institutional framework are of crucial importance.

This is essentially the line taken by Dahl. A system with periodical elections and competition between political parties, he suggests, does not result in majority rule, but it does vastly increase the size, number and variety of minorities whose preferences must be taken into account by leaders in making policy choices (Dahl 1956: 132). The normal American process is an example where an 'active and legitimate group' can make itself heard effectively, the criterion for which is that officials expect to suffer in some significant way if they do not placate the group. Hence, government decisions rest not on majority — the numerical majority is incapable of any co-ordinated action — but on 'the steady appeasement of relatively small groups' (*ibid.*: 145-6). And it is, of course, a feature of such a system that the group which rules in the strict sense may fail to appease sufficient other groups, to a sufficient degree, to remain in power when the next periodical election comes round — further clear proof, it is thought, of the residue of power which remains with the electorate.

Now to describe matters in this way is to put a particular kind of gloss on elite theory. It is to imply that when it constructs a model involving competition between small groups for the purpose of attaining power it does so *faute de mieux,* as a regrettable necessity in the real world, but where nevertheless as much power as possible is to remain in the hands of the populace at large. It would be misleading not to make clear, however, that much elite theory is very different in tone, manifesting considerable mistrust of the populace, and portraying its ignorance and apathy in very unflattering terms.

For example, in the influential *Voting* (Berelson 1954), empirical investigations suggested little political debate among the populace at large, very weak motivation to become involved in the political process and indifference towards the result. The considerable amount of 'don't know' encountered was thought more often than not to signify 'don't care' (*ibid.*: 309), and the requirement of active participation in decision-making was held to be more appropriate for the opinion leaders in the society *(ibid.*: 322-3).

This view of the electorate was reinforced by subsequent

empirical studies on both sides of the Atlantic. Campbell *et al.* held in the US context that sheer ignorance of the existence of major social and economic problems was one of the main limitations on civic participation (Campbell 1960: 170). Their measures, they believed, had shown that the public's understanding of policy issues was poorly developed. Drawing a distinction between 'the typical voter' and 'more sophisticated individuals', they concluded that the former had only a modest understanding, or might even be quite ignorant, as compared with the latter (*ibid.*: 542). In relation to Britain, Abrams and Rose took the view that probably only one-tenth of the electorate was sufficiently well-informed on most issues to be able to state reasons for and against particular policies. The electorate, they concluded, was not only uninformed but also uninterested (Abrams and Rose 1969: 73).

However, though these descriptions of the electorate might be unflattering, they were not thought by some elite theorists to represent an undesirable state of affairs. On the contrary, since active participation centred around highly charged issues, it threatened the stability and basic consensus which were essential for the survival of democracy. Hence, apathy and restricted participation were actually beneficial for the system. As Berelson put it, 'an individual "inadequacy" provides a positive service for the system' (Berelson 1954: 316). On that view of the matter, a high degree of active participation was not just unfeasible but undesirable. The news that elections told us little about the voters' preferences with regard to specific policies was met with relief rather than regret.

3   THE THEORY ASSESSED

There is one possible criticism of elite theory which I wish to put aside. That is the criticism that it gets off on the wrong foot at the outset because it is formulated in reaction to a 'classical democratic theory' which is itself a myth, a mixture of different theories not held by any one author (cf. Pateman 1970: 17-21). That criticism may be justified, but it is not relevant to an assessment of the merits of elite theory itself. It is worth mentioning, however, since a similar complaint might be levelled against my own outline of elite theory. Any of the authors cited in the previous section might complain that I have associated views which they do express with others which they do not, others which are expressed only by separate theorists. That is perfectly correct, but I hope none would take it amiss if I said that it is no individual writer as such that I am concerned with in assessing elite theory. A climate of thought may be created by the work of a number of theorists in such a way that an accurate description of that climate may well fail as an accurate description of any given, single theorist. Such a climate of thought clearly was created by the theorists discussed in the previous section, whatever differences of opinion there may be among them, and that is what I wish to examine.

In at least one respect elite theory is developed in terms which are congenial with those employed towards the end of the discussion in Part One. It works with an ontology of pressure groups, political parties and the like. True, it comes to this via a description of contemporary political reality rather than via abstract theorising of the kind contained in chapter 6. Nevertheless, the net result is the same — that a theory of democratic decision-making should accord independent importance to entities in which individual human beings as such are merely constituents. Some of these entities will be groups and collectives in the senses defined in chapter 6, sections 3 and 4.

At the same time, the unfinished business of chapter 6 remains unfinished in this new context. We still have the question which groups and collectives it is rational for individual human beings to identify with. At best, that question is simply not raised in elite theory. At worst, there is a tacit assumption that what is beneficial for the political system as a whole is beneficial for the individuals within it. This is not necessarily true. If the stability of the system depended on apathy among the mass of citizens and if, for example, that apathy depended on their occupying a subservient and impoverished position, then there would be little reason for such citizens to identify with the needs of the system. To put it another way, stability is an ambiguous value. Whether you have reason to prize it will turn on the nature of the set of social relations being stabilised and your position within them.

Elite theory also provides a salutary reminder that the conception of autonomous, rational agents is an ideal which is lived up to only imperfectly, with momentous consequences in the realm of human intercourse generally and political life in particular. Questions then arise about where we go from there. In what respects does this require amendment of democratic theory? Is it a state of affairs capable of significant alteration? On the face of it, elite theory does not provide explicit answers to these questions (though we shall have to consider in the next section whether that appearance is correct). A precondition for answering them, however, is an adequate diagnosis of present imperfections in the attainment of rational, autonomous agency. Elite theory does provide such a diagnosis, but there is serious doubt whether it is accurate.

Take, for example, the issue of the empirical evidence for the conclusions about the high level of apathy and ignorance among the mass of the electorate. A considerable body of data and research has been accumulated whose findings stand in opposition to those of elite theory. One crucial work of this kind was *The Responsible Electorate* (Key 1966), whose author sought to establish 'the perverse and unorthodox argument ... that voters are not fools', but rather are moved by concern with central questions of public policy (*ibid*.: vii). They behaved rationally and responsibly, he suggested, within the limits set by the alternatives offered and the information available. Other studies (many of them described in Pennock 1979: 288-93) came to similar conclusions, and a different picture of voters came to be offered, therefore, one which made their contribution to political decisions a good deal less suspect. They were depicted as better informed and far more disposed to align their voting behaviour with their preferences, as opposed to voting in a particular way out of blind habit or tradition (cf. Pomper 1972).

This is not the place for a full-scale evaluation of the rival empirical hypotheses concerning the nature of the electorate, but two points may be made. First, it pays to be cautious in embracing generalisations about 'the voter' or 'the citizen' on the basis of very particular and local empirical data. The subject of Berelson's original research had been one community on one electoral occasion (though an appendix contains a summary of apparently similar findings from other election studies. Cf. Berelson 1954: 327-47). Berelson himself was alive to the dangers here (cf. *ibid*.: xiii), but other theorists may not have been so careful. Key's work, in contrast, covers US presidential elections from 1936 to 1960, and Pomper's from 1956 to 1968. Secondly, it may well be that the original picture of the average voter as apathetic and ignorant was more plausible for a particular stretch of historical time. The 1950s were a notoriously apathetic decade, politically speaking, and the generalisation about the apathy of the electorate looked far more suspect by the end of the 1960s than it would have at the beginning of them.

Still, there is a detectable degree of inactivity on the part of the general populace in the official political sphere, and speculation or theorising is called for to account for it. One suggestion, not to be lightly dismissed, is that for less privileged groups, among whom apathy is generally held to be concentrated, a relatively high cost is attached to political activity which they are in the worst position to afford. As Barry puts it, their apparent apathy may reflect the fact that they cannot afford the luxury of collective political action (Barry 1970: 34). A slightly different way of looking at it is to suggest that if these citizens correctly perceive that they do not belong to the most powerful organised interest groups, and that in consequence any efforts they will make will be relatively ineffectual, then it is wrong to characterise their apathy as irrational (cf. Margolis 1983: 127-8). Yet a third option would be the idea that the observed level of inactivity need not denote apathy — it might be an index of frustration, for example — but that nevertheless it is irrational, since those worst off cannot afford the luxury of *not* having anything to do with politics.

Without even attempting to choose among these options, we can see that one and the same set of empirical data about people's behaviour can be open to quite different interpretations; and the interpretation adopted will depend, among other things, on more general political theories and values. In this regard there has been some justified criticism of elite theory, on the grounds that the particular interpretation which it offers amounts to an undefended celebration of existing social arrangements. The idea that ruling elites are kept within bounds where they must periodically compete for election, and that the interests of people in general are looked after by virtue of groups bringing pressure to bear on such ruling elites, it has been objected, takes too little notice of the surrounding social context in which these activities take place (cf. Bachrach 1967: 36-8).

An analogy is often drawn between the workings of democracy as seen in elite theory and the workings of market society. It is fair to point out that, just as a market economy measures only demand which has money to back it, so the apparatus of an indirect system of democracy, based on political parties, bureaucracies and the like, measures only political demands with the power (including the economic power) to back them. Even if individuals are properly organised into a pressure group, they may have no means of bringing effective pressure to bear on a ruling elite if they are devoid of power. To take an example, the unemployed, however well organised, cannot lay down threats to government of either of the kinds which big business or organised labour can. A general failing, we might therefore say, of elite theory is that it ignores the kind of lesson learnt in the discussion of liberty in chapter 3. Schumpeter asserts that everyone is free to compete for political leadership in a democracy just in the same sense in which everyone is free to start another textile mill (Schumpeter 1943: 272 n.6). If that is so, then a worthwhile ideal of liberty is not being conformed to, and there is as yet little cause for self-congratulation.

Consider next the claims in elite theory about the average citizen's reduced sense of reality and sense of responsibility when approaching large-scale political questions, as against the immediate and local issues of personal life. I shall discuss in more detail in the next chapter the objection that it is precisely because the mass of people are excluded from any significant, active participation in decision-making that they do not perform particularly well at it. If that objection can be sustained, then it allows the further proposal, in the spirit of some of the views expressed by John Stuart Mill in *Representative Government,* that drawing them into a fuller participation in public decisions will itself have an educative effect, force them to widen their horizons and improve the quality of their performance (cf. Pateman 1970: 29-31).

Even if that objection were accepted, however, there is one aspect of the elite theory's argument which it would fail to touch. That is the point that in private life there is immediate perception of the consequences of one's decisions, immediate feedback which establishes clear lines of responsibility. It is arguable that here elite theory is correct not only in its description of contemporary reality, but also with regard to the different state of affairs envisaged by the advocate of greater participation. For, it may be said, whereas a member of a very small elite, and most of all a president or a prime minister, may experience a similarly immediate feedback with regard to his or her public decisions, that immediate experience ceases to be possible for any given individual at all where participation is very widespread. The lines of causal influence are spread wider and correspondingly thinner, so that no one ends up feeling a clear responsibility for the outcome.

I believe this suggestion is plausible, but not in the end persuasive. It concerns several questions: what the facts of causal responsibility actually are; how people are likely to respond to those facts; and, perhaps implicitly, how it is appropriate or desirable for them to respond. We have already seen some of the complications attending the first question, at an abstract level, in chapter 6, sections 2 and 3. It is, I suggested, an oversimplification of the forms of influence operating on the individual, and also an oversimplification of the nature of social action, to suppose that what I bring about is entirely the consequence of my own isolated decisions and efforts. Schumpeter himself makes essentially the same point at a less abstract level, as we have seen, when he observes that even a dictator must rely on the co-operation of large numbers of other people to bring plans to fruition. In consequence, a feeling that one is solely responsible for the outcome of one's decisions is actually a misperception, and one which in some cases (no doubt including some presidents and prime ministers) will amount to clinical megalomania. Whether it is appropriate or desirable for anyone to labour under such an illusion must be at least problematic.

In contrast, where decisions are taken by a collective of the type described in chapter 6, section 3, it will be much more evident that causal responsibility is dispersed. Suppose, then, that the population were directly involved in making political decisions in the context of such a collective, rather than, as at present, being peripherally and indirectly involved by virtue of electing members of a small elite, who themselves make such decisions. It is a matter for speculation how the members of that population would view their responsibility in those new circumstances. Certainly we might surmise, as Wolff does concerning a similar situation, that there would be a flowering of interest and a level of informed responsibility quite unlike anything previously encountered (Wolff 1976: 34-7).

More than this would need to be settled, however, if we wished to answer the further question which state of affairs was preferable. We should need to decide not only whether members of an elite are sufficiently awed by their perception of their responsibilities to behave with greater decency than a mass of 'ordinary' citizens would; we should also have to decide whether it was compatible with the values implicit in democratic theory that so much power should be concentrated in so few hands. Ideally, of course, we should observe a directly participating mass in action to see what sense of responsibility they could muster, before passing to the difficult task of comparing this with rule by an elite.

But at this stage it may be objected that we have reached the realms of fantasy. In view of those conditions of life encapsulated in the previous section under the slogan 'size, time and complexity', it may be claimed, the comparison required here is not even in principle capable of being carried out. Elite theory will win the argument by default, as it were, since it just is not possible for everyone standing outside the elites to take on power in their place.

Let us pursue the fantasy, if that is what it is. Wolff makes his comments about responsibility in the context of a proposal for the introduction of 'instant direct democracy', a proposal which he describes as being meant 'a good deal more than half in earnest' Wolff 1976: 34). This is that news programmes on television be replaced by briefing sessions, debates, and the like, on matters requiring social decisions. Experts would be commissioned to provide relevant data and make recommendations. Then once a week there would be a voting session by telephone, in which the whole populace voted on the current issues. I am not concerned to evaluate Wolff's speculation about the resulting level of responsibility. What I do think is noteworthy is that in one respect this is not a fantasy at all. That is that there are no technological obstacles to the state of affairs described by Wolff coming into being.

That is a significant point. We have seen in Part One the importance of rational debate to a defensible conception of democracy, and there have been crucial developments in the twentieth century, in the means of disseminating and collecting information, which facilitate such debate among the population. The development of computer technology and cable television allowing a two-way flow are of clear relevance, for example. The exact significance of the point can no doubt be misunderstood or exaggerated, but it still has application. It can forestall any very simple objection that the high degree of participation characteristic of democracy in its original setting of ancient Greece is impossible of attainment merely because of the size of modern populations. No doubt difficult questions arise about how debates could be organised and run, and how questions for decision were to be framed; and it is obvious that some system of delegation would be unavoidable. But it will not do simply to argue that the populace cannot all be got into a public forum large enough to hold them. Technology, in short, makes a difference to the ways in which, and the extent to which, a given ideal can be embodied in actual social relations. If you have to send someone round on horseback to collect the votes, it is not possible to consult an entire population over matters requiring speedy action; with computer technology, it is.

What this forces us to do is clarify the thoughts behind the slogan 'size, time and complexity', and in particular to determine how much of the problem so denoted is due to brute material arrangements and how much to 'human nature' or human frailty of one kind or another. One recent writer is in no doubt. In connexion with the political possibilities opened up by a two-way cable television network in Columbus, Ohio, he concedes that there is no longer a problem about the technical feasibility of direct democracy at the level of the large-scale nation state: the problem is rather about the 'quality of the preferences' which would then control policy (Fishkin 1982: 6).

We have seen that there are opposing views on that question. What must now be added is that if elite theory relies too heavily on an argument from the poor quality of the preferences of the general public, it is in danger of undercutting itself.

If those preferences are so bad and unreliable when it is a matter of issues of policy, why suppose that they will be any better when it is a matter of selecting leaders? It will not do to reply that all the populace needs to do, in the cyclical process of selecting leaders, is to judge whether a given elite has achieved its aims and is therefore worthy to continue in power. An elite may achieve its aims despite, rather than because of, its own efforts, if there are sufficient compensating factors present in the circumstances in which it is operating. It will take a fine judgment of causal chains to decide whether this is so or not in a given case. What is far more likely in political reality, of course, is that an elite fails to achieve at least some of its aims, and is ready with plausible explanations for its failure. Again, a similar expertise in judgment of causal connexions will be needed to assess the explanations.

We may then be led to wonder whether competence in selecting leaders and competence in selecting policies are really separable at all. After all, a precondition of making a rational choice of leaders will be the capacity to judge which of them have sound plans for achieving given objectives, and this will be inseparable from a capacity to judge that particular plans actually are sound. But then the fall-back position, that the masses should be confined to choosing leaders as a kind of damage-limitation exercise, because of their incompetence in political judgment, becomes an untenable one.

This is a very serious matter for an elite theory. If consistency requires that the doubts about ordinary citizens' competence to judge policies be extended to their ability to select leaders, elite theory is in danger of ceasing to be a theory of democracy at all. For it is, of course, their supposed lack of competence in the first area which justifies their exclusion from policy decision-making. And if so, then why should their incompetence in the second area — which turns out to be part of the very same incompetence — not equally justify their exclusion from selecting leaders? But then the extent to which they can be regarded as ruling themselves has shrunk to zero. The minimal demand on any theory of democracy is that it should conform to some interpretation of 'rule by the people', and an elite theory which pursued this apparently consistent line would not even meet that demand.

There are, naturally, rejoinders which might be made on behalf of elite theory at this point. One, which we shall consider in the next section, would be to deny that it is in the business of justification at all. Another would be to resist the implication of the last few paragraphs, that exclusion from policy decisions must be accounted for by an exhaustive choice between facts about technology or dismal facts about human frailty. Rather, it may be held that it is facts about human *organisation,* or social structure which dictate exclusion for all but a few. In other words, it may be insisted that we take seriously the idea that the existence of oligarchies really is ruled by an iron law, that there is something in the nature of social life which, leaving aside all questions of technology and human wickedness or ignorance, calls forth ruling groups. A plausible candidate for such a factor would be the need for social differentiation in contemporary society, with resulting disparities in kind and degree of expertise which different citizens possess (cf. Dunn 1979: 18-19). Given that we cannot simply abandon and take on new roles at will, the social division of labour puts a brake on aspirations of political equality. Someone, we may feel, just has to do the political work, and it cannot be everyone. That conclusion may be further bolstered by a challenge to find any society or group bearing a significant resemblance to our own which does not manifest the same tendency for particular groups within it to take on the role of political elite or leadership.

This latter challenge carries echoes of our earlier discussion of political equality in chapter 4, section 3. As in that earlier context, I should argue that the inability to point to examples which embody some favoured state of affairs is a disadvantage, but not a fatal one. What would compensate for it would be a plausible theory which not only explained why elites flourish as they do, but was also able to postulate circumstances in which they would cease to do so. There is no absence of candidates for such a theory. Thus, it can be argued that it is inequalities in such variables as wealth or education which produce elites; that those inequalities are themselves socially produced rather than being the result of nature; and that it is possible to evolve forms of social organisation in which those features are absent. Whether these arguments can be sustained is a question to be taken up in later chapters. All we can say at this stage is that the issue between elite theorist and critic remains open. The widespread existence of elites in modern society is no more than a weak presumption in favour of their inevitability, but it is a presumption which has to be rebutted.

4 THE STATUS OF ELITE THEORY

Virtually all items of literature which can be regarded as contributions to elite theory purport not merely to describe but also to *explain* the systems they deal with. To that extent at least, the confinement of political decision-making to a relatively small number of people will be viewed as not accidental or arbitrary; and in many cases, the stronger and more definite position is adopted that such confinement is necessary or inevitable. As I have indicated, it is less clear how far there is a definite commitment to the view that it is desirable. For the understanding of that issue it is pertinent to mention the intellectual climate attending the formation of elite theory.

I referred briefly in chapter 1 to the tradition, stemming from David Hume, which holds that there is an unbridgeable gulf between statements of fact and statements of value. That tradition received strong reinforcement in the 1930s with the growth of logical positivism, according to which statements of value are not merely separated from factual statements about the nature of the world — so that they cannot be supported by evidence in any straightforward way — but are not properly expressive of coherent thoughts at all. Normative judgments or judgments of value were, in the terminology made popular by

Ayer (1936), merely emotive, serving to express and arouse feelings but not being susceptible of truth or falsity.

This view of the matter had (and, I should argue, continues to have) a profound impact not just in philosophy but in social scientific disciplines. It served to confirm in their views those theorists who were already suspicious of the murky nature of normative judgments, and to induce an uneasiness in others that making them was engaging in a form of discourse which could not conform to normal standards of rigour and rationality. The upshot in either case was an aspiration to engage in 'value-free' theorising, producing work which was scientific and objective, and free of tainted normative commitments. Much (though not all) elite democratic theory must be understood in this way. It does not merely involve the rejection of particular normative positions, in the way I suggested earlier in this chapter that Schumpeter rejected the importance attached to consensus in some democratic theory. Rather, the intention is to avoid normative commitment altogether, in favour of producing a purely empirical theory.

Doubts can be raised whether it is a feasible project at all to produce value-free social scientific theories, and many critics have held that in any case elite theory fails to do so. Specifically, it has been claimed that theories of this type are normatively conservative, since they involve an uncritical acceptance and justification of the existing political system (cf. Duncan and Lukes 1963, Walker 1965).

Now this charge must be handled with care. It is certainly difficult to read the work of elite theorists and believe that they have no views on the desirability of the present system. Indeed, on occasion they express these explicitly. Berelson argues that the existing system 'not only works on the most difficult and complex questions but often works with distinction' (Berelson 1954: 312). Dahl regards it as no mean thing that the American system provides a high probability that any active and legitimate group will make itself heard effectively, a 'relatively efficient system for reinforcing agreement, encouraging moderation and maintaining social peace . . .' (Dahl 1956: 150-1). However, this does not necessarily vitiate or in any way contaminate their original descriptive and explanatory theories themselves. These normative views expressed by the theorists could be regarded as simply optional extras, as it were, which they have appended.

Is there any more integral way in which elite theory is inescapably normative? Consider two possibilities. In an argument briefly described in chapter 2, section 3, David Miller observes that the original theories are intended to be explanatory of 'how democratic systems do in fact work as opposed to how they are supposed to work according to the familiar rhetoric of democratic politics' (Miller 1983: 135). But the model developed to explain this is also normative, he suggests: if it shows that a system of competition between elites produces a result in line with the people's wishes then a democrat must, other things being equal, approve of that system. Hence, he concludes, 'it makes no sense to divorce the explanatory and normative aspects' of such theories (*ibid.*).

Leaving aside any other possible difficulties in Miller's argument, however, it still does not show that any normative commitment is actually integral to elite theory. For example, we might note that, by the same token, if the theory showed the system produced a result in line with people's wishes, then an *anti*-democrat must *dis*approve of the system. What this reveals is that the normative commitment would be located in a reader's response to the theory rather than in the theorist's own assertions. It is still not in the theory itself.

A second possibility is provided by Quentin Skinner. Basing his claim on facts about the use of the term 'democracy', he suggests that it has the dual role of *describing* a more or less determinate set of characteristics of a system, and also of *commending* the system (Skinner 1973: 298). The set of characteristics is only more or less determinate, since differing views are possible of what constitutes rule by the people. On the other hand, it is held to be a 'non-contingent fact' that to describe a system as a democracy is to endorse, commend or approve of it. Accordingly, when elite theorists offer their own account of how competition between elites may constitute rule by the people, this is held to be a straightforward empirical claim. Nevertheless, it cannot be presented in the guise of normatively neutral analysis, since we are obliged to accept it as commendable (*ibid.*: 297, 299).

This is a complex issue which I have tried to unravel elsewhere

(Graham 1985). The nature of the commendatory force attaching to the term 'democracy' needs further elaboration. For one thing, as Skinner himself is aware, it is only in relatively recent historical times that the term has come to carry a positive, rather than negative, commendatory force. More importantly, it is perfectly possible explicitly to dissociate oneself from this force, without contradiction, by announcing one's opposition to democracy. This certainly raises a doubt about whether it is a non-contingent fact that to describe a system as a democracy is (usually) to commend it.

Despite this, however, something close to the substance of Skinner's point seems to me correct. In the political culture we are concerned with and live in, the description of a system as democratic may reasonably be taken to be an expression of approval, in the absence of any special disclaimers to the contrary. Equally, and for similar reasons, it may *elicit* approval (though whether it in fact does so may depend crucially on exactly what is so described). The problem with elite theory is then that, with its commitment to 'realistic' empirical investigation from the outset, it involves making assumptions — rather than producing arguments — about which systems are properly to be identified as democratic.

That is the deeper fault in the approach of elite theory, and it exists independently of any question of the normative or commendatory force of the term 'democracy'. We can allow that if the term has a normative aspect even roughly of the kind Skinner posits, then elite theory itself has a normative aspect. But even if this were not so, theories of this kind would still be incomplete and inadequately defended, for reasons put forward in chapter 1, section 1. Elite theory, like any theory about anything, carries conceptual assumptions as well as making empirical claims. It carries conceptual assumptions about how the objects of its investigations are to be identified, or what systems are to count as democratic. Unlike some theories in other areas, however, theories of democracy are not uncontroversial in the assumptions they make on that question. There are rival claimants for the term democracy, opposing views on its application. Therefore, as I argued in chapter 1, philosophical arguments are called for — explanations of the principles behind a particular use of the term and the purpose it is designed to serve — rather than just empirical claims.

In consequence, the task of justifying the application of the epithet 'democratic' to a particular kind of system cannot be avoided. And the fact that the term is, as a matter of fact, applied by people in a given way does not remove the need for such justification. We still need to defend the view that what we call democracy really is democracy. Critics of elite theory have rightly felt that the data unearthed by it about the systems normally called democratic have made that task harder rather than easier.

5 CONCLUSION

I remarked earlier on the recognition in elite theory of the existence and importance of groups and collectives. In this vein, for example, Berelson criticises 'classical' theory for its excessive concern with the individual citizen, at the expense of collective properties of the electorate as a whole (Berelson 1954: 312). In the same vein, consensus receives emphasis, especially when the value of stability in a political system is being endorsed. However, it should be clear from the discussion of this chapter that the notion of consensus is very different from that which evolved in Part One. It amounts effectively to acceptance of the rules of the game in a representative system (the metaphor which recurs in the literature of elite theory is that of underlying consensus topped with surface conflict). And, consistently with the writing-out of most citizens from substantive decision-making, the requirement of consensus is itself sometimes confined to 'a predominant portion of the politically active members' (Dahl 1956: 132). In any event, the business of conflict and opposition is central, since it is competition between elites for the popular vote in recurrent elections which is taken to be distinctive of democracy.

The division into leaders and led, elites and masses, government and populace ensures that the degree of political equality obtaining in a democracy, which was left an open question in chapter 4, is very severely confined. Political power is necessarily very unequally distributed in that major way, whatever subsidiary inequalities there are. The liberty of rational agents to conceive and execute their plans and projects is also curtailed if political decisions have a significant impact on the range of possible options open to such agents. And it is reasonable to assume that they do. Virtually any aspiration depends for its fulfilment on prevailing social conditions in many ways — even going for a walk generally calls for shoes and the co-operative effort needed to produce and distribute them — and those conditions in their turn are influenced by political decisions.

Of course, it might be replied that the political arrangements described and implicitly defended in elite theory do affect these matters, but affect them for the better. Leave the politics to other people and I, as a rational agent, can get on with the things I regard as worthwhile: my ability to do so is enhanced by the social stability which is a feature of elite systems. That is a reply which needs to be handled with care. First, we should need to fix the implicit standard of comparison involved. The possibilities might be enhanced as compared with a situation of chaos, but not as compared with some very different but feasible set of political arrangements. Secondly, if a result is secured which is congenial to rational agents, but without their influencing that result directly, there are grounds for saying that they are acquiescing in a state of affairs which is inimical to their own status and treats them, rather, as passive recipients.

Now the departure of elite theory from the values of equality, liberty and consensus as discussed in Part One may prompt the conclusion that it is based on some alternative conception of those values, within the overarching conception of democracy as rule by the people which we have taken as a fixed point throughout our discussion. As a variant on that conclusion, Skinner interprets elite theory (at least in its later forms) as making an empirical claim that the conditions for rule by the people have traditionally been too narrowly drawn (Skinner 1973: 297). Serious doubt can be cast on this interpretation, however. If it is small groups which acquire the power to decide political questions, and if they have only to seek an accommodation with minorities, Dahl's 'appeasement of relatively small groups' (Dahl 1956: 146), then it looks as though there is no sense left in which the people do rule (cf. Graham 1985: 31).

In other words, on the facts as presented in elite theory, it is difficult to see why the inference is not drawn that there is no democracy, or that the existing system falls desperately short of the ideal, rather than simply labelling as democracy the system which those facts describe. The question might then further be raised: if the facts are as described in elite theory, what can be done to improve the situation by way of education, better dissemination of information, and so on. Elite theories either do not address themselves to that question or, as I have suggested, are informed by the assumption that things cannot change substantially from the position of rule by elites.

This has led one critic to lament that we have a choice between the 'dismally ideological' elite theory or a 'fairly blatant utopian' alternative which reinstates some notion of effective rule by the people (Dunn 1979: 26-7). But before we can allow that depressing conclusion to stand, more argument is required. Elite theory in the stronger, modalised form — not merely that elites do rule but that they must — has to be construed as elliptical for the claim that this is what must happen, given that certain other features of our life remain constant. We still have to assess rival theories which hold that those other features need not and perhaps should not remain constant.

In the confrontation which I have presented between elite theory and the more abstract theorising of Part One, elite theory is revealed to be, in a sense, curiously untheoretical. It presents the abstract theory with facts about real people's actual behaviour which are alleged to be ignored in those more heady, abstract regions. Yet the facts so presented are themselves inadequately assimilated into a theoretical framework. We must therefore look at some of the other options in theorising those facts.

FURTHER READING

Other works, not discussed, which are characteristic of what I have identified as elite theory include Lipset 1960, Almond and

Applied Theory

Verba 1963, and Eckstein 1966. Bachrach 1967 offers the classic critique. Hampshire 1978 contains a number of papers considering what sense of responsibility we can and should expect of politicians. Margolis 1979 and Valinas 1978 address the relevance of technology to democratic practice. Bottomore 1966 questions the inevitability of elites, and Taylor 1967 the possibility of value-free political science.

8 Participation theory

1 INTRODUCTION

If 'apathy' was the political watchword of the 1950s, then 'participation' played the same role for the 1960s. In the latter decade, moreover, the single date 1968 came to have far more than merely chronological significance, with its echoes of the Prague Spring and the subsequent Russian invasion, the turmoil of student protest all over the world and other striking political events. This is not the appropriate place to attempt an analysis of those political events themselves. One thing which emerged from them, however, was a renewed interest in models of democracy where the degree of participation on the part of the ordinary person was immeasurably higher than that specified in elite theory.

I should stress that my procedure in this chapter is the same as in the previous one. When I refer to participation theory I am not referring to a theory which necessarily matches in all particulars the pronouncements of any individual writer. My aim is to identify a core of theory to which the writings of individual theorists approximate more or less closely. That common core comprises a conception of democracy with no fundamental dichotomy between active leaders and a passive, inert mass; and, much more explicitly than the corresponding elements in elite theory, arguments about the extent to which the removal of such a dichotomy is both possible and desirable.

Any democratic system must by its nature involve *some* degree of participation. By this stage of our discussion we can recognise that the issue for a theory of democracy is where to fix that degree, between total exclusion from any influence over social decisions and total involvement at every stage of every decision. To the extent that elite theory genuinely offers no more than a description of prevailing practices, participation theory need have no quarrel with it. It may allow that there is currently a high degree of apathy among citizens and that 'size, time and complexity' present a problem. But participation theory provides its own suggestions as to the conditions which produce that result, and the steps which may and ought to be taken to produce a different result, a result where widespread participation in political decisions is more likely to occur.

In that last endeavour, participation theory exemplifies the fact that theorising in this area need not be confined to passive description or diagnosis. It embodies recommendations for change, and those recommendations may themselves be well or ill supported by argument. We therefore have to reach an assessment of participation theory in that regard. Among the issues to be discussed are the soundness of the idea of participation which is employed; the plausibility of the claims about how participation is to be increased; the problem of breaking the vicious circle of self-sustaining apathy; and the connexion between the proposed context of participation and the wider social structure.

2 THE THEORY STATED

We encountered two general problems facing a theory of democracy if it is to be applied to the real world whilst still maintaining contact with the principles discussed in Part One. These were, first, the failure of people to conform with anything like perfection to the ideal of rational, autonomous agents; and, secondly, the futility of talk of consensus in circumstances where we are dealing with very large numbers of very disparate people. One way of regarding participation theory is as an attempt to come to grips with these two problems. The fundamental idea is that people can *learn* to become effective political agents on the basis of experience in more limited contexts, and that this will provide them with the capacity to act in the wider political domain, as well as inducing a tendency to identify with the group in which they actively participate, thus reducing the problem of disparate views and conflicts of will. This theme is present as one strand in J.S. Mill's *Representative Government*, written at a time when the entry of the mass of people into the political process was under way and therefore a matter of immediate and current concern. It is also present in the guild socialism of G.D.H. Cole (e.g. Cole 1920), and, in the more recent context, in Carole Pateman's *Participation and Democratic Theory* (Pateman 1970).

Broadly speaking, the two limited contexts where increased participation has been advocated are *industry* and the *local community*. The industrial context, it is suggested, is central in many people's lives — it is where they spend much of their time — and provides 'an education in the management of collective affairs' which it is difficult to parallel elsewhere (Pateman 1970: 43). Schemes for participation, or 'workers' control', or 'industrial democracy', have therefore been advocated with those considerations in mind. It is perhaps even more obvious that existence in a local community of some sort is a central part of people's lives. But of course it does not follow that the major decisions affecting the nature of that community must themselves emanate from within it, and frequently they do not. They come, instead, from some central authority whose knowledge of the community in question may be relatively poor. The demand for decentralisation and community control of various aspects of community life is one guise which the demand for greater participation can take. It was exemplified by the movement for neighbourhood control of schools, police, planning and similar institutions; and the US federal government's Community Action Programmes inaugurated in 1964 were themselves couched in a rhetoric which answered to the demand for greater participation.

In chapter 2, section 1 I introduced a rough classification of the different kinds of grounds on which democracy might be favoured. It might be favoured just for the type of system which it is *intrinsically,* regardless of its particular effects; or it might be favoured precisely for its *consequences*, which might be described either in *non-moral* or in *moral* terms. In effect, the various supporting arguments surrounding participation theory cover all the classifications mentioned.

Where the claim is that participatory democracy implies a recognition of the dignity and worth of the individual, and therefore of the appropriateness of according him or her an active role in the decision-making process, an intrinsic justification is being offered. The idea that participation in decision-making at the work-place constitutes a less alienated form of labour than simply obeying orders, because it is a more fitting relation for a human being to enter into, can be viewed in a similar light. On the other hand, the grounds offered for this view may be that as alienation decreases and job satisfaction increases, so there grows a feeling of competence in shaping one's destiny and a capacity to take effective action in one's own interest. In that case, a justification is being put forward which rests on claims about the consequences of such a system described in non-moral terms. Finally, the argument may be couched in different terms. It may be suggested that participation produces a sense of community for individuals which, given the circumstances of modern mass society, is not otherwise easily achieved, and fosters an identification with a collective and its enterprises (cf. Bachrach 1975: 40), with the result that contributions to decision-making are more public-spirited and less selfish than they would otherwise be. Democracy is then being framed by reference to its consequences described in moral terms.

I also indicated in chapter 1, section 1 that there are difficulties in making a sharp distinction between conceptual and empirical claims. To whatever extent some such distinction can be made, however, both kinds of claim are in play in participation theory. It can be held that participation theory is an articulation of the conceptual truth that in a democracy people rule themselves rather than some being ruled by others, in that the theory merely allots to them the active role required by this definition. But the theory also involves claims about the *effects* of people having such a role, and the truth of those claims will turn much more on contingent facts about what actually happens in the world when the appropriate circumstances for participation obtain. Here, in other words, it is more a matter of turning to look at the evidence. This has been done by a number of participation theorists, and they have contributed to producing a theory which, like elite theory, contains a significant empirical component. In the case of participation theory, however, no one could suppose that it was presenting 'merely' empirical claims.

A major source of empirical research to which participation theorists have frequently referred is Almond and Verba's *The Civic Culture* (Almond and Verba 1963), though the authors do not themselves draw the conclusions of participation theory from their studies. They investigated political attitudes in the United States, Britain, Germany, Italy and Mexico, and were particularly concerned with 'the ordinary man's perception of his own influence' (*ibid.*: 181). Their argument was that citizens' confidence in their ability to have an effect on government derived in part from opportunities to exercise an influence in smaller authority structures such as the family, the school and the work-place (*ibid.*: 189; cf. 323-74). In fact, they argued that the gap between family and polity was so wide that experiences in other structures closer to the political system were likely to be more influential (*ibid.*: 371-3), and the work-place was taken as the most significant (*ibid.*: 294). One finding which held uniformly through the studies was that those belonging to political organisations scored higher on the subjective competence scale than those belonging only to non-political organisations, who in turn still scored higher than those reporting membership of no organisations at all (*ibid.*: 307-9).

No doubt findings of this kind are open to a variety of interpretation, but they at least leave room for the possibility that it is participation in organisation which itself fosters the requisite confidence, rather than vice versa. This in turn can provide the impetus for the view that present low levels of participation need not simply be accepted, and that the work-place constitutes a suitable location for the training in participation which even participation theorists would agree must be achieved before there can be any useful substantive contribution on the part of the ordinary citizen at the national level.

Fragments of support for this general approach have been collected together in Blumberg's *Industrial Democracy* (Blumberg 1968). Studies of workers' participation in industry tend to deal with small-scale experiments, but to balance this there is the point noticed by Blumberg that studies of participation in general cover a wide variety of institutional settings and types of people (*ibid.*: 73). His own main concern is with the relation between participation and work satisfaction, and after surveying the relevant literature he contends that there is a remarkable consistency in findings, across all the diversity in the subjects of study, the theoretical background and design of the research projects, and so on. There is hardly a study, he suggests, which fails to show that a genuine increase in workers' participation is attended by an increase in satisfaction and well-being (*ibid.*: 123).

Typical is the famous experiment carried out at the Harwood Company. Similar changes in job routines were introduced for four groups of workers, but the manner of their introduction was very dissimilar. One group was simply informed of the changes. In a second, elected representatives from among operative workers were charged with introducing the changes, explaining them to fellow operators and guiding them in the necessary training. The remaining two groups were 'total-participation' groups where, instead of delegating decisions, all operatives shared in the task of redesigning the job. Broadly, the experimenters found that 'success', measured both in terms of worker satisfaction and subsequent productivity levels, was directly proportional to the amount of worker participation. This finding was confirmed when members of the 'no participation' group were dispersed throughout the factory and subsequently reconvened into a 'total-participation' group (*ibid.*: 81–4).

In another experiment, participation in decision-making was systematically increased for two groups of a company's workers and decreased for two others. Control was gained and lost respectively over such matters as work methods, recess periods and dealing with lateness. The finding here was that in every case where employees' power over decision-making was increased, the evidence of the questionnaires they completed suggested that they were likely to be more satisfied with their job, their company and their supervisors, with the opposite result in the contrasting case (*ibid.*: 87-90).

Further optimistic conclusions are drawn by Blumberg.

There is evidence to suggest a significant desire for greater participation on the part of employees. In one study, over half the employees said they wanted more say in how work was done, despite considerable perceived obstacles to having an influence. In another, 70 per cent said they would like to make more decisions on their jobs (*ibid.*: 115). This desire contrasts markedly with the apathy earlier found to prevail in the general political sphere by elite theorists. The optimism it occasions is further bolstered by the finding that individual's behaviour itself varies according to the climate of the group, so that 'the organisation that permits participation ultimately produces individuals who are responsible (*sic*) to participation' (*ibid.*: 109).

We should note here that in the midst of a very wide range of different empirical studies from which these findings are taken, the idea of participation is in fact used in a variety of different ways. Blumberg, for instance, explicitly employs it to cover everything from a situation where workers simply receive information from management to a situation where they completely determine an issue, without sharing joint decision-making with any other group. Such a wide usage obviously creates problems when one is framing and amassing support for hypotheses about participation and its attendant circumstances. By contrast, Pateman, although she quotes extensively from Blumberg and Almond and Verba in constructing a case in favour of participation theory, employs the term in a more confined way. She distinguishes as *pseudo participation* the case where employees are encouraged to discuss and question the decisions of a supervisor but have no effective control over them, on the grounds that the whole point of industrial participation is to modify the situation where decision is the prerogative of management and the workers are excluded (*ibid.*: 68-9). *Partial participation* is defined as the case where one party does have influence over another but the *final* power rests with the latter — these roles again typically being taken by 'men' and 'management' respectively in industry (*ibid.*: 70). *Full participation* has a familiar ring to it and is defined as 'a process where each individual member of a decision-making body has equal power to determine the outcome of decision' (*ibid.*: 71).

The arguments of participation theory, as they occur in writers like Blumberg and Pateman, encourage a disposition not simply to take as given the current attitudes of a group or the structure within which they are expressed. The nature of the evidence they call on, however, does raise the question how far their findings can be transferred across to the wider political context. Pateman concedes that much of the available evidence is about participation at a low level, concerning immediate work arrangements (*ibid*.: 70), whereas evidence about the effects of participation at a higher level, concerning the general running of an enterprise, would be much more salient for the wider context. The problem is that such evidence is scarce, since very few enterprises *are* run with widespread higher-level participation. Experiments in 'workers' self-management' in Yugoslavia are relevant but ambiguous, and even a committed participation theorist like Pateman is only able to draw from them the negative and qualified conclusion, that they do not show the democratisation of industrial authority structures to be impossible (*ibid*.: 102).

The question of the transfer from limited industrial experience to the wider political realm is one we shall have to return to in assessing participation theory. In the meantime we should note, however, that at least so far as the organisational aspects of the wider context are concerned, models are available which form a natural complement to the argument mentioned so far. G.D.H. Cole, for instance, proposed an extremely elaborate system of guilds which involved maximum participation and face-to-face discussion at the basic level, with representatives elected to subsequent layers of decision-making up to a National Commune. Their role was far removed from that of representatives in our own system, however, in that they represented their electors in some respect or other, rather than totally, and they would be subject to recall (Cole 1920: 32-3, 133-4). Similarly, the National Commune was to be a co-ordinating body only, in contrast to the state as we know it (*ibid*.: 137). In the United States, Mary Parker Follett employed a like notion of layering, based on neighbourhood groups similar to town meetings, with a notion of accountability similar to Cole's (Follett 1918: 189-257). More recently, C.B. Macpherson has suggested the model of a 'pyramidal system', which has 'direct democracy' at the base and 'delegate democracy' at every level above that (Macpherson 1977: 108). Since he assumes that political parties with parliamentary or presidential/congressional government must continue to exist, however, he believes that pyramidal participation would have to be adopted within the parties themselves (*ibid.*: 113).

We may or may not judge these suggestions to be too innocent in relation to the world as we know it to be. But they do constitute the beginning of an attempt to specify decision-making structures in which the degree of individuals' control over decisions is considerably greater than at present, whilst avoiding the absurdity of involving every individual directly in every decision. They also indicate that within models of delegation and representation, the direction of dominance between delegates or representatives, on the one hand, and populace, on the other, may run in the opposite direction from the one we encounter in our own systems of representation. But since they are theoretical models they cannot establish more than that. They cannot advance the speculative claim that within such a structure consensus would be much more likely to emerge, nor can they show that it is possible to engender the will and the competence required for widespread participation in politics in the wider sphere. Their role is simply to illustrate the possibility of thinking beyond existing structures.

In brief, what we have encountered in this section is an evident desire to bring political arrangements more into line with some of the principles discussed in Part One. This desire is backed up by a theory built around data collected from a significant area of many people's lives, data which purport to show the scope for improvement in competence in decision-making, and the existence of a wish for greater involvement in it at least in that significant area. No doubt caution must be exercised in drawing any sweeping conclusions from the data themselves, but there is certainly no reason in principle why they should not be used to extend one's theorising about political organisation beyond what already surrounds us.

3 THE THEORY ASSESSED

It is prudent not to take too rosy a view of the evidence put forward in support of participation theory (as some participation theorists themselves realise), just as it was prudent not to take too complacent a view of the evidence put forward in support of elite theory. Much of it is based on what respondents *say*, and this may fail to correspond with how things actually are. For example, Almond and Verba measure *subjective* confidence, the strength of one's *belief* that one has political influence, since they are primarily interested in individuals' *perception* of their own influence. That is an important factor since, as they point out, the level of confidence in one's power may have an effect on what one tries to do. In a similar way, decision-makers may act differently depending on what they believe the powers of the ordinary citizen to be (Almond and Verba 1963: 181-2). This is an area where self-fulfilling beliefs are possible, and evidence of this kind is useful if it demonstrates that one particular obstacle to more widespread participation is removable. If one's level of confidence is variable and can be increased with good effect, from the point of view of participation in decision-making, that is a fact worth establishing.

Subjective attitudes are only one factor, however, in determining the extent of people's power and control, and there are dangers in this way of establishing the facts. In Almond and Verba's research, only a small proportion of those who said they believed that they could influence political decisions reported that they had actually tried to do so. Shocks, indeed, might have been in store for others who tried, since 40 per cent of US respondents and 24 per cent of British thought there was some likelihood that an attempt on their part to influence national legislation would be successful (*ibid.*: 480). We might say, therefore, that an increase in subjective competence is not necessarily an increase in real competence. There is a similar danger in relying on evidence of this kind to establish the claim that there is a widespread *desire* for political participation. For although 51 per cent of US respondents expressed the view that the ordinary person should take an active part in the community, only 10 per cent mentioned activities which could be classified in that way when they were asked what they did with their spare time (*ibid.*: 480).

The problem which arises for participation theory is partly one of motivation and partly one of expertise and social organisation. The motivational problem is not the one discussed in Part One, of how to interest an abstract individual in the principles of democracy as abstractly conceived there. Rather, it is how to interest real individuals, in concrete circumstances, in a particular form of democratic procedure. Granting that there is a strong wish to have more control over one's work, that is a far cry from a wish to become seriously involved in wider political processes. Hence, even on the most favourable outcome, that greater participation at work does increase one's level of competence in a general way, this will make no difference in the absence of the appropriate desire and determination to employ one's increased competence politically.

At that point participation theory necessarily becomes speculative, and it is possible to offer counter-speculation. People's level of job-satisfaction and competence may be altered, but in a world where the main part of their lives is devoted to earning enough to satisfy their material and other needs, it is unlikely that they will develop a deep interest in public affairs. That, we might surmise, will largely be left to those with the leisure and the resources to become expert in the matter, or those whose job it is to do so, while the rest of the populace will continue to interest themselves in various forms of relaxation in the hours when they are not earning their living. But even if they did not do so, there is something absurd, it may be felt, in the idea that they might equip themselves successively, in all the different areas where expertise is required, with the knowledge needed for any meaningful contribution to decision-making. Over a large area of our lives, it may be concluded, we simply have no alternative but to defer to experts. That is why there is a problem for participation theory not only with respect to motivation but also with respect to expertise and social organisation.

The point about expertise ought not to go unchallenged by participation theorists. It is, of course, true that all kinds of expert knowledge must be relied upon in making decisions about all sorts of arrangements in a modern society, and no one could acquire all of it. It is an occasion for relief and gratitude that such knowledge is there to be called upon. But, as I have already argued in chapter 4, section 3, it is highly problematic what the political implications of this obvious fact are. Technical expertise is not the same thing as political expertise — indeed, there may be no such thing as political expertise, in the required sense. Hence, there is as yet no argument here for allotting any specifically political role to technical experts. There is no reason why non-experts should not make the best assessment they can of the options open to them in the light of expert opinion (which is likely very often to be divided in any case), and retain for themselves the prerogative of deciding which option to follow. That, after all, is what elected representatives in a representative democracy must do. The core of participation theory contains the idea of the ordinary citizen's taking part in political decisions to a far greater degree than at present, but with no attempt to quantify the precise degree of involvement. It is not obvious that the impossibility of becoming a polymath implies the impossibility of far greater involvement.

The motivational problem is perceived as a serious one by C.B. Macpherson. He argues that the main problem is not how to run a participatory democracy but how to reach it, on the grounds that the changes which have to be envisaged for us to reach such a form of democracy are themselves such as to make us capable of running it (Macpherson 1977: 98). But a system of minimal participation, in his view, is precisely what holds present society together, and this produces a kind of vicious circle. We should need a different kind of society for widespread participation to be a genuine option, yet it is probably only through widespread participation that such a society could come into being. Macpherson's own response is to look for factors which constitute a partial change in one area or the other, and which may continue to operate with cumulative and reciprocal effect (*ibid*.: 101-2).

A distinct but very similar response is to argue that the changes implied by participation theory are not something separate from wider social change but are integral to it. In this vein, Pateman argues that one reason for making industrial participation central is that abolishing the distinction between 'managers' and 'men' would go a large way towards the economic equality required for equal participation (Pateman 1970: 43). Similarly, Blumberg complains that, despite evidence on the favourable effects of participation, there is a general reluctance to face the question how far private ownership and control of industry act as a brake on fostering it (Blumberg 1968: 129-30). The drift of these remarks is to make participation theory much more clearly committed to 'workers' control'. It is suggestive of the scheme described by Bottomore, in which political authority is devolved on local associations wherever possible, and enterprises are owned or effectively controlled by those working in them, subject to controls in the interests of a national economic plan (Bottomore 1966: 139-40).

In a way, responses of this kind displace the problem rather than solving it, for we can now raise the question what grounds there are for supposing widespread support for participation understood in this clearly more radical sense. Macpherson, it is true, tentatively tries to find such grounds, in what he regards as a growing tendency for people to question the cost of economic growth, the costs of political apathy, and the ability of corporate capitalism to meet consumer expectations (Macpherson 1977: 102-6). An argument of that kind, however, rests on highly challengeable views about the extent to which people's current political and industrial activities constitute a fundamental calling into question of existing political and social arrangements. In the absence of anything more compelling, the problem of motivation simply re-emerges.

What these responses do throw into sharp relief, however, is a series of questions which arise concerning relations between units of participation and the wider society. There will always be a range of issues for decision, from health policy to control of pollution to relations between different localities, which transcend the limited context of particular enterprises in which people work. What implications for the making of such decisions follow from the existence of smaller units of participation?

None of the participation theorists mentioned appears to

envisage the disappearance of government as such, in something approaching its present form. This already places a limit on the realisation of equal power in decision-making, but it also raises what we might call the Eckstein problem. Harry Eckstein has put forward the hypothesis that stability requires a congruence between authority patterns in government and those in other social institutions, since otherwise a kind of psychological strain results from being subjected to conflicting normative demands in different contexts (Eckstein 1966: 234, 255-6). His own view is that since institutions close to government, notably economic ones, cannot be democratised, government itself must remain to a significant extent impure, so far as democratic practice is concerned (*ibid.*: 237, 261-2).

If Eckstein's hypothesis is correct, this is a serious matter for participation theory. Of course, it may not be correct; and the difficulty of judging that question is the same difficulty as judging between elite and participation theory when they go beyond a mere analysis of present circumstances and make, respectively, the claims that an existing state of affairs is inevitable and that a not-yet existing state of affairs is possible. But, whether correct or not, it prompts another worry about the relation between participatory unit and wider society. This concerns the aspiration to consensus.

I noted in section 2 that participation theory might be seen as offering a contribution to meeting the general difficulty of talking in terms of consensus, where very large numbers of disparate people are concerned. A feeling of significance and effectiveness within a small unit might foster an identification with its interests and a reduction of conflict between individual wills. The worry this may provoke, however, is that any move towards consensus within a small unit is likely to be achieved at the expense of a sharpening conflict outside or between units. Pennock, for example, uses this point in criticism of participatory democracy and in favour of representative democracy: a territorial representative has to represent so many different interests that there is a bias towards compromise from the start in the larger arena; but this is not likely to occur with members of a small self-governing unit, at least if they identify with the interests of that unit (Pennock 1979: 459).

We may then begin to wonder how secure the participatory model is from the point of view of normative principles. In chapter 1, section 2 we saw the strong appeal of the basic principle that all those affected by a given decision ought to have a say in its making (at least if competent to do so). But consider then the position in the wider community of an enterprise owned and run by those who work in it. If enterprises have anything like their present function of producing goods and services for sale, then the range of those affected is much wider than those who make decisions within it. The latter will, admittedly, be the ones affected by the decisions to do directly with the process of production in the enterprise. But if their control over the enterprise is to be total, then many other decisions will be taken, affecting, for example, the environment, and therefore people who otherwise have no connexion with the enterprise. Those who rely on the supply of goods or services, or wish to avail themselves of them, will also be affected by the decisions.

The lines of influence will not run all one way, from units of participation to the wider context, of course. The context will itself set severe limits on any plans which members of the enterprise might wish to bring to fruition. The experience of the Meriden motorcycle co-operative in England is germane here, since it was a prototype of the participatory model, owned and run by those who worked in it. It fell prey to market forces and reached a crisis, however, which necessitated the calling in of business efficiency experts. They recommended the unpalatable step of redundancy for some of the workers. The advice was followed, but even this was insufficient to solve the co-operative's difficulties, and eventually it was wound up.

It may be replied that this is an isolated case in a context where generally there is not worker-ownership of industry, and that things would work out very differently where such was the rule rather than the exception. This may very well be true, and it indicates what is really needed here. When participation theory has been strengthened to the point of involving a commitment to 'workers' control', what is further required is an account of how enterprises of the kind envisaged would fit into the rest of market society, or how indeed that form of society is itself to be superseded, if that is also envisaged.

Lurking beneath the surface here is the complicated issue of the relation between ownership and control. These can fall apart in contemporary society, on one level at least, when internal control of a firm is in the hands of managers, though the firm itself is owned by shareholders. Some or all managers may be shareholders as well, but these are distinct roles and they may be occupied by entirely separate groups of people. This is an important consideration, for a number of reasons. If shareholders have the power to dismiss managers whose performance they disapprove of, or if through some other medium they can determine the conditions in which managers operate, then a residue of *ultimate* control remains with them. In any case, the possession of sufficiently large shareholdings will ensure correspondingly large reserves of wealth for such people, and we have explored in Part One the connexion between material circumstances and degrees of liberty. Yet *this* comparison slips from view when participation theorists concentrate on the division between 'men' and 'management' within enterprises. Members of the latter two groups are obviously in very different positions from each other so far as internal control is concerned, yet in relation to at least major shareholders it may be reasonable to regard them as belonging to one and the same group — for example, by virtue of their need, unlike major shareholders, to put themselves into the industrial context in the first place, in order to earn a living.

In fact, it seems to me that concentration on the industrial context in participation theory constitutes both its strengths and its weaknesses. On the one hand, it calls attention to a major source of diminished autonomy in many people's lives, and it provides some evidence to suggest that this is not a state of affairs in which they acquiesce happily. It also makes clear the importance for democratic theory of examining structures which are not themselves part of the official politics of a society. On the other hand, it does not follow that this is the most appropriate site for developing participatory democracy either in theory or in practice. We should notice that many people do not spend their lives in enterprises of the designated kind — the retired, the unemployed, and full-time housewives, for example. (For that matter, are hospitals, schools and colleges enterprises in the required sense?) If any one place has to be

selected as the most apposite place to begin building a more
participatory form of society, then a political movement might
be a better candidate than industrial enterprises. Entry would
be voluntary, an enthusiasm for wider participation could be
its aim, and the genuineness of this enthusiasm could be
displayed in practice, or explanations found for why this was
not possible.

But certainly as far as developing a conception of participatory democracy is concerned, it would be better not to
think in terms of starting with one particular kind of institution
at all. We saw in Part One the general argument that freedom
and equal effectiveness in decision-making rest on a whole
nexus of factors in addition to formal provision. Participation
theory shares that view, and advocates substantive
involvement. But when we carry the general point across to
contemporary social reality, there are grounds for thinking
that the terms of reference of participation theory have been
too narrowly drawn. The interconnexions between different
types of institution are such that we ought to begin to think in
terms of increased participation in a democratic *society*,
permeated throughout with the appropriate practices.

Now if the price of a participatory theory is to be raised so
high, it may be felt that the project would be better
abandoned. After all, there are those who enjoy political
activity and those who do not. Should we be justified in
instituting large changes in people's lives, and setting up
institutions they might feel bound to participate in, when they
might be chemists or astronomers or church workers living a
life of selfless pursuit of knowledge or others' welfare who
would in any case prefer to leave politicking to others (cf.
Pennock 1979: 463-4)? We might note in this connexion a
poignant passage in a later work by G.D.H. Cole, in which he
retracts many of his earlier views. He had, he confessed,
constructed a 'politically minded person's Utopia', insensitive
to the fact that most people have other fish to fry (Cole 1929:
160-1). Why, then, go to all this trouble, rather than leaving
politics to the politicians?

This criticism is one which I believe participation theory
should reject. It serves as a salutary reminder, to be sure, that
there would be something suspect in attempting to *impose*

participatory democracy, as there is in the idea of forcing people to be free. But chemists and church workers do not exist in a vacuum, and even if they are not interested in politics, politics will be interested in them. They live in a complex society where individuals are highly interdependent, and the decisions taken by those who do engage in politics have major repercussions on everyone else. If, therefore, large numbers of people regard politics as 'not for them', an interest amongst others which may or may not be indulged in, that should give cause for concern over the way politics is conducted and regarded, rather than acting as an endorsement of a system of professional politicians and bureaucrats. To have no active interest in decisions which determine how you live (they may even determine *whether* you live) is to be, in a very straightforward sense, alienated from your own status as a rational autonomous agent.

4 CONCLUSION

The impulse, as it were, behind participation theory fits fairly well with the principles discussed in Part One. The theory focuses on the individual in the context of co-operative effort with others, and engages in an attempt to find concrete means of fulfilling the ideal of self-rule which is at the heart of the concept of democracy. Unlike elite theory, it does not stop short at analysing and explaining the visible degree of incompetence or apathy manifested by people in their contribution to collective decision-making: it attempts to provide suggestions for remedying that state of affairs. It therefore contrasts with elite theory in being necessarily a theory built around the idea of change, rather than around a description of what already exists.

It also serves a useful function in drawing into the debate institutions which are not themselves part of the official political sphere. There are many important connexions and analogies between political and non-political institutions. The analogies make it entirely appropriate to speak of, say, the politics of industry, the family, the school, committees, and so on. The connexions indicate that we shall have only a partial understanding of any of these institutions if we take them in isolation from the others. Hence, the importance of drawing some of these other institutions into the debate, both for an understanding of current political attitudes and the circumstances attending their formation, and for any plausible ideas about how an alternative state of affairs might function.

We might categorise the problems that participation theory has to contend with, in building up a proposal for much wider participation in decision-making, as *psychological* and *structural.* Given the apparent apathy and acquiescence in a state of affairs where there is relatively little participation, a psychological argument must be constructed. It must be shown that, despite appearances, there is a strong desire for participation, or a theory must be provided which explains how such a desire will arise, or a recipe must be given for actually creating it. More than this, it must be shown that any such desire can be matched by an adequate capacity for participation. The strongest desire in the world would be of no avail if, for example, we believed that political questions were so complex that they were beyond the sophistication of the average person (a position taken by Macpherson 1977: 95-6 — rather surprisingly, given his sympathy for participation theory). In a rapidly changing world, however, it is perhaps wise not to take average degree of sophistication, or educational attainment, as a constant.

Even if the psychological case were made out, there is still the structural requirement. It is not sufficient that most people are able to participate and wish to do so: the position they occupy in society and the nature of their lives is currently such that serious and sustained participation in the political process is not a real option. For it to become so, either the volume of political decision-making would have to be drastically reduced or most people would have to have significantly more time available than at present for participation. What is advocated by participation theory is not some superficial change that can be easily superimposed on a way of life which is already a going concern, and in many ways militates against the goal of that theory.

As will perhaps be clear from my discussion, I think that it is not out of the question that participation theory should meet all these requirements, but that as things stand it has not yet done so. Indeed, it would have to be transformed into a much wider theory of society and social change before it could do so. Because the change it envisages is such a radical one, no existing features of society should remain outside the melting pot unless we have strong reason to believe that they must continue in their present form.

The wider implications present in the original idea of participation are clearly recognised by some theorists, as we have seen. Yet it is noteworthy what features of contemporary society they will allow to go unquestioned and unexamined on occasion. Macpherson believes that political parties must be assumed to continue in existence in his model of participatory democracy (Macpherson 1977: 112), and Bottomore shelves the question whether they are necessary for democracy, on the grounds that it is 'unavoidably speculative' (Bottomore 1966: 119). Pateman admits to saying little about the question of ownership of industry, despite recognising the importance of economic inequality (Pateman 1970: 43, 108n). Yet political parties are heavily implicated by their role in a highly non-participatory system, and it seems reasonable to demand that their nature, origin and function be examined, to see what purposes they serve and under what circumstances they might be transformed or replaced. Similarly, given the connexions between wealth and opportunities to contribute to public life, it might be thought a pressing matter to discuss patterns of ownership of substantial resources.

A critic might readily agree that *if* participation theory is to be sustained then it must presuppose, or at least be prepared to consider, radically changed social conditions, and therefore raise questions of this much wider order; but add that, since many of the features of our own society cannot be altered, that is the end of the theory. That conclusion would be premature, however, before considering the most controversial, and perhaps the most challenging, theory of society and social change in modern times. We must therefore now turn to Marx.

FURTHER READING

Useful collections on participation theory are Cook and
Morgan 1971, Parry 1972, and Pennock and Chapman 1975.
Blumberg 1968 and Pateman 1970 both discuss the empirical
evidence from Yugoslavia. Verba, Nie and Kim 1978 builds
upon the original work of Almond and Verba 1963 and is also
cross-cultural. Mansbridge 1980 discusses sympathetically
some of the practical problems of participation in the context
of town meetings, while Dahl 1970 offers a sobering reminder
of practical problems in the wider context. Workers' control is
the subject of Coates 1968. Clegg 1960 gives a very different
view of industrial relations.

9   Marxist theory

1 INTRODUCTION

To some readers the suggestion will come as a surprise that
Marxism should have anything to contribute (except
negatively) to a discussion of democracy. After all, it is in that
name that some of the most oppressive and authoritarian
regimes of this century have been set up and sustained. Since
Marxist practice is the very antithesis of the democratic
practice implied by the principles discussed earlier, should we
not conclude that Marxist theory is similarly antithetical?

I entirely endorse the assessment that regimes *claiming* the
Marxist title have been oppressive and authoritarian. The
implication this holds for Marxist theory is more complicated,
however. First, paraphrasing Macintyre, we might say that the
regimes in question tell us no more about the essence of
Marxism than the reign of a Borgia pope does about the essence
of Christianity (Macintyre 1981: 243). We shall see, however,
that the implicit separation here of theory from practice is not
so easily made in the case of Marxism. Secondly, we might
argue that, just as there are regimes, so there are *theories* which
claim the Marxist label without justification. Whilst I believe
this is true, it would be a tedious business to work out what the
precise standards are to which a theory must measure up before
it earns that label. Accordingly, I shall proceed in a slightly
different way.

I shall distinguish between *strictly defined* and *broadly
defined* Marxism. By strictly defined Marxist theory I mean
theory whose substance is directly traceable to the writings of
Karl Marx and his lifelong collaborator Friedrich Engels. By
broadly defined Marxist theory I mean theory which takes, or

170

purports to take, its inspiration in some looser way from that source. The subject of this chapter is strictly defined Marxism, and if I refer to it at some points in the chapter as Marxism, without qualification, it should nevertheless be clear that I am referring to the views of Marx and Engels. (Broadly defined Marxism in some forms, and particularly the historically most influential Leninist form, will occupy our attention in chapter 10.) My procedure in this chapter is therefore the reverse of that adopted in the discussion of elite and participation theory. In those cases, individual theorists came into view only by virtue of contributing to a common core theory, which might not even be attributable in its entirety to one single theorist. In the present case, it is precisely a single theorist, or at least a pair of co-theorists, that we shall be concerned with. I believe that that single source has much to offer, but has been much misunderstood; and I hope I shall be forgiven by elite and participation theorists if I say that no single one of them has the same stature or has given rise to as much trouble.

In one way, the discussion of Marxist theory is continuous with that of participation theory: it is a theory of — or more precisely a theorised proposal for — change, rather than merely a description and explanation of existing reality. In another way, however, there is a break with all the earlier discussion. Both in Part One and hitherto in Part Two, the context has been the familiar one of liberal individualist political thought of the kind identified in the Introduction; and many of the arguments and positions which have been discussed are a commonly encountered part of the surrounding political culture. The same cannot be said of Marx's theories. They form no part of the received wisdom in our culture; they involve the employment of a distinct and rather unfamiliar set of concepts; and they allot a particular and unfamiliar role to theory itself, bringing in an historical dimension as a necessity in a way which has not been assumed in preceding chapters. For these reasons there is an especial need in this instance to fill in the background which makes Marx's views on democratic theory intelligible. They must be located in a much wider set of proposals for social change. I must therefore ask the reader's patience while laying out some of the basic elements in Marx's general theories as a prelude to identifying his contribution specifically to democratic theory.

Because Marx's theory is not in the first instance a theory *of* democracy, but rather of a complete and basic change in the whole fabric of society, questions can be raised about its relation to democracy at two points. We need to consider both Marx's views on how the change he advocates is to be achieved, what relations should obtain among those he designates as the agents of that change, and also his views on the type of decision-procedure to be adopted after the change and the establishment of the new society.

I shall suggest that there is a plausible reading of Marx which brings his position on both of these issues close to the democratic principles developed so far in this book. What he has to say about the nature of classes, the means of emancipation which must be adopted by the working class, and the connexion between political life and other, material aspects of society, all suggest a concrete application of the concept of collective decision-making by free, rational agents, and an application worthy of serious consideration. I hope to establish that limited conclusion, rather than offering a full defence of Marx's position. For it goes without saying that, in the space available, massive oversimplification, both exegetically and of the issues themselves, is virtually unavoidable.

2 THE THEORY STATED

Elite theory represented the first attempt in Part Two to embed democratic principles in concrete reality, with a corresponding modification of those principles so as to accommodate them to features of concrete reality which were accepted as given. Marxism can be viewed as a very much broader and more theoretically articulated attempt of the same kind. Indeed, it is no exaggeration to say that for Marx *everything* must be embedded in concrete reality, since it follows from his *materialist conception of history* that everything must be viewed in historical and material context.

That conception is most famously summarised in Marx's Preface to his *Critique of Political Economy* (Marx 1859).

There he argues that political forms, amongst other things, cannot be comprehended by themselves but originate in 'the material conditions of life' (*ibid.*: 20). Two technical terms are crucial in the identification of the material conditions of life: *productive forces* and *production relations*. Productive forces are such things as raw materials, instruments of production (tools, machinery, whole factories would be examples), and also the human energy and skills required to produce wealth. Production relations are such relations as owning, or in an appropriate way having the use of, some productive force.

People enter into particular production relations in the course of producing their material life, relations which on the one hand are appropriate to the stage which their productive forces have reached, and on the other hand constitute the 'real foundation' on which arises a legal and political super-structure. A particular dynamic is then posited, relating the different factors mentioned here. There comes a point at which existing production relations cease to foster further development of the productive forces and become a hindrance to such development. Revolutionary changes then ensue which result in a transformation of the economic foundation and eventually of the entire superstructure. A new set of production relations is then generated, appropriate for further development of the productive forces.

People fall into *classes* depending on the nature of their relation to the forces of production. It then becomes possible to re-state the dynamic of large-scale social change, as Marx does in the *Communist Manifesto*, in terms of class. 'The history of all past society has consisted in the development of class antagonisms, antagonisms that assumed different forms at different epochs' (Marx and Engels 1848: 86). All had in common the exploitation of one part of society by another, but this exploitation would take a different form depending on the nature of the relation between classes, whether freeman and slave, lord and serf, capitalist and worker, or whatever (*ibid.*: 68).

In the architectural metaphor of foundation and superstructure, which has been rejected as misleading by some critics and subjected to complex interpretation by others, Marx is gesturing toward the primacy of material aspects of human existence. First, given the sort of creatures we are, the satisfaction of a need for food, clothing, shelter and similar things is a precondition of any kind of life at all, and these needs must be met not once but recurrently. Secondly, given the kind of environment we have inhabited, the activities associated with meeting those material needs have occupied a significant rather than marginal role in people's existence. Many people have had to spend a lot of time wresting the necessaries of life from a relatively inhospitable earth, rather than plucking fruit from the trees in a Garden of Eden.

Now it may be objected that neither of these truths is any more than a truism, and therefore neither is adequate as the basis for anything which might be termed a conception of history. In a sense, this is correct. No one is actually likely to dissent from them when they are stated explicitly. It is another matter, however, for such truths to inform the actual study of history, and it is certainly possible implicitly to ignore them in that endeavour. A study of history, for example, which dealt only with the acts of 'great men', such as kings and prime ministers, but yet purported to be a history of human society would be deficient in just that way.

On the other hand, it should be conceded that Marx must and does assert the primacy of material life in some further sense, in order to make some possible contribution to our understanding of the nature of human history. At its crudest, this would be taken by both follower and opponent alike to consist in some idea that the material, economic arrangements of a society mechanically and irresistibly determine its other features. A more defensible interpretation, and one which emerges very naturally from the kinds of primacy already mentioned, is this. Given the place which the satisfaction of material needs occupies in our lives, it is a plausible hypothesis worth exploring that the influence of this fact will make itself felt in relation to other parts of our life — our culture, our theories, the ways in which we relate to each other when we are not working to satisfy material needs, and so forth — in a variety of ways which would have to be specified. Two ways which are suggested by Marx's Preface are, first, that the facts of material life at any given time will constrain other facts of life, that non-material institutions and practices will flourish or have marginal significance or atrophy altogether, depending on the degree to which they are suitable for facilitating the functioning and development of the prevailing material institutions. Secondly, and closely connected, it may be argued that the material has *explanatory* primacy, in that the surest way to an understanding of the significance of non-material institutions is by relating them in some systematic way back to their material base (cf. Marx 1867: 175n.).

There are difficulties in determining the exact role which Marx allots to ideas and theories in this conception of history, corresponding to the difficulties in determining the nature of the primacy of material life. The simplest and crudest interpretation would again be to suppose that ideas are a mere residue or epiphenomenon, with no role of their own to play. Such an interpretation may gain a vestige of plausibility from his reference, in the Preface, to 'the legal, political, religious, artistic or philosophic — in short, ideological forms' in which people become conscious of the conflict between productive forces and existing production relations, and his insistence that to judge such a period from its own consciousness would be like judging an individual by what he thinks about himself (Marx 1859: 21).

This is a complicated issue, as we shall see, but it would be erroneous to conclude that for Marx theorising is simply unimportant, or that human history is bound to move in a certain direction regardless of the thought or conscious actions of human beings. On the contrary, as he famously remarked elsewhere, 'Men make their own history', but it was important to add, 'not under circumstances they themselves have chosen but under the given and inherited circumstances with which they are directly confronted' (Marx 1869: 146). Their ideological consciousness itself must be explained by reference to the conflicts in material life, but it is nevertheless in those ideological forms that they fight out the basic conflict between forces and relations of production (Marx 1859: 21).

It would be difficult to make sense of Marx's own theorising, or indeed his life, if it were not allowed that ideas, and action grounded in theory, can make a difference to things. Rather, Marx should be taken as warning against the treatment of ideas and theory in a vacuum. That is why, in exegetical fairness, his own views on democratic theory must be seen in a much wider context. We should note, too, that Marx himself makes no exception of communist theory in this respect, observing that unless the *material* elements of a complete revolution are present it makes no difference if the *idea* of communism has been expressed a hundred times (Marx and Engels 1846: 50-1).

Marx distinguished a number of successive epochs by reference to their mode of producing material life — Asiatic, ancient, feudal and modern bourgeois. It is the last of these, the epoch of capitalism, which now concerns us: its nature, its mooted demise and replacement with a new form of society, and then the implications of all this for democracy.

In the very first sentence of the *magnum opus, Capital,* capitalism is identified as that mode of production in which wealth appears in the form of an immense collection of commodities (Marx 1867: 125). Commodities are themselves identified as objects which satisfy some human need and are produced for the purpose of exchange (*ibid.*: 166). In that respect they would differ, for example, from goods which were produced for the immediate consumption of the producers. Commodities may appear in various types of society, but it is only in capitalism that products *predominate* in that form (*ibid.*: 273). A major theme in volume one of *Capital* is the tracing of the consequences which follow if a society's wealth generally takes the form of commodities: the need for one commodity to function as money, the eventual appearance of the money-commodity as capital (money which is advanced for the purpose of making more money), and the gradual divorce of the two sides of commodities — their existence as objects which meet some need and as objects for exchange. We should note, therefore, that for Marx 'capitalism' is not some loose term of abuse, nor even primarily a political term. It denotes a particular type of society by reference to the form which its wealth takes.

Identification of capitalism in this way serves to indicate the production relations which are distinctive of that epoch. Already implicit in the idea of a commodity are the roles of buyer and seller. For Marx it is a central fact about a developed capitalist society that a large — an increasingly large — number of people have no commodity of any significance to sell except their own mental and physical energies, their ability to work. Their position is unlike that of, say, a peasant who has immediate access to the means of subsistence: they must therefore sell themselves, piecemeal, to those who do own the raw materials, instruments of labour and means of subsistence, for the wherewithal which will enable them to live. In return they must labour for a given number of hours in productive activities which constitute a means of life but are not regarded by them as part of their life proper. That begins when work ceases (cf. Marx 1849: 82-3).

In these considerations we have the initial specification of the two classes distinctive of the capitalist epoch: the bourgeoisie, or capitalist class, 'owners of the means of social production and employers of wage labour' and the proletariat, or working class, 'who, having no means of production of their own, are reduced to selling their labour power in order to live' (Marx and Engels 1848: 67n. — clarificatory note added by Engels, for the 1888 English edition). Society, Marx argues, is splitting up more and more into these 'two great hostile camps' (Marx and Engels 1848: 68; cf. Marx 1867: 899).

Why should this relation be characterised as an opposition? It is only a partial answer to say that it is a buying-selling relation. It is true that buyers and sellers have opposed interests so far as concerns the price they agree in striking a bargain, but both sides may stand to gain from the transaction in a way in which they would not if it did not take place at all. They may both end up with something they desire which they would not otherwise have. It is more important to notice what the subject of this particular transaction is. Human energy, the ability to work is bound up with the human being in such a way that its sale has momentous consequences for the seller. It is not an object I can take along to the buyer and then leave. It is inseparable from me, and therefore my life is taken over for a certain time when that commodity is bought. If I am under a constraint to enter into such a transaction, and if it results in a significant part of my life taking on a character quite different from anything I should choose if I were not under such a constraint, then it becomes pertinent to speak, as Marx does, of the enslavement of the proletariat. Most important of all for Marx, however, is the use to which the buyer is able to put this particular commodity. It is the source of the surplus which accrues to the capitalist class, the owners of the means of production, and therefore in working for them the members of the working class actually reinforce and intensify that condition which is responsible for their enslavement and which constitutes their exploitation (Marx 1867: 270-80).

If political and other institutions are to be understood on the basis of the nature of prevailing productive forces and production relations, we now have a sufficient sketch of Marx's view of production to begin to understand his view of politics. The first thing we should notice is that, as a result of his account of a class-divided society, the role of the state and the political decision-making process in general is conceived of very differently from the way familiar to us from liberal theory. These institutions do not constitute neutral ground on which contingent conflicts between people can be worked through and resolved; they do not constitute a concentrated means of keeping in check the wayward impulses of individuals, in the interests of the community. On the contrary, they function in circumstances where there is integral, inherent and ineradicable conflict between classes, and they function in the interest of the ruling class. In the crisp formulation of the *Communist Manifesto*, 'The executive of the modern state is but a committee for managing the common affairs of the whole bourgeoisie' (Marx and Engels 1848: 69).

Such a thesis is prone to excessively crude construal (once again, by both opponents and adherents of Marxism): it may, for instance, be interpreted as a simple conspiracy theory. But there is sufficient subtlety in Marx's (and Engels's) thought to resist this. It is recognised that the state may act independently of the ruling class. In the case of the Bonapartist state, for example, the suggestion appears to be that the dictatorial rule of an individual, depriving the bourgeoisie of its political powers, was what was required actually to further that class's interests at that time (cf. Marx 1869: 238). Certainly there is no notion of state agents taking orders from the ruling class. There will be conflicts of interest within that class, as well as differences of opinion on the best policies to be pursued, and a certain distance between the state and the class will be necessary for the state to perform its function successfully.

Equally, there need be no hint of conscious awareness that sectional interests are being pursued at the expense of those of another class: they may be sincerely pursued under the guise of 'the national interest', for instance, without the realisation that this masks a fundamental opposition of interests. Indeed, it is a notoriously recurrent theme in Marx's writings that a network of misleading appearances is generated by the relations of capitalist society, and that a powerful theory is needed for those appearances to be penetrated (cf, Marx 1867: 163-7). In its absence, much that goes on in capitalism goes on 'behind the backs' of all the actors concerned.

Marx considers himself to be armed with just such a theory, however, and this provides us with views about the social change to be effected and its relation to democratic procedure. The general tension described earlier between production relations and the development of productive forces manifests itself in capitalist society, and the proletariat has a key role to play in its resolution. The progressive achievement of capitalism is to have developed productive potential to a colossal degree. But within the framework of the relations of capitalism it is a potential which cannot be released, since wealth is produced only for sale and exchange. It falls to the class which is propertyless and exploited in this system to bring about a fundamental transformation. Its task is to abolish that relation which defines it as a class. The two sides of that relation are the ownership of capital by the bourgeoisie and the position of wage-slavery of the proletariat. Hence its task is 'the abolishing of bourgeois property' (Marx and Engels 1848: 80). In its place, 'capital is converted into common property, into the property of all members of society' (*ibid.*: 81). Nothing less than this will suffice, and Marx insists, 'Instead of the *conservative* motto, "A fair day's wage for a fair day's work!" they (the working class) ought to inscribe on their banner the *revolutionary* watchword, "*Abolition of the wages system!*"' (Marx 1865: 446; italics in original). The resources of society, then, are to be owned in common by all members of society, rather than by a privileged class within it.

Given the centrality and primacy allotted to material considerations in Marx's conception of history, this proposal for a fundamental transformation of production relations implies a transformation in the *whole* of social relations. When we raise the question how that protracted social revolution is to be achieved, then we directly enter on the question of Marx's political stance and his relation to democracy in the light of his other theories.

A political revolution — a fundamental change in the power relations of society — is necessary for the inauguration of the more protracted social revolution. What are the conditions for its occurrence? Marx makes an important distinction between previous revolutions and the revolution to establish communal ownership of the means of wealth production. Previously, new minority ruling classes had emerged to consolidate their particular form of appropriating wealth, whereas the proletariat, in abolishing the specifically capitalist form of appropriation, abolishes wealth appropriation altogether, since it itself has no characteristic form of appropriation to consolidate. 'All previous historical movements were movements of minorities, in the interest of minorities. The proletarian movement is the self-conscious independent movement of the immense majority, in the interest of the immense majority' (Marx and Engels 1848: 78). As he puts the point later in *Capital*, previously 'it was a matter of the expropriation of the mass of the people by a few usurpers: but in this case, we have the expropriation of a few usurpers by the mass of the people' (Marx 1867: 930).

Marx believed that the dynamics of capitalism itself fostered the growth of this 'self-conscious, independent movement'. As the proletariat increases in numbers and in misery, at the same time its unity and organisation are enhanced by the co-operative effort required for production in capitalism (Marx and Engels 1848: 75-6; cf. Marx 1867: 929). The first step in the revolution is then, as he puts it, 'to raise the proletariat to the position of ruling class, to win the battle of democracy' (Marx and Engels 1848: 86). That political ascendancy is then to be used to concentrate the means of production in the hands of the state, so as to facilitate their further development as rapidly as possible. Thereafter, when production is 'in the hands of a vast association of the nation' and there are no longer any class divisions, political power as the power of one class to oppress another will no longer exist (*ibid.*: 87).

The optimism of the relatively early *Communist Manifesto*

period may subsequently have been tempered in various ways, and there were certainly changes in Marx's views. For example, as we shall see in a moment, the idea of centralisation is replaced by strong statements in favour of dispersal of power. But there is no reason to think Marx ever changed his opinion on the crucial point that the revolution to emancipate the working class from their condition had to be achieved by the working class themselves. He makes that point at the beginning of the provisional rules which he drafted for the First International (Marx 1864: 82). In a letter to the leaders of the German Social-Democratic Workers' Party, he and Engels call attention to the fact that this is their view, and dissociate themselves from 'people who openly declare that the workers are too uneducated to free themselves and must first be liberated from above by philanthropic big bourgeois and petty bourgeois' (Marx and Engels 1879: 375). And Engels repeats the point in his preface to the 1888 English translation of the *Communist Manifesto*.

It is a natural corollary to this to set store, as Marx does, by a system of universal suffrage. In an article on the Chartists he suggests that its establishment would be 'a far more socialistic measure than anything which has been honoured with that name on the Continent' and that its inevitable result would be 'the political supremacy of the working class'; and these claims are linked with the fact that the proletariat formed the large majority of the population and had gained a clear consciousness of its position as a class (Marx 1852: 264). Much later he urged that universal suffrage be 'transformed from the instrument of fraud that it has been up till now into an instrument of emancipation' (Marx 1880: 376-7), and in a speech made in 1872 he explicitly linked the possibility of non-violent revolution to 'victory through the polls' (cf. Evans 1975: 137). Engels, too, points out the obvious advantages of universal suffrage for a strategy of effecting a revolution by the mass support of the majority of the population: it provides an index of the degree of the support which has been won, thus warning against untimely action (or inaction), as well as providing an excellent means of propaganda and forcing the opposition to justify their stance (Engels 1895: 129-30; cf. Engels 1884: 322).

Where institutions such as universal suffrage are not available, and the working class are therefore excluded from legitimate politics, Marx is prepared to envisage the use of violence for the attainment of political ends. Even where they are available, however, it would be an error to conclude that the Marxist recipe for political revolution is to employ all the institutions of liberal democracy in just the way that any other group of political agents would. On the contrary, Marx declares (and sees fit to repeat) that 'the working class cannot simply lay hold of the ready-made state machine, and wield it for its own purposes' (Marx 1871: 206; cf. Marx and Engels 1848: 66). We should recall that the political revolution is to initiate a wider social revolution, and that political institutions are, on Marx's view, systematically related to the material base of a given society. In the light of that, we should expect that political institutions would themselves need to change in the new society.

What, then, are Marx's commitments concerning political organisation in the new society? Here we encounter a difficulty. Associated with that question is a notorious phrase which Marx used a number of times: *the dictatorship of the proletariat* (e.g. Marx 1875: 355). Given the stress (and more importantly, the interpretation) placed on this expression in broadly defined Marxism, it would be easy to conclude that Marx's concern with democracy at an earlier stage has been displaced. After all, in twentieth-century politics dictatorship is the natural antithesis of democracy. The problem is that Marx himself never gives an explicit account of what he understands by the phrase.

On the other hand, Engels suggested that in order to know what the dictatorship of the proletariat looked like we should look at the Paris Commune (Engels 1891: 485). It is therefore of some interest to note what political features of the Commune Marx himself thought worthy of mention in his eulogy of it. He points out that the municipal councillors were elected by universal suffrage, and, like other public officials, worked only for workmen's wages and were revocable at short notice. Revocability and accountability, rather than representation, are stressed. The plan for national organisation was to be based on tiers of elected delegates, revocable and bound by written instructions. 'Instead of deciding once in three or six years which member of the ruling class was to misrepresent the people in parliament, universal suffrage was to serve the people, constituted in communes, as individual suffrage serves every other employer in the search for workmen and managers in his business' (Marx 1871: 210). In both contexts, mistakes can be rectified as long as control is retained over those so selected. The 'merely repressive organs of the old governmental power' were to be abolished, and the few legitimate functions of central government would be restored to the 'responsible agents of society' (*ibid.*).

We see, then, some of the reasoning behind the remark about the working class not laying hold of the ready-made state machine and wielding it for its own purpose. Very different institutions and practices are to be called into being in the social transformation. This is partly a reflexion of the fact that the working class's own purpose is something wider than just political practice. The Commune 'supplied the republic with the basis of really democratic institutions' but the 'true republic' was not its ultimate aim. Rather, it provided 'the political form at last discovered under which to work out the economical emancipation of labour' (*ibid.*: 212). The wider aim of a fundamental change in material relations itself therefore influences the political stance to be adopted. A society of 'free and associated labour' (*ibid.*: 213), created and sustained by a populace which has chosen to initiate and run a society on such a basis, presupposes political arrangements where responsibility is not handed over to a few who act in the name of the many.

In the interests of scholarly accuracy we should bear in mind that these were the type of political arrangements which Marx praised. It is sounder to work back from them to a conclusion about what he must have had in mind when speaking of the dictatorship of the proletariat, rather than investing that expression with an interpretation plainly at odds with the political forms sponsored by Marx. On that principle, it is clear that 'dictatorship' here has little in common with what is conjured up by that term in the twentieth-century mind. Marx took seriously the notion of an entire *class* ruling; and though this leaves him open to obvious objection, if we are to reject strictly defined Marxism it is important that we do so on the proper grounds.

3 THE THEORY ASSESSED

There are obviously a number of different subsidiary theories which go to make up strictly defined Marxist theory as a whole, and this leaves it vulnerable to criticism at many different points. In the context of the present discussion it is not possible even to describe, much less evaluate, all such criticisms. What we must eventually do is reach an assessment of it as an applied theory, and consider whether it fares any better than elite theory and participation theory in relation to the real world. Before that, however, I want to give preliminary consideration to the question how far a theory of this *sort* will accord with the principles discussed in Part One.

A recurrent theme in Part One was the artificiality of preserving democratic procedures only for an official decision-making sphere. I argued there that the most acceptable grounds for placing value on the ideal of self-rule — the nature of human beings as autonomous, rational agents — also constitute grounds for extending provision for self-rule beyond mere formal or legal enablement. If what is important is the absence of interference with rational decisions, then *any* source of such interference should be taken into account. Wealth, or its absence, was taken as the most obvious example of a consideration which can easily play a major role in interfering with the plans which a rational agent might otherwise bring to fruition.

That is a point which can be made, and was made, in the context of liberal democratic theory. Marx, however, makes a similar point in a far more systematic and, so to speak, theorised way. In his materialist conception of history he attempts to trace the influence of the material arrangements of our life over other aspects in an ambitiously wide explanatory theory. If I was right in my claim, in Part One, that a commitment to the realisation of the value of self-rule implies a commitment to the removal of obstacles to its realisation from whatever source, and if Marx is right in his explanatory theory, then he will also be providing important information about the conditions in which democratic practice can be embedded. He *will* be contributing to an understanding of what is required for the principles of democracy to be applied in the actual world, if his analysis of class society and its effects is accurate.

Moreover, though it is impossible to evaluate Marx's whole explanatory theory in the present context, there is one strand in it which sets it apart from theorising in the liberal tradition and which has a high degree of plausibility. Generally speaking, when attention is paid in liberal theory to the effect of material considerations on, say, the ability to exercise an equal influence in decision-making, then it is such questions as the *distribution* of wealth which get discussed. But wealth is available for distribution only when it has already been *produced*. The mode of production is in that sense more fundamental, and there is plausibility in supposing that it may also be more fundamental in other ways — in the degree and nature of its influence, for example, over the rest of a community's activities. And that, of course, is one of the theses on which Marx's view of history is founded. Merely to recognise, therefore, the importance of economic factors is not yet to subscribe to any specifically Marxist thesis. Discussion of the mode of producing wealth is almost entirely absent in much liberal political theory, and Marx makes good that deficiency by calling attention to the very central role played in one's life by one's position in a network of productive relations. The autonomous, rational agent of Part One may, in the real world, be a tycoon or a propertyless worker, and it will make a great deal of difference to their potential *as* such agents which of these positions they occupy.

However, we should also recall from Part One the limitation on the idea of a moral world consisting only of individual autonomous agents, and the corresponding limitation on a conception of democracy based on such a premise. We noticed, first, that these agents do not live an isolated existence. The plans and projects conceived by any one individual agent invariably impinge on those of others, and that is what renders problematic the notion that such agents ought to be accorded a high degree of non-interference when simply pursuing their own goals. Mutual interference is, as it were, already the order of the day. But the major limitation introduced in Part One lay in the fact that other, *collective*, agents had to be recognised as part of the moral world, and that part of the identity of any individual was linked to that of the different collectives to which he or she belonged. This does not of itself make it rational for an individual to identify *with* a collective purely by virtue of membership of it, and it is unfinished business remaining from the arguments of Part One to give any general account of the conditions under which such identification would be rational or otherwise.

In his own response to the limits of individualism it seems to me that Marx expresses views which contribute usefully to these issues. The mutual interference of individuals, and their mutual dependence, is something he insists on. He suggests, in fact, that the picture of the isolated individual arises in a particular historical epoch. The further back in history we go, the more the individual appears to be part of a larger whole. It is not until bourgeois society that the social texture appears to confront the individual as something external: and the irony of this is that it is precisely at this time that the individual is most a social being. The idea of such an individual carrying on production outside of society is preposterous (Marx 1859: 189). From this standpoint the idea of privacy *should* appear problematic. The pursuit of *any* goals presupposes the background existence of a particular network of social relations and is therefore not the sole business of the individual agent who wishes to pursue those goals.

The positive side of the coin is that Marx gives concrete historical content to the idea of the reality of collectives, and the subsumption of individuals under them. The capitalist mode of production presupposes the employment of a relatively large number of individuals, working in co-operation. This gives rise to an intrinsically *collective* power, with new skills not possessed by any individual who goes to make up what Marx refers to as the collective labourer (Marx 1867: 468-9; cf. *ibid.*: 443). The notion of a productive worker itself then gets transferred. It is no longer a matter of the individual putting his hand to the object being produced, but rather of performing one of the subordinate functions of the collective labourer (*ibid.*: 643-4). By the same token, the mechanism of capitalist production which brings workers together in a huge co-operative effort also serves to train, unite and organise them for their role as the agents of the overthrow of capitalism (*ibid.*: 929).

Implicit in this is a claim about a set of circumstances where it is rational for an individual to identify with a collective. In chapter 6, section 4 I discussed the simple model where an individual voluntarily joins with others to form a collective for specific purposes, and suggested that there the case for identification was strong. In effect, Marx is suggesting that the concerted political action on the part of the working class which he recommends would fall under that rubric.

Membership of the working class itself is anything but a voluntary affair: individuals qualify by virtue of the negative condition of being propertyless and forced to sell their ability to work. But in the terminology which I employed in chapter 6 this does make them a *group*, by virtue of their sharing a significant common feature. The materialist conception of history is, amongst other things, an attempt to show just *how* significant that common feature is. Workers also, as we have seen, belong to collectives by virtue of being constituents of a 'collective labourer', whose function is to produce the wealth which is owned as a monopoly by the capitalist class. This means that they constitute, again in my earlier terminology, an *interest group*, a collection of individuals with a significant common interest, namely the reclaiming of the wealth they produce and its conversion into commonly held property in the context of a classless society. Not only that, but on Marx's account if they formed themselves into an overall collective they would have the corporate potential to achieve that end. They therefore have a reason to constitute themselves into just such a collective and to identify with its aims. They share a common, undesirable condition; it is in their interest to eradicate it, and it would be precisely through the corporate power provided by a collective composed of the members of the working class that they would be able to eradicate it.

Now this line of argument is not free from difficulties, some peculiarly its own and some simply particularised versions of more general difficulties. Of the latter type would be the objection that it fails to cope with the 'free rider' problem: if every member of the proletariat will gain from that class's constituting itself into a collective to bring about a revolution, but not every single member is needed to achieve the desired result, why should any single member not take a free ride at the expense of the others and leave the effort to them (cf. Buchanan 1979)? Now this question recalls the general motivational problem discussed at various points in Part One, of how to interest a rational creature in democratic procedures and provide considerations in favour of accepting them when they run contrary to that creature's own wishes. In setting up both problems it is sometimes assumed that rational motivation must connect with the egoistic concerns of an individual. I have already suggested that that assumption can be challenged (cf. chapter 2, section 4); and I should argue that one of the consequences of establishing in chapter 6 that individuals are not exhausted in their individuality is that this changes somewhat the terms in which problems like these must be posed. I shall not pursue that point any further, however. My claim is the more limited one that the components of strictly defined Marxism are in important respects the right *sort* of theories for conforming to the principles which, on the account in Part One, underlie an acceptable theory of democracy. How far they are not merely this but also the right theories is a far wider question.

It needs to be said with the greatest possible emphasis, however, that Marx himself would be profoundly unimpressed by the qualified praise being offered. Part One contained a discussion of principles which were normative, comparatively abstract and apparently timeless. In contrast, Marx insists again and again on the importance of 'historical specificity'. His own proposals are proposals for a particular juncture in human history; and, given his beliefs about the sort of role that theory plays in human affairs, it is entirely natural that he should wish the proposals to be judged by reference to their usefulness at that juncture. In other words, whereas my announced interest is in the contribution which strictly defined Marxism can make to an intellectual debate about the nature of democracy, it follows from the content of that doctrine (including its claims about the place of theory) that it itself must stand or fall according to its successful application, or otherwise, in human history.

Now this places the doctrine in a peculiarly vulnerable position. It means that, on its own terms, we cannot keep neatly separated the idea that its proposals have not been taken up and the idea that it suffers from theoretical deficiencies. If its proposals are not taken up or turn out to be disastrous, then it looks as though they are not appropriate for the material circumstances, and then the doctrine is by its own criteria deficient. And the fact is that, despite the availability of Marxist theory, we do not live in a world where private ownership of the means of production, buying and selling, the wages system have all been abolished, in favour of communal ownership of the earth's resources. The question does indeed therefore become pressing whether Marxist theory can fare any better as an applied theory than elite or participation theory.

Broadly speaking, Marx and Engels provide us with an objective, and a particular means of reaching it. If we wish to probe their suggestions for weakness it is open to us to do it at either or both of these points.

On the face of it, the objective seems morally elevated enough. The 'association of free men, working with the means of production held in common, and expanding their many different forms of labour power in full self-awareness as one single social labour force' (Marx 1867: 171) has an attractive ring. So does the idea that 'in place of the old bourgeois society, with its classes and class antagonisms, we shall have an association in which the free development of each is the condition for the free development of all' (Marx and Engels 1848: 87). These descriptions are suggestive of a state of affairs where consensus obtains and where there is an opportunity for rational identification with the collective, rather than some institutionalised arrangement for allowing the will of some individuals to override that of others. So far, that still sounds a suitable conception for democratic theory.

But does it have application? Many critics have felt that it is precisely at this stage that the theoretical rot sets in. First, there is nothing like a detailed specification from Marx of the new form of society, and it may be objected that it is irrational and reckless to propose a fundamental uprooting of known institutions, with all their imperfections, in the absence of a very clear set of alternative proposals which we have strong reason to believe will be superior. This is not, of course, an accidental omission on Marx's part. He argues that the working class 'have no ready-made utopias to introduce' and that they 'will have to pass through long struggles, through a series of historic processes, transforming circumstances and men' (Marx 1871: 213). He clearly thought it quite inappropriate, given this, to produce detailed blueprints, as opposed to sketching the general principles of the new society.

This gives rise to a second criticism, however, that where it *is* possible to pinpoint Marx's conception of the new society it proves to be unrealistic. For example, the talk of a free association, and the well-known phrase about the government of people being replaced by the administration of things, involves a failure to recognise that in any human community public policy decisions must be taken. Someone, for instance, must decide where new airports or power stations are to be built. This requires some form of government, whether we care to call it by that name or not, and some measure of coercion. The notion that conflict and the politics which goes with it can disappear is simply untenable.

It is true that in his description of the Paris Commune Marx attempts, as we have seen, to call attention to modes of decision-making quite different from those which we normally associate with government, familiar from our acquaintance with existing systems. But it may be felt that there is a similar lack of realism there. The idea that executive tasks can be spread amongst the population presupposes that political and administrative decisions are simple enough for anyone to make them, whereas they rely on a good deal of knowledge and expertise. In a similar vein, talk of delegates acting under written instructions and recallable on demand may sound attractive, but it is clearly unworkable for all but the tiniest of bodies.

How should we assess the issues here? There is certainly an absence of concrete detail in Marx's specification of his objective, beyond a skeletal description of the distribution of the means of wealth production and an account of some of the favoured principles of decision-making. But for a number of reasons it would not be easy to remedy this. Since the goal is a world-wide society of common ownership, there is not the theoretical possibility of providing a concrete example in a geographically circumscribed area (though exponents of broadly defined Marxism agonise over the possibility or actuality of 'socialism in one country'). Since the transformation of society urged by him would be in a number of respects a unique one, there is only limited evidence and example available from past history. The revolution, as we saw, was to be the work of a self-conscious majority rather than a minority, and was to inaugurate a classless society rather than establishing a new dominant class. It follows from this that the question of the precise form which decision-making takes must itself remain in the hands of the majority. This may deflect the objection that the doctrine is reckless in proposing to sweep away the devil we know in favour of one we do not, because until the majority has itself formulated a concrete embodiment of the objective the time is in any case not ripe for any sweeping away. But by the same token it does mean that there is likely to be dissatisfaction from our own vantage point at the lack of concrete detail in the specification of the objective.

On the question of realism, my view is that it is not obvious that the case against Marx has been established. The mere fact of the need for public decisions does not establish that there must be a group of decision-makers with coercive power; nor does the fact, of itself, that different kinds of expertise must be called on in reaching decisions which affect human society. Marx's conception of the democratic, classless society does, it is true, presuppose a citizenry which is immeasurably better informed and more involved in public decisions, as well as having much greater time at its disposal to exercise its citizenship, than at present. But it would take a solidly-established theory to show that such changes are impossible. We have already seen enough variation in the data produced by elite and participation theorists on the question of apathy, for example, to justify caution in reaching such conclusions.

The objections to Marxist theory from a position of commonsense realism may or may not turn out in the end to be well-founded. In the short run, however, they do serve two useful functions. One is to demonstrate once again that the proposed transformation of society is a profound and revolutionary one. If we imagine a quite different form of decision-making just grafted on to our existing way of life the result is very implausible indeed. But if we are to be fair to Marx we must also imagine social relations changing in many other ways — a drastic move away from the consumer mentality, for example, and a massive reduction in the time spent by people at work, as well as a transformation of the relations in workplaces themselves. It is no objection to Marx's conception of a system where citizens rule themselves that it fails to fit in with prevailing circumstances. On the contrary, that is his point.

The second function follows naturally from this, namely to reinforce the point that Marx's views on democracy cannot be taken and assessed separately from his other views. To take the example just mentioned, it matters greatly to our assessment whether he is correct in his claim that the productive forces have been sufficiently developed by capitalist society that a massive reduction in the working day *is* a possibility. No final verdict on 'Marx on democracy' is possible, therefore, without a much wider assessment of his theories, which plainly cannot be undertaken here. That may be irritating for the development of my argument in this book, but no doubt the conclusion would gratify Marx.

At this point let us turn from discussion of objectives to discussion of means. As we have seen, Marx had definite views on the mechanisms which would lead society in his favoured direction. The increasing polarization into capitalists and proletarians, the growing misery and exploitation of the latter, together with their increased co-operation and organisation, lead to a growth in revolutionary class consciousness. Capitalism, in the notorious phrase, produces its own grave-diggers. In the light of the survival of capitalism one hundred years after Marx's death, and the course it has taken, it is not surprising that these views have produced misgivings in sympathetic as well as hostile critics.

For one thing, it is argued that the class structure of society has not become simplified in the appropriate way. Quite apart from problems presented by the existence of a peasantry in parts of the world affected by revolution, we have seen the growth of a huge 'middle class', so that there is a problem for Marxist theory about the class location of people as diverse as technicians, supervisors, teachers, civil servants and salesmen (cf. Blackburn 1976: 39). For another thing, competition on the labour market puts groups of workers into competition with one another and encourages differentiation on grounds other than class, such as sex, religion, language, race and so on (*ibid*.). Indeed, it has been claimed that lines of cleavage according to characteristics like these, rather than those of class, may constitute the primary source of social antagonism (Parkin 1979: 5).

Generally speaking, therefore, strictly defined Marxism is left with the embarrassing problem of 'how to account for the awkward discrepancies between classes defined as embodiments of productive relations and classes as active political agencies' (*ibid*.: 25). It has been felt that, not only has the postulated class consciousness not materialised, but the prospects of its doing so in the future must be equally bleak. Suspicion is felt over the idea that the crushed victims of capitalism would somehow have the capacity to build a better world (cf. Dunn 1979: 98-9; Macintyre 1981: 244). That enterprise would surely require the skills and aptitudes of the middle class, and the problem then is that 'all the precedents suggest that the political allegiance of these white-collar groups would be less than wholehearted' (Parkin 1979: 178).

Once these flaws in the account of the growth of class consciousness are admitted, then further damage to Marx's original position may follow. If there are permanent and intractable divisions within the working class then any political movement which faithfully reflected those divisions would probably be doomed to ineffectiveness. But in that case Marx's proposal that the working class should itself make the revolution will have to be abandoned, in favour of some kind of 'substitutism'. This fact may, indeed, be welcomed, on the grounds that, even though revolutions may enjoy the support of majorities, they must remain the work of minorities (cf. Miliband 1977: 126-7, 130).

Problems like these have resulted in forms of broadly defined Marxism very different from Marx's own position, especially with regard to the centrality of material, economic considerations, as against general cultural ones, in shaping political consciousness and action. I should argue, however, that abandonment of this aspect of his theories is premature and is often founded on a misunderstanding of the nature and import of his theory of class.

To begin with, we must distinguish the criteria used to *identify* classes from the various substantive claims made about the groups of people so identified, and the courses of action which they are urged to adopt. On the score of identification there is no problem for Marx in the growth of the 'middle class'. Supervisors, teachers and the rest meet the criterion of having no significant means of production of their own, and in consequence needing to sell their labour power in order to live. The growth in white collar occupations is of itself no threat to the thesis that capitalism produces a polarization of classes, if the test of class membership turns on one's relation to the means of production. If we do not normally think of people who fall into the white collar categories as belonging to the working class, that merely shows that we are employing a conception of class different from that of Marx.

But, it will be said, if such people *do not think of themselves* as members of the working class, does that not vitiate the thesis of the growth of working class consciousness in Marx's sense? He is at liberty to identify the working class according to any criteria he chooses; but what is the point in doing so, if his substantive thesis about the entity so defined turns out to be false?

Now there is absolutely no denying the failure of class consciousness to grow along the postulated lines. What we must decide, however, is whether this reflects a theoretical weakness or merely a contingently optimistic attitude on Marx's part. Many people take their primary political self-description from religion, race, sex, or from a conception of class differently grounded from Marx's — one based on income level, or type of occupation, or cultural attributes, for example, rather than on relation to the means of production. But even though this is true, and even though it may be instrumental in shaping their political behaviour, it does not necessarily constitute a rebuttal of Marxist theory.

We should recall Marx's observation that people become

conscious of the conflict between productive forces and productive relations in *ideological* forms (Marx 1859: 21), as well as the recurrent theme of the distortion of people's perception of their own social relations, a distortion for the removal of which a sound theory is needed. It would be in conformity with one kind of primacy of material life to be able to show that, where people's lives are dominated by conceptions other than those of class as defined in Marxist theory, nevertheless important expressions of their resulting political consciousness occur in the material realm. Thus, where religious conceptions predominate, bigotry directed against Catholics might gain its most important expression in such facts as their being *denied jobs*. It would be in conformity with another kind of primacy to be able to show that the possession of some ideological and distorted set of perceptions was itself functionally useful for sustaining a given set of productive relations. Thus, self-identification by reference to nationality might produce a sense of community with and loyalty towards the capitalist class of one's own nation, coupled with a hostile attitude to both capitalists and workers of some other country.

To the extent that Marxist theory is an explanatory one, if the sorts of possibility described here can be made good in concrete historical cases there is no reason to abandon it. But of course the theory has other aspects than the explanatory: it seeks not merely to interpret the world but to change it. In that respect it aspires not just to explain the dislocation between the conceptions and actions of the working class, on the one hand, and their political interests, on the other. It aspires also to bring actions and political interests into line with each other.

Strictly defined Marxism must be judged to be a failure to date in that last endeavour. Nevertheless, once again we should not conclude too hastily that the rational response is to abandon it. For one thing, Marx dealt in historical epochs — large units of time — and in that context the failure to achieve a massive objective in one hundred years is not yet a damning indictment. Something so close to a miracle may take a little longer. More importantly, however, we should after all resist a crude equation of acceptability as a theory with practical success. Even leaving aside its explanatory aspects and judging

Marxism just *as* a practical proposal, we have to assess it by other criteria than just that.

One question will be how cogent an account it gives of where different individuals' interests lie. It presents us with a relatively unfamiliar idea: that a very broad band of the population — those people who have to sell their mental and physical energies — share a common interest in ending that condition, despite the many differences of status, income, cultural background, and so forth, which they display. It argues that case by reference to the undesirability of the common condition which they share. A very large part of their life is, in an importantly literal sense, no longer their own, and takes a shape which they would not otherwise choose to give it; and they are prone to suffer the effects of the social system which surrounds the relation they are involved in, in a way unlike the relatively small proportion of the population who are under no such constraints and are in fact the purchasers of labour power. The case is further buttressed by the (essentially economic) theory that this broad band of people is properly regarded as a corporate entity which, by means of its many talents, produces the surplus which accrues to the capitalist class. By the same token the corporate entity can act to build a new set of social relations.

If Marxist theory is construed in this way then it avoids some of the more obvious criticisms mentioned earlier. It does not, for example, urge that a narrow band of manual or factory workers are capable of reconstructing society without the aid and talents of 'white collar' workers of various kinds. It also offers resistance to the idea of 'substitutism'. Intractable divisions there may well be between different sections of the working class, and conflicting interests too, as long as the thinking and the behaviour of those sections remain within the confines of capitalist society. But precisely what Marx is urging is that they look beyond sectional interests and beyond the confines of capitalist society. He proposes that they look to a more fundamental level where they share a common interest, and act to convert productive resources into the common possession of all. The enormity as well as the nature of such a programme positively calls for the participation of the majority, rather than mere passive support.

In that respect and many others Marx's theory calls for developments unique in human history. But that hardly constitutes an objection to it, since he could very well reply that the problems of capitalism also call for developments unique in human history. The general tension between production relations and productive forces here appears itself in a unique form: privations occur despite the prodigious feats of production which the technology of capitalism makes possible; and the complex co-operative effort which goes into producing wealth cannot be matched by any co-operative decisions regarding either its disposal or social arrangements in general. If we also bear in mind the extent to which Marx's theory takes a form consonant with the abstract principles of Part One, then I believe the upshot is an applied theory with a strong democratic commitment which is well worth serious consideration.

But it may still be felt — indeed, historically has been felt, with tragic results — that there are quicker, if rougher, routes available to the desired destination which would be sanctioned on Marx's own premises. Members of the proletariat, it has been allowed, have not developed a revolutionary class consciousness, and the ideological distortions to which they are subjected in capitalism exercise a profound influence on the development of their consciousness. But, it may be said, the Marxist analysis reveals the 'true interests' of the proletariat, regardless of whether the workers recognise them as such and choose to pursue them. Why not conclude, therefore, that it is unnecessary to test opinion and abide by its expression, and not only that but that it may be positively misleading in the circumstances to put oneself under that kind of constraint? Why not simply act in what is, according to the theory, in the real interests of the mass of people even if they fail, as the theory might itself predict, to recognise them?

This is a line of argument which will occupy our attention further in chapter 10. If it were cogent, its effect would obviously be to make the connexion between Marxist objectives, on the one hand, and commitment to democratic procedures, on the other, far more tenuous than I have tried to establish. But we may doubt whether it is cogent. Certainly any account of the ideological distortions of capitalism must leave room for the self-evident fact that some people, including some workers, manage to escape them and embrace Marxism. Perhaps those who do so have superior cognitive powers or something of the kind. But unless that or some better explanation is forthcoming, we can ask why it is not possible for many more to do so, thus avoiding the need for a pre-empting of their own views on where their interests lie.

Consider the matter from the side of democracy. In chapter 2 I argued that we ought not simply to equate people's interests with their subjective preferences, that it is perfectly possible for someone to be mistaken about what is in their interests and for another person to be in a better position to judge. I cannot therefore reject the present line of argument on the grounds that the only way of specifying someone's interests is by finding out what *they* think they are. But at the same time, it does not automatically follow that acting against someone's preferences but in their interests is justified. A theme of several chapters in Part One was precisely that other considerations come into the reckoning when it is a question of the fitting ways of treating human beings, considerations which place a limit on benevolent interference in their lives. The attraction of democracy was located in its treating people in a way appropriate to their nature, rather than in its necessarily maximising their interests. It is a reasonable position to hold that it is important for people to be able to decide things for themselves, even if they do not always decide for the best. And that position does offer a point of leverage against the present line of argument.

However, it offers a point of leverage only if there is a prior commitment to democracy, and that may increase the feeling that we are now confronted with a choice between Marxism and democracy. After all, I have already pointed out that Marx would not rest any argument on an appeal to abstract, timeless principles to do with the nature of human beings and their status as rational, autonomous agents. For that reason it is important to be able to show that there are reasons internal to Marxism itself which point to a similar conclusion about the impermissibility of imposing what is in someone's interests when they themselves resist it.

What is the nature of the transformation which, according

to Marx, it is the role of the proletariat to bring about? In place of the compulsion to work which is characteristic of their position in capitalism, there will be a free association of people. In place of the exploitation of one section by another there will be common ownership of the means of production. In place of the political domination of a bureaucratic elite there will be widespread participation and revocable delegation. Leaving aside all question of the realism of Marx's proposals, these are the arrangements which he regards as meeting the real interests of the proletariat. *But these are arrangements which in their very description are incapable of attainment without the voluntary co-operation of the proletariat itself.* Whereas you can make people do what they do not wish to do, you cannot make them adopt a set of social relations which require their voluntary co-operation if they do not voluntarily co-operate. Admittedly, you might hope that by acting against someone's wishes *now* you would be able to create a state of affairs *later* where they were happy to conform to what had originally been forced upon them. But, as I shall try to show in chapter 10, where it is an entirely new system of society which is at issue, and one having the kind of characteristics outlined, something more than hope is required, and nothing more than hope has been offered in the most historically influential strand of broadly defined Marxism.

In the absence of anything more than hope, there is sound sense in Marx's repeated insistence that the proletariat must emancipate itself, and his resistance to the idea that this can be achieved by some philanthropic agency on the proletariat's behalf. In other words, the *content* of the real interests of the proletariat, on Marx's account, dictates a limitation on effective action designed to realise those interests. Such action must be consonant with the proletariat's wishes, and therefore the focus for change must be those wishes themselves. That is why Marx insists that a revolutionary consciousness, as well as the appropriate material conditions, is a prerequisite for the revolution.

If political movements acting in Marx's name have ignored this and opted for short-cuts involving brutal suppression of the proletariat's own wishes, that is a matter for condemnation and explanation. But neither will be aided by placing the responsibility on Marx's theory, when it is precisely a departure from that theory which has produced such a result.

4 CONCLUSION

In its relation to democracy, strictly defined Marxism has certain affinities with both participation theory and elite theory, as well as obvious differences.

It shares with participation theory a mistrust of the gap between rhetoric and practice in existing representative systems, and an aspiration to a much fuller participation in decision-making by the whole populace, an aspiration to give content to the idea of self-rule as something distinct from merely some ruling others. It is clearly much wider and more ambitious in scope than participation theory, in attempting to give an analysis of the entire social structure in which decision-making occurs and providing proposals for correspondingly wide changes. In that respect it provides explanations at points where I suggested participation theory was vulnerable. It offers motivational grounds for embarking on a programme of transforming society, by attempting to establish a systematic connexion between one's exclusion from substantive decision-making and one's position in a whole network of social relations, which brings with it disadvantages of many different kinds. It takes on the Eckstein problem — that stability requires congruence between authority patterns in governmental and other institutions — by the radical strategy of a willingness to advocate change in authority patterns throughout society, and to envisage the disappearance of government in its present form altogether. Finally, it takes on the dilemma facing participation theory, that the structure of most people's working lives is such as to rule out sustained participation, by once again adopting a radical strategy. It proposes a social system where people's lives would no longer be dominated by work and where all the political activity produced by class division would disappear. In other words, it proposes a joint solution which consists partly in affording people far more time for controlling the conditions of their own existence instead of working to enrich a minority, and partly in establishing material conditions where there is a drastic reduction in the volume of what would now be regarded as political issues.

Marxism shares with elite theory a realistic appraisal of the extent of unequal influence over decision-making in contemporary society, and the degree to which the entire system of society would have to change for that to be otherwise. (Indeed, on my account Marx makes the preconditions for social transformation far more stringent than many forms of broadly defined Marxism.) Marxism and elite theory part company on the question whether an entire transformation is either possible or desirable.

One of the grounds for elite theory's negative position on that question was that the ordinary citizen does and must suffer a reduced sense of responsibility in the political realm, where there is not such an obvious and direct connexion between decision and consequences (chapter 7, section 3). Elite theory makes much of the lack of interest and incapacity which the masses have for running society, just as participation theory makes much of the possibility of increasing people's feelings of efficacy at least in a circumscribed area. In one way elite theory has the better argument, in that the wider decision-making is spread, the less can individuals feel that there is a direct connexion between *their* decision and the outcome. But in another way Marx provides a perspective preferable to both theories on this point.

On the normative principles discussed in Part One, it is difficult to square with the requirements of democracy a situation where members of a small elite, or a president or prime minister, experience direct feedback on the effectiveness of their decisions. Circumstances where they are able to do so offend against standards of liberty and equality in the form which these must take in an acceptable conception of democracy. Marx takes the argument away from such cases by concentrating on *collective* efficacy. With his stress on *corporate* action and his ontology of classes, he brings into focus the possibility of large numbers of individuals having rational grounds for identifying with large collectives, entities which *as* collectives may achieve a great deal and have a great impact on the world. This furnishes the possibility of recognising that *we* are effective, in ways in which an ordinary individual could not feel that *he* or *she* was. Moreover, in the case of the corporate labourer described by Marx this possibility is furnished simply as a consequence of a shift in conception. Such corporate efficacy exists, but in the absence of Marx's analysis is not appreciated for what it is.

Throughout this chapter I have stressed that its topic is the theoretical legacy of Marx rather than the broadly defined Marxism which has informed much practical politics. Marx provides a model for consensus in decision-making amongst social equals, but insists that the great divide between class and classless society must be bridged before any approximation to the model can be achieved. There need be no implication here of a utopian conception where the entire population of the world acts as one, with all conflict eradicated. Rather, Marx calls attention to the major source of structurally-produced, inevitable conflict in contemporary reality. Differences and disagreements would obviously survive the removal of that source. But they would occur in a social climate where rational deference to collective decisions, as described in chapter 6, section 4, would be a possibility, because of the rational and voluntary subscription required to bring about that climate in the first place. All of this is the antithesis of the one-party states and bureaucratic elites taking Marx's name, and this licenses the conclusion that the theory described in this chapter has, so to speak, been lost to history. My aim has been to show that, if we have a regard for democracy, we should not acquiesce in that loss too readily.

Much of the theory as I have presented it in this chapter might well be strongly opposed from the standpoint of broadly defined Marxism (and not on grounds wholly different from those of anti-Marxism). In the form described here, it might be said, the theory *deserves* to be lost to history, since it is so obviously in need of reconstruction. It is utopian in its supposition that the political consciousness of the majority can be revolutionised by ordinary means when, as Marx himself insisted, the ruling ideas of an epoch are those of the ruling class. If the prevailing ideology is functional for prevailing production relations, then it is unrealistic to suppose that revolution can be fomented by activity at the ideological level.

Equally unrealistic and unspecific, it may be said, is the idea of an entire class, rather than some smaller and more effective unit, taking significant political action.

These criticisms point in the direction of a rather different political theory from strictly defined Marxism, and must be taken up in the remaining chapter. For it is, of course, an oversimplification to say that the theory of the present chapter was lost to history. The full fact is, I shall argue, that a *deformation* of it became historically influential. Or to put it another way, the terrible fate which befell Marx was that he was Leninised.

FURTHER READING

Many of Marx's political writings are usefully gathered together in Fernbach 1973a, 1973b and 1974. His commitment to democracy is explored in Hunt 1975. Cohen 1978 set entirely new standards for philosophical commentary on Marx, and these have been sustained in Elster 1985. A useful introduction to the politics of both Marx and broadly defined Marxism is Miliband 1977. Rees 1971, Kolakowski 1978 and Dunn 1979 all in different ways question the coherence of the objectives set by Marx.

10 Leninist theory

1 INTRODUCTION

For many years it was common both in practical politics and in academic discussion for reference to be made to the theories of 'Marxism–Leninism'. It was almost as if the theories thus referred to so obviously formed a seamless whole that they might have been the work of one man with a double-barrelled name. Such a form of reference is less common than it was in the academic sphere, largely as a result of an increasingly serious interest in Marx's writings and the observance of standards of scholarship which would automatically prevail in the case of any less controversial theorist. Reference to 'Marxism–Leninism' is still common, however, in the political sphere. It was partly to avoid the misleading assumptions behind this label that I introduced the terminological distinction between strictly defined and broadly defined Marxism at the beginning of chapter 9. In that terminology Leninism is itself one species of broadly defined Marxism, though a sufficiently distinctive one to have acquired its own name.

In the present chapter I shall argue that not only is Leninism distinctive, but there is a considerable theoretical distance between Marx and Lenin, with important repercussions for their respective attitudes to democracy. I believe that a failure to recognise this theoretical distance has carried with it momentous political consequences, but that is not what I am centrally concerned to argue. For example, for anyone who regards the political legacy of Lenin as a disaster, at least two different images of him are available. One would cast him as a ruthless and unscrupulous schemer, the other as an honest but tragic figure trapped in wholly unpropitious historical circumstances. I shall not attempt to adjudicate between them, simply because I wish to concentrate on Lenin's contribution to theory rather than on his character as a political agent.

Of course, this distinction is not a very sharp one, since there is bound to be *some* connexion between deeds and theoretical stance. And it might be argued that it is inappropriate to look to Lenin for a web of theory separate from his reaction to actual, particular political contexts. After all, he was caught up in momentous events in world history to a far greater extent than Marx, and was consequently less in a position to provide grand general theories.

This observation may be correct, but if my argument in chapter 1 was sound it should not deter the kind of assessment of Lenin's position which I wish to undertake. He proposes particular courses of political action which he clearly regards as desirable and justifiable. A justification will necessitate pointing to features they possess which reveal their desirability, defending them against possible objections, and the like, and will be to that extent general. In however temporising a political stance, we may look for or attempt to reconstruct the material of such a justification. We should note, too, that Lenin himself thought that certain features of Bolshevism had universal application and significance, and he wrote a pamphlet calling attention to those features in the belief that 'on certain very important questions of the proletarian revolution, *all* countries will inevitably have to do what Russia has done' (Lenin 1920a: 16; italics in original. Cf. *ibid*.: 32). In the end, therefore, there is nothing to prevent us from asking of Lenin, as we did of Marx, how far his objectives and his proposed means of achieving them are sound, and how far they are consistent with acceptable democratic principles of the kind discussed in Part One.

No doubt in carrying out such an assessment we must take due note of changes in Lenin's theoretical position which occurred precisely under the impetus of political events. The most obvious instance is the view he took of the possibility of an imminent revolution to establish socialism. In 1905 he argued that the 'degree of Russia's economic development (an objective condition), and the degree of class consciousness and

organisation of the broad masses of the proletariat (a
subjective condition inseparably bound up with the objective
condition) make the immediate and complete emancipation of
the working class impossible' (Lenin 1905: 28). But by 1918,
taking the view that the international proletarian revolution
was clearly maturing, he summed up the results of the
experience of the Russian revolution in the belief that it was to
be understood 'as a link in a chain of socialist proletarian
revolutions being called forth by the imperialist war' (Lenin
1918a: 2).

It will be necessary to document changing assumptions, as
well as underlying assumptions which persist. The latter, I shall
suggest, provide evidence of the distance between Lenin and
Marx. The two problems we were left with in our discussion of
Marx concerned doubts about the likelihood of a growth in
class consciousness and doubts about the possibility of an
entire class acting as an effective political agent. There is
remarkably little in Marx's writings about the role of a political
party in all of this. I shall seek to show that the underlying
assumptions which account for the role that Lenin allots to the
Party, and the agencies within it, are a constant in his views.
They consist in different types of *vanguardism*, the doctrine
that a given group's emancipation depends crucially on some
other, much smaller group's leadership, guidance, or
domination in some stronger form. I shall relate these
assumptions to Lenin's stance on such questions as what to do
about the state apparatus, the role of parliament and suffrage,
and the dictatorship of the proletariat.

2 THE THEORY STATED

We began our discussion of Marx by noting that for him
questions of politics and democracy must be dealt with in the
wider context of the material, economic organisation of life.
His programme is for a fundamental transformation of that
economic organisation; and because of the role which political
institutions play in sustaining economic relations, this of
necessity calls for action at the political level. In *What is to be
Done?* Lenin makes a related point. Engels, in praising the

contribution of German workers to revolutionary struggle, had made a tripartite division, suggesting that 'For the first time since a workers' movement has existed, the struggle is being conducted pursuant to its three sides — the theoretical, the political, and the practical-economic (resistance to the capitalists) . . .' (Engels 1875: 653, cited in Lenin 1902: 28).

Lenin makes much of this, and with regard to the category of the theoretical, observes that the appropriate consciousness for revolution could not exist among the workers. The history of all countries, he suggests, shows that the working class, exclusively by its own effort, is able to develop only 'trade union consciousness', that is a conviction that it is necessary to combine in unions, fight the employers, and conduct similar struggles within the framework of the existing social structure (*ibid*.: 31-2). The absence of adequate theory amongst the workers, and their resulting non-revolutionary consciousness, affects their politics: 'working-class trade-unionist politics is precisely working-class bourgeois politics' (*ibid*.: 94). Where, then, is revolution to come from? The appropriate consciousness must be brought to the workers 'from without' (*ibid*.: 31). Specifically, the sound theory associated with sound politics, the theory of socialism, emanates from intellectuals, of whom Marx and Engels are themselves examples (*ibid*.: 32).

We have here early signs of Lenin's vanguardism, the singling out of a small group who hold the key to the emancipation of some larger group. The doctrine has both extensive and intensive versions, as it were. In the extensive versions the Russian proletariat might have a vanguard role in relation to all oppressed classes in Russia, or in relation to the international proletariat. Lenin thought that the Russian proletariat might aspire to the 'honourable title' of vanguard of the international proletariat (Lenin 1902: 29). In this he differs from Engels, who thought it 'not at all in the interest of this movement that the workers of any particular country should march at its head' (Engels 1875: 654).

It is the intensive versions of vanguardism, however, allotting a similar role to various smaller agencies *vis-à-vis* the proletariat itself, which are crucial to Lenin's theoretical stance. They emerge in his criticism of 'economism', the concentration on economic struggle in the context of the relation between employer and employee. In amplification of his earlier remark, Lenin argues that 'class political consciousness can be brought to the workers *only from without,* that is, only from outside the economic struggle, from outside the sphere of relations between workers and employers' (Lenin 1902: 78-9; italics in original). It was necessary, he held, for bringing political knowledge to the workers to 'go among all classes of the population' (*ibid.*: 79). As for political organisation, whereas the workers' 'economistic' trade union organisations should be as broadly-based and public as possible, 'the organisation of the revolutionaries must consist first and foremost of people who make revolutionary activity their profession' and 'must perforce not be very extensive and must be as secret as possible' (*ibid.*: 109).

Now it is of course vital to bear in mind the historical context in which Lenin was formulating his theories. Marx's prediction had been that, as capitalism emerged as the dominant world system, so the proletariat would come to prevail as the majority class. But early twentieth-century Russia, with its vast peasantry and only isolated pockets of industry, was a long way from conforming to this description. Any theorist wishing to include Russia within the scope of the theory associated with Marx's prediction would, therefore, certainly need to take into account this fact about its class composition. Equally, Russia was an absolutist state. The civil liberties whose importance I discussed in chapter 3, section 2 were entirely non-existent. A political theory would also have to take that into account, and in *those* circumstances the idea of a secret, exclusive organisation may have more appeal than it would for us, in our very different circumstances.

Moreover, it may be felt that there is nothing particularly objectionable in the form of vanguardism apparent here. Lenin simply asserts the need for 'an organisation of revolutionaries capable of guiding the *entire* proletarian struggle for emancipation' (*ibid.*: 114; italics in original), his grounds being that 'without the "dozen" tried and talented leaders (and talented men are not born by the hundreds), professionally trained, schooled by long experience, and working in perfect harmony, no class in modern society can wage a determined struggle' (*ibid.*: 118-19).

As a salutary example, Lenin cites the Webbs' account of early English trade unionists, with their naive belief in 'primitive democracy', in which all questions were decided by the vote of all the members and all official duties were fulfilled by all members in turn. 'A long period of historical experience', he comments, 'was required for workers to realise the absurdity of such a conception of democracy' and recognise the need for representatives and full-time officials (*ibid.*: 138). In any case, concentrating secret functions

in the hands of as small a number of professional revolutionaries as possible does not mean that the latter will 'do the thinking for all' and that the rank and file will not take an active part in the *movement*. On the contrary, the membership will promote increasing numbers of the professional revolutionaries from its ranks . . .   (*ibid.*: 122; italics in original)

However, before we conclude that in taking this line Lenin is simply giving more realistic content to the idea of a class taking political action than Marx did, we should consider how the line developed and persisted in his thought, even when there was no longer a Tsar around to be blamed if there was absolutism in Russia.

In *The State and Revolution* (actually written in 1917 but published the following year) the extensive and intensive versions of vanguardism are still present. The proletariat is again depicted as 'capable of being the leader of *all* the working and exploited masses' (Lenin 1918a: 31; italics in original). But it is the *vanguard* of the proletariat, rather than the proletariat itself, 'which is capable of taking power and *of leading the whole people* to socialism . . . (*ibid.*: 32; italics in original). And in *'Left-Wing' Communism, an Infantile Disorder* further indications are given why a vanguard should be thought necessary and what its role is to be. Urging the need for compromise in political dealings, Lenin suggests that it is one of the functions of a party organisation and of party leaders to acquire the knowledge, experience and flair needed to solve complex political problems correctly (Lenin 1920a: 53-4). These problems may involve nothing less than the capture of political power. For it cannot be captured until the struggle has reached a certain stage, which will be different in different circumstances and 'can be correctly gauged only by thoughtful, experienced and knowledgeable political leaders of the proletariat in each particular country' (*ibid.*: 37).

In this spirit Lenin expresses apprehension over excessive growth of the Party, and points out that it was directed by a Central Committee of nineteen, from whom still smaller bodies carried out work in Moscow. 'No important political or organisational question is decided by any state institution in our republic without the guidance of the Party's Central Committee' (*ibid.*: 33).

From the extensive to the intensive versions of vanguardism we see a progressive narrowing of the vanguard agency: the whole proletariat, the Party, the Central Committee. The terminal point would be one individual. We know that as a matter of history this is what occurred in Russia, and this is a possibility which Lenin himself allowed for. 'That in the history of revolutionary movements the dictatorship of individuals was very often the expression, the vehicle, the channel of the dictatorship of the revolutionary classes has been shown by the irrefutable experience of history' (Lenin 1918b: 267). Similarly, he pointed out that the Central Committee itself endorsed the view that 'the will of a class may sometimes be carried out by a dictator, who sometimes does more alone and is frequently more necessary' (Lenin 1920b: 476). This is perhaps the logical outcome of that 'absolute centralisation and rigorous discipline' which he regarded as 'an essential condition of victory over the bourgeoisie' (Lenin 1920a: 10).

Lenin's attitude to political change and democracy must be understood against the backcloth of this vanguardism. On the nature of the state we find, initially, echoes of some of Marx's views. It is seen not as a neutral agency but as a force against the oppressed class (Lenin 1918a: 22-4). Hence, although Lenin is 'in favour of a democratic republic as the best form of the state for the proletariat under capitalism', he insists that their lot is still wage-slavery (*ibid.*: 24). Hence, although 'we have a more or less complete democracy in the democratic republic' it is 'always hemmed in by the narrow limits set by capitalist exploitation' (*ibid.*: 105). It remains democracy for the rich, since the poor are too crushed by poverty to be bothered with politics.

We should notice here Lenin's tendency to *identify* democracy with a particular form of the state, one which 'recognises the subordination of the minority to the majority' (*ibid.*: 99) and also 'signifies the formal recognition of equality of citizens' (*ibid.*: 121). But as a state, it is also based on the systematic use of violence (*ibid.*: 99). This identification explains why Lenin should talk of democracy 'withering away'. Revolution is to put an end to the bourgeois state, and when the state in general withers away then so does democracy (*ibid.*: 109).

But what is to replace those state institutions and how is an alternative system of society to be reached? In Lenin's conception of an alternative form of society, without a state apparatus, we also find, at least for a time, echoes of Marx, and a similar celebration of commune or soviet organisation. The armed people replace the standing army, and the majority fulfil all the functions previously carried out by a privileged minority — a state of affairs made possible by the degree to which capitalism, with its large-scale production, communications, and so on, has rendered the functions of state power much simpler to carry out (Lenin 1918a: 52-3). The aspiration is to a society where people '*become accustomed* to observing the elementary conditions of social life *without violence* and *without subordination*' (*ibid.*: 99; italics in original. Cf. *ibid.*: 108-9). There is an express desire to see many more ordinary citizens brought into active participation in the process of transforming society (cf. Lenin 1917a: 61), and an insistence that people recognise only bodies set up by themselves, as opposed to those appointed from above. 'The idea of "direction" by officials "appointed" from above is essentially false and undemocratic . . .' (Lenin 1917b: 322). 'Socialism cannot be decreed from above. Its spirit rejects the mechanical bureaucratic approach; living, creative socialism is the product of the masses themselves' (Lenin 1917c: 288).

Now these sentiments belong to a particular period. Lenin's talk of the commune as a form of organisation becomes less frequent after 1917, virtually disappearing by 1920, with a coincident increase in his discussion of the *dictatorship of the proletariat* (cf. Harding 1981: 201). No doubt this signals an increased recognition on Lenin's part of the complexity of large organisations. No doubt, too, the circumstances surrounding the Russian revolution — the invasion by hostile powers, the famine and devastation — play a part in determining his views as to the means appropriate for re-shaping society. Equally, however, the vanguardism he subscribed to must be taken into account in understanding the stress he placed on, and the interpretation he gave to, the idea of the dictatorship of the proletariat.

For Lenin, a recognition of the dictatorship of the proletariat is definitive of Marxism (Lenin 1918a: 42). That dictatorship 'will for the first time create democracy for the people, for the majority, along with the necessary suppression of the minority — the exploiters' (*ibid.*: 109). Suppression is to be taken seriously. Lenin criticises broadly defined Marxists such as Kautsky, who dream of the socialist transformation 'not as the overthrow of the rule of the exploiting class, but as the peaceful submission of the minority to the majority which has become aware of its aims' (*ibid.*: 31). 'Major questions in the life of nations', he had earlier asserted, 'are settled only by force' (Lenin 1905: 132). Hence the repeated insistence that the state is to be *smashed* (Lenin 1918a: 34-5, 46-7).

There are two ironies here. First, although the state as an instrument of class oppression is to be smashed, it has first to be *strengthened* in the form of the dictatorship of the proletariat (cf. Harding 1981: 201). Secondly, although the latter has been defined as democracy for the majority, it is in fact the dictatorship of the vanguard. 'Yes', Lenin declared, 'the dictatorship of one party! We stand upon it and cannot depart from this ground, since this is the party which in the course of decades has won for itself the position of vanguard of the whole factory and industrial proletariat' (Carr 1950: 230). Owing to the 'low cultural level' of the working people 'the Soviets, which by virtue of their programme are organs of government *by the working people,* are in fact organs of government *for the working people* by the advanced section of the proletariat, but not by the working people as a whole' (Lenin 1919a: 183; italics in original). Not that Lenin is embarrassed by this fact. On the contrary, he is critical of those

German communists who had suggested that there was a choice between dictatorship of leaders or dictatorship of a class, and had declared themselves in favour of the latter. Lenin insists that this is a false dilemma.

The mere presentation of the question — 'dictatorship of the party *or* dictatorship of the class: dictatorship (party) of the leaders, *or* dictatorship (party) of the masses?' — testifies to most incredibly and hopelessly muddled thinking . . . It is common knowledge that the masses are divided into classes . . . that as a rule and in most cases — at least in present-day civilised countries — classes are led by political parties; that political parties, as a general rule, are run by more or less stable groups composed of the most authoritative, influential and experienced members, who are elected to the most responsible positions, and are called leaders. All this is elementary. Why replace it with some kind of rigmarole . . .? (Lenin 1920a: 26-7).

Avinieri has observed that the term 'dictatorship of the proletariat' occurs relatively infrequently in Marx's writings, and that it does not there have the ideological centrality or indeed the particular connotation which it subsequently acquired (Avinieri 1976: 38). In my discussion of Marx, I pointed out that any interpretation of that idea in his thought must square with his firm commitment to the need for the proletariat to rely on its own efforts for its emancipation, and connectedly with his acceptance of majoritarianism and the importance he attaches to suffrage (chapter 9, section 2). It is interesting to contrast Lenin's position on all three issues.

Lenin's vanguardism, as we have already seen, leads to a position at some distance from Marx's self-emancipation thesis. The workers cannot achieve revolutionary conscious-ness by their own efforts; this must come from outside. That stance has implications for Lenin's attitude to majoritarianism. At best he is majoritarian with regard to the *vanguard,* and at times he appears not to recognise that this might create a problem with regard to the majority view within the *working class*. Notice, for example, the crucial telescoping of the two entities when he says that 'revolution is impossible without a change in the views of the majority of the working class', but then goes on to state that 'for a revolution to take place, it is essential, first, that a majority of the workers (*or at least a majority of the class-conscious, thinking and politically active* workers) should fully realise that revolution is necessary . . .' (Lenin 1920a: 69; italics added).

When it comes to the seizure of power by the vanguard, however, it is clear that this does not leave room for serious regard for the views of the majority of workers overall. The workers 'have preserved a good deal of the traditional mentality of capitalist society' (Lenin 1919c: 424). Indeed, the 'ignorant masses fall to every bait' (Lenin 1919b: 301). Hence, 'we can count on the politically conscious workers alone; the remaining mass, the bourgeoisie and the petty proprietors are against us' (Lenin 1918c: 402). Yet, notwithstanding this opposition, 'The politically conscious worker must know that he is a representative of his class' (*ibid.*: 403). And the communist's correct understanding of his tasks

> consists in correctly gauging the conditions and the moment when the *vanguard* of the proletariat can successfully assume power, when it is able — *during and after* the seizure of power — to win adequate support from sufficiently broad strata of the working class and the non-proletarian working masses, and when it is able thereafter to maintain, consolidate and extend *its* rule . . .   (Lenin 1920a: 36; all italics added)

In these comments, not only is it clear that it is the vanguard rather than the class which is to rule, but it is equally plain that the vanguard need not (perhaps even cannot) concern itself with establishing majority support prior to seizure of power.

On the question of suffrage Lenin's views are slightly less straightforward. We have seen his views on the state, and the need to smash it and its institutions. But 'It is necessary to link the strictest devotion to the ideas of communism with the ability to effect all the necessary practical compromises, tacks, conciliatory manoeuvres, zigzags, retreats and so on . . .' (*ibid.*: 79). A boycott of parliament in Russia in 1905 gave the proletariat valuable experience, for example, whereas later boycotts were a mistake (*ibid.*: 21). On the other hand, Lenin urges revolutionaries to work for the return of a Labour government in Britain, precisely because he thinks this is not in the interest of the working class, and that the chastening experience of it may be turned to account in revolutionising them (*ibid.*: 70). In effect, therefore, it is part of Lenin's theory that *tactics* should dictate the decision to boycott or participate in parliamentary practices. There is no suggestion, as there is in the case of Marx and Engels, that any of those practices might, in themselves, be of positive benefit for revolutionary purposes.

3 THE THEORY ASSESSED

For anyone schooled in liberal values of the kind discussed in Part One, Lenin's position is likely to produce a reaction approximating to horror. In particular, the lack of recognition that there might be principled constraints on how the goal is to be achieved, the lack of provision for dissenting opinions to be heard, and the 'tactical' attitude to parliamentary institutions, all offend liberal standards. What defence, it may be asked, does this give to those who happen not to agree with Lenin over the chosen goals? In chapters 3 and 4, I offered a critique of liberal values. I argued against a formal interpretation of them, which gained expression in legal and similar provision for certain kinds of liberty and equality but ignored wider material and social circumstances. This, I suggested, would be insufficient to do justice to the importance attached to the values themselves. But it was no part of that critique to argue that these types of provision were unnecessary or unimportant. It may be felt that Leninism is vulnerable precisely because it rests on the assumption that they are.

I have no wish to discourage a reaction of horror to Leninism, but I believe this very natural objection fails to bring out the important theoretical issues. It is open to the rejoinder, for example, that the appalling consequences of capitalist society, including its *moral* consequences, are so evil that drastic action is necessary to eradicate them, and that niceties about civil liberties and the like cannot be allowed to stand in the way. A Leninist might argue, with some justification, that this position is no different in principle from that occupied by many a liberal. It is, after all, common enough to encounter among liberals the view that ordinary moral qualms must be put aside when a matter of sufficient moral magnitude is at stake. It is often thought, for example, that we should condone in members of governments a duplicity in their public role which would be reprehensible if practised in their private lives; and many liberals have thought it defensible to acquiesce in the killing of innocent civilians of another country in time of war. The only difference, it might be said, is that for a Leninist capitalism is always in a state of war.

The natural objection to Leninism also fails to bring out the fact that, within broadly defined Marxism itself, the question of the appropriate and legitimate means to the chosen goal has been a matter of long and complex controversy. This is explained partly, no doubt, by the fact that Marx's own legacy on that question is a complicated one, as I tried to bring out in the previous chapter.

The debate in that tradition has been couched in more than one pair of terms. Sometimes the notion of an organic growth within capitalism towards the new society is opposed to the violent smashing of the institutions of capitalist society; sometimes reformism, the attempt to reach the new society by working within the political framework of capitalism, is opposed to insurrectionary means. The issues here are complex, turning on theoretical questions about historical continuity and discontinuity, the inevitability or otherwise of socialism, and much else. In this context I can touch on the debate only where it has a point of contact with our own discussion of democracy, and that occurs at what might be called the question of *constitutionalism.* How far can existing political arrangements themselves be employed as the vehicle of a wholesale social transformation, and how far would those arrangements themselves need abolition and replacement either prior to or as part of such a transformation (cf. Miliband 1977: 178)?

We have seen that Lenin himself speaks with a slightly forked tongue on the question, distancing himself from those who would oppose on principle participation in institutions like a parliament, and taking the view that at least for tactical reasons such participation may be necessary. There can be little doubt, however, that the position which predominates in his theory is that existing institutions are to be smashed. The alternative position, occupied by his contemporary Kautsky in the wider debate, raises arguments of direct relevance to our concern with democracy.

Kautsky, who tends to use the term 'democracy' as a label for the institutions of a parliamentary system in much the same way as Lenin, is insistent that democracy itself cannot solve the problems of capitalism. But he is equally insistent that 'Socialism as a means to the emancipation of the proletariat, without democracy, is unthinkable' (Kautsky 1918: 5); and for him that means capture of political power by parliamentary and other legal means. He echoes Engels's point that democracy in this sense provides a clear indication, both to the proletariat and to those who oppose it, what strength of support the proletarian movement has (*ibid.*: 36). He argues, further, that it would be suicide to cast aside the support of universal suffrage when it is 'a powerful source of moral authority' (*ibid.*: 47). Where the movement is in a majority it can claim legitimacy by the criteria of such a system; where it is in a minority such a system affords its best means of protection (*ibid.*: 133). This is important because the superior armed might of the modern state makes a nonsense of the idea of proletarian revolution through violence: democracy paves the way for a peaceful transition (*ibid.*: 38).

On the one hand, some of the reasoning underlying this endorsement of the institutions of a parliamentary system is familiar from Marx's arguments, and whatever plausibility was found in them in that earlier context will apply here too. Certainly it is a fact that such institutions have continued to have a very wide appeal for members of the proletariat. On the other hand, there are opposing considerations which would explain why Kautsky's name in Leninist circles always carries the prefix 'the renegade'. It may be argued that in a parliamentary electoral system any party must make the winning of elections and staying in power its priority. In consequence of this, and the need to make compromises and enter into allegiances with parties of different, non-revolutionary, views, a revolutionary party is likely to lose sight of its original long-term objective and become bogged down in reforms and palliatives. And if history has demonstrated the proletariat's affection for the parliamentary system, it has just as surely demonstrated that system's ability to absorb and neutralise revolutionary parties which try to act through it.

Now it may be that there is something faulty in the way the general choice here is being presented. Miliband observes, for instance, in the realm of practical politics that after the 1930s the Communist International progressively abandoned insurrectionary for constitutional politics, whatever Leninist rhetoric it may have employed (Miliband 1977: 172-3). He suggests that in fact 'smashing' the state is not a real option at all, since seizure of power for revolutionary purposes is just the time when a strong state is needed, to carry through difficult tasks in the face of both internal and external opposition (*ibid.*: 180-1). We might then see the relatively recent development of Eurocommunism as a belated theoretical acknowledgment of the fact that Leninism must carry a far more thoroughgoing commitment to the constitutionalism of parliamentary and electoral politics than might at first be thought.

Yet this serves, in its turn, only to highlight the original dilemma. Suppose that the realities of a revolutionary situation temper the Leninist zeal for smashing, that existing political institutions are themselves necessary for revolutionary action, and therefore could not be abolished during such a time. That may dictate a constitutionalist line, but it will hardly be helpful news for revolutionary theory if it is also true that following that line will result in abandonment of revolutionary objectives. And the dilemma is particularly acute if, as Parkin argues, there is no third option between constitutionalism and violent seizure of power (Parkin 1979: 194).

Clearly we are dealing with a speculative question here. We might wonder whether participation in a parliamentary system must always, in all circumstances, lead to a deflection from revolutionary objectives; and, if not, what circumstances might be required to prevent such deflection. In that connexion, there are theoretical resources available in Marx's own scenario which are lacking in the ways of setting up the dilemma presently under consideration.

What I have in mind is the commitment to the self-emancipation thesis and the associated support for majoritarianism discussed in chapter 9, section 2. In effect, Marx's position is that revolution — or at least the revolution he advocates, involving the abolition of classes and the conversion of the means of production into the common property of society — is impossible without a revolutionary proletariat. I argued in chapter 9 that this position exhibits a relatively high consonance with democratic principles. In the present context I think it importantly changes the shape of the speculation we are concerned with. In Marx's scenario, any speculated opposition at the point of revolution must necessarily be less than it might be in Lenin's. According to Marx, capitalism becomes established as the dominant world system; the majority of people come to assume the status of workers, those who have to sell their energies in order to gain access to the means of life; and a revolutionary class consciousness is forged as the conditions of capitalism foster their recognition of the interests which unite them. I am not concerned at this juncture with the plausibility of this scenario, but with what is implied by it. Opposition to a revolutionary transformation, certainly, is possible: but since the transformation is to be carried through by a politically conscious majority, opposition must *ex hypothesi* be less than active support. A balance in favour of opposition would simply render the revolutionary project inoperable until that condition changed.

Marx's presuppositions enable a distinctive challenge to be made to the two alternative positions on the question of constitutionalism as we have been considering them. In one way, the most important political development for Marx takes place *prior* to any revolution and *outside* parliamentary institutions, namely in the growth of working-class consciousness. This is distinct from Kautsky's parliamentary constitutionalism, where the entry of a party into parliament, which may form alliances with non-revolutionary groups and the like, is seen as the chief means to revolution. We saw in chapter 9 that Marx insisted on the impossibility of the working class simply laying hold of the ready-made state machine and wielding it for its own purposes (Marx 1871: 206), and singled out the Paris Commune, with institutions very different from those of a parliamentary system, as providing 'the political form at last discovered under which to work out the economical emancipation of labour' (*ibid.*: 212). On the other hand, Marx's position is distinct from Lenin's. The state is not to be smashed but taken control of, so that it cannot be used *against* a revolutionary working class; and *some* of the institutions of a parliamentary system, notably universal suffrage, will be something to foster for a majoritarian like Marx, though not for a vanguardist like Lenin.

In the light of Marx's presuppositions, there do seem to be oversimplifications in the terms used to express the original dilemma of the route to the new society. There need be no straightforward, exclusive and exhaustive choice between constitutionalism and violent seizure of power. Certain elements within existing institutions may be valued, and action taken in conformity with them, while others may not. Connectedly, the aspiration to a peaceful transition need not be identified with an attempt to effect it by piecemeal means, an identification which both Kautsky and Lenin are prone to make. It is consistent with Marx's presuppositions to recognise parliament as an institution geared to the needs of capitalism, and therefore inappropriate as the *vehicle* for a fundamental transformation, but yet to regard its connected electoral practices as coinciding, to some extent, with the principles governing that transformation, and to that extent aiding the possibility of a peaceful transition. This is not tantamount to the view parodied by Lenin as the expectation that the ruling class will meekly submit to the working class, as minority to majority. It does, however, limit violence to the role of *counter*-violence in the event of resistance when a clear majority for revolutionary change is apparent, rather than seeing the use of violence as itself a primary means of change, even in the absence of majority support.

It goes without saying that this clarification of Marx's version of the scenario for radical social change carries many problems with it. It perhaps makes even plainer than the earlier discussion in chapter 9 that Marx's preconditions for revolution are very stringent indeed. It also raises the question how a movement could use an electoral system based on principles only *some* of which it approved of. How would it be possible for revolutionaries to demonstrate the strength of support for their programme through the ballot box *without* becoming involved in compromises and a loss of their revolutionary perspective? Most seriously of all, nothing is said about how to reach that state of affairs where the majority of the working class opts for revolution, except for hypothesising that capitalism itself encourages that process.

But this brings us back again to Lenin's vanguardism, which may be thought to replace that problem by arguing the pointlessness or impossibility of waiting for such majority support *before* beginning the political revolution. The people's choices in present conditions are not those of rational, autonomous agents: they are manipulated, subjected to gross ideological distortions. Accordingly, choices must be made *for* them, choices which will result in a set of circumstances more favourable to their subsequently taking a greater degree of control over their lives thereafter.

Now the starting point for these Leninist reflexions, taken at its broadest, is shared by a large number of theorists who may be in all other respects far removed from any version of broadly defined Marxism. If people always behaved like perfectly rational agents, then a large part of the need for Part Two of this book would disappear. We could move straight to a consideration of the best way of incorporating in concrete social arrangements procedures which conformed to the principles discussed in Part One. But, as I indicated in the Interlude following Part One, theories have to be built around the fact that people do not always behave in that way. Applied theories of democracy then begin to diverge from each other, as they move away from this agreed datum to tackle such questions as the chief sources of irrationality, the extent to which and the ease with which they are eliminable, and in consequence the forms of democratic organisation which are practically worth considering.

On questions of this order all versions of Marxism are distinguished from some other theories by virtue of the depth and pervasiveness which they ascribe to the sources of irrationality. Large numbers of people do not merely fail to form, and act on, wants and preferences which it would be rational for them to do: they are actually prevented from doing so, because the preferences which would express their real interests are, for reasons to do with their perception of their own social relations, unavailable to them.

For anyone who subscribes to a theory of this kind but also has a commitment to democratic values, there arises the *paradox of emancipation* (Benton 1982: 14-15). Either, action to remedy this undesirable state of affairs requires the consent of those affected, in which case such action is ruled out; or action is taken without consent, in which case the commitment to democratic values has been abandoned. What I believe needs to be stressed is how far Marx and Lenin diverge from *each other* in their handling of this problem.

Marx, I suggested, attempts to breach the resistance offered by the first half of the dilemma. He constructs a theory which explains ideological illusions and can itself inform the political activity designed to bring about a change in political consciousness, thus securing consent. If this effort, combined with the influences at work within the dynamic of capitalist society itself, is not successful, then the desired change — to a state of affairs characterised by voluntary and harmonious co-operation — is in any case postponed. Lenin, by contrast, exhibits impatience with such temporising. The proletariat, he insists, can attract other working groups to its side 'only *after* it has achieved a victory, only after it has won state power . . . and emancipated *all* working people from the yoke of capital and *shown* them in practice the benefits (the benefits of freedom from the exploiters) accruing from proletarian state power' (Lenin 1920c: 339-40; italics in original).

A view of this kind will be repugnant to liberal democratic theory because it envisages a departure from the principle of self-rule, in favour of a paternalistic attitude, allowing a powerful role to the elect who are in the privileged position of being able to judge when others are not in a fit condition for ruling themselves. But it will be equally repugnant to strictly defined Marxism, though for a slightly different sort of reason. It will not be so much that abstract principles place a constraint on the pursuit of a particular goal; rather, that the nature of the goal itself carries implications for the manner of its pursuit. Where self-rule is part of the very objective, self-rule must *in some sense* figure in the process of bringing about that objective, for in its absence the constituents of the new society will be in no state to endow it with the features it is supposed to have.

Even more important, perhaps, are other dangers which a view like Lenin's carries. As the vehicle of vanguardism becomes narrowed, so this licenses a yet more powerful role to the keepers of orthodoxy, who are in a position to discern and secure what is in the interests of others who cannot see or do this for themselves (cf. Miliband 1977: 35-6, Parkin 1979: 153-4). The very terms of the theory exclude the possibility of *rational* opposition to the plans formulated by the vanguard, and certainly sound, class-conscious opposition is a non-starter. This perhaps explains why dissenters in regimes paying allegiance to Leninism are not merely brutally suppressed but run the risk of ending up in a psychiatric ward.

With prophetic insight, Kautsky complained that a strategy of this kind endangered the very objective of transforming social relations. When a minority vanguard failed to initiate the monumental task of ushering in a new society, with a politically unprepared population, then success-worshippers would 'not enquire from what causes it did not succeed. They would not seek for the explanation in the unfavourable or unripe conditions, but in Socialism itself, and would conclude that Socialism is realisable under no circumstances' (Kautsky 1918: 89).

That was precisely the conclusion which Michels came to, around the same time. The dictatorship of the proletariat, he suggested, would be less euphemistically described as a dictatorship 'in the hands of those leaders who have been sufficiently astute and sufficiently powerful to grasp the sceptre of dominion in the name of socialism' (Michels 1915: 384). But it is 'extremely probable that a social group which had secured control of the instruments of collective power would do all that was possible to retain that control' (*ibid.*: 385). The difference between individual and group dictatorship, he suggests, is minimal, and both are inimical to democracy. Hence, his general belief in the inevitability of oligarchy is strengthened by 'the manner in which, according to the Marxist conception of the revolution, the social transformation is to be effected' (*ibid.*: 384).

If the strictly defined Marxist conception fitted Michels's description, or if the vanguardism of the Leninist conception were more plausible, then Michels would have a point. But neither of these is true. As I mentioned in section 2, Lenin stresses that theories of modern socialism were formed in the minds of the bourgeois intelligentsia, rather than workers, endorsing Kautsky's earlier claim to that effect (Lenin 1902:

31-2, 39-40). Yet what follows if this claim about the origin of socialist theories is true? Certainly not that assent to those theories, once formed, will be forthcoming from one group rather than the other. Of course, it may well be that an intellectual appreciation of the detailed functioning of capitalism is more prominent amongst intellectual workers than amongst non-intellectual workers (and we should bear in mind that, by and large, intellectuals *are* workers on the criterion of strictly defined Marxism). But that is of dubious relevance to the issue. Growth in class consciousness is a prerequisite for the transformation to a classless society, and theory must play a role in the creation of that consciousness because of the power of ideology. But the plausible gloss on that idea is that one element in revolutionary political consciousness is an intellectual appreciation of the *general* functioning of capitalist society. This would not give intellectuals any special role, certainly not a special political role, to play.

In any case, a more important element will be a preparedness to change social relations, a preparedness, both in effecting the transformation and in the subsequent society of co-operative common ownership of resources, to take a very much less passive role in social life than is presently suffered by the mass of people. So far as that element is concerned, there are no grounds for making a special case of intellectuals or anyone else. On the contrary, the pressure is to make the acquisition of this element of political consciousness a necessity for all those different groups whose skills and active assent are required for the successful running of a society of this kind.

In fostering that element it is difficult to see how vanguardism can be anything but a hindrance. It requires from the mass of people a deference in political matters to those privileged enough to be able to see where the mass's interests lie, a trust that they can be carried to a future non-benighted state at present unavailable to them. If I were a member of the mass rather than the vanguard, I should want to be told a convincing story to show that anything so passive *could* prepare me for a much more participatory role in a new form of society. If I were a member of the vanguard rather than the mass, I suppose I might be tempted to try the argument that the vanguard can begin the business of educating the mass for a more active role and then slowly dismantle itself as the education bears fruit. I hope, however, that I should resist that temptation — not just because I should hear Michels's words ringing in my ears, but also because of the case built up by Marx, especially in *Capital,* to show that many features of capitalist society are inescapable, despite good intentions on anyone's part, short of the fundamental transformation to the society of common ownership which rule by a vanguard cannot itself produce. It would probably be better, therefore, if as a member of the vanguard I simply asked the masses to trust me, rather than expecting that I could offer an intellectual justification of my position.

Lenin's vanguardism has deep roots, and the erroneous assumptions which lead him to it are made early. They are present in his response to Engels's claim that the struggle for social transformation needs to be pursued in economic, political and theoretical spheres, discussed at the beginning of section 2. When Lenin argues against 'economism' and spontaneity, he is conforming to Engels's own strictures and indeed to strictly defined Marxism. As we saw, Marx draws attention to the limited value of resisting the encroachments of capitalism whilst staying within the wage relation (what Engels explicitly identifies as the economic struggle); and he urges the need instead to abolish that relation, the prerequisite for which is a political movement guided by an adequate theory, placing that relation in the perspective of capitalism viewed as an entire social system. But where Lenin departs from strictly defined Marxism, good sense and respect for democratic values, is in his assumption that a *separate group of people* must take responsibility for providing a revolutionary theoretical perspective and leading a revolutionary political movement. Significantly, he fails to notice that it is the German *workers* whom Engels credits with having 'retained that sense of theory which the so-called "educated" classes of Germany have almost completely lost' (Engels 1875: 652, cited in Lenin 1902: 27). His vanguardism is a complete departure from Marx's and Engels's repeated insistence that the workers must emancipate themselves, that 'We cannot ally ourselves, therefore, with people who openly declare that the workers are too uneducated to free themselves . . .' (Marx and Engels 1879: 375).

Perhaps the most important upshot for the course of our own discussion is this. I was prepared to give credence to a large part of Marx's theory, as being a useful one for understanding the severe limits on the degree of control which most people have over decisions affecting their lives in major ways. But Marx appeared to paint himself into a corner when he allotted to bourgeois ideology a strong role in sustaining illusions about the existing state of things, and he gave insufficient guidance on how an entire social class could initiate and retain control of a political movement. Leninism, it was thought, might make good some of these deficiencies by taking a more realistic view, recognising the need for party organisation and the like. However, one of its most prominent features is a preparedness to allow a minority to suppress the wishes and even the views of a majority. This, as we have seen, can be challenged from the standpoints of abstract democratic principle and of strictly defined Marxism. But when we bear in mind how Leninism justifies this position it becomes clear that the theory has a further flaw.

The justification is that those suffering from the illusions born of capitalist society will subsequently come to see that the suppression managed in the dictatorship of the vanguard was for their benefit, and will come to throw off those illusions. But that involves an appeal to considerations whose strength cannot, in the nature of the case, be assessed in the present. In just that respect in which it was thought that it might be superior to strictly defined Marxism, therefore, Leninism fails. Lenin the realist takes on the guise of Lenin the idealist, staking all on a speculative belief in some future regeneration of autonomy and rationality in those on behalf of whom he and his vanguard would act. Whatever the circumstances of 1917 and its aftermath, which may or may not exonerate Lenin as a practical political agent, his theory is vitiated by its vanguardist assumptions. By contrast, Marx claims that a society of fully participating agents can be reached only via a political movement in which agents themselves do, precisely, fully participate as equals. That claim is not only more plausible and more morally appealing. In its demand for practical proof now rather than in the future, in the form of a mass political movement of participating agents, it is considerably less dangerous.

4 CONCLUSION

We began Part Two by considering a form of applied theory, elite theory, which recognises the fallibility, irrationality and apathy of many members of society, and relates these data to the existence of political systems where the degree of political control in the hands of such members is confined to periodic election of decision-makers. We then examined other applied theories, which do not in the same way implicitly endorse such political systems or the lack of any very thorough or widespread participation on which they rest. In one way, Leninism is a continuation of that development to a new extreme, since it involves a rejection of more of the institutions of representative, majoritarian parliamentary democracy than do participation theory or strictly defined Marxism (or at least an acceptance of those institutions only where it is tactically advantageous).

Yet, taken in another way, Leninism brings the discussion of Part Two full circle. The underlying view of the human material presently available for political projects is remarkably similar to that contained in elite theory: the unreliability and malleability of the masses, for example, is common ground between Lenin and Schumpeter. There are more detailed echoes, too. When Lenin insists on far greater powers for professional revolutionaries than the masses, but gives the assurance that increasing numbers will be 'promoted' (Lenin 1902: 122), then in *one* respect his point is reminiscent of Dahl's suggestion that elections and political competition increase the number of minorities which can influence decisions taken by leaders (Dahl 1956: 132). In both cases there is a failure to perceive that the very structure which embodies such gross inequalities of power may itself be offensive to democratic principles.

Of course, the parallel does not hold across the whole range of the two theories. Apologists for Leninism will point out that

Lenin's interest lay ultimately in a wholly new set of social relations, just as apologists for elite theory will point out that their views rest on the importance of giving a voice to opposing groups rather than suppressing them. These responses are justified, and they tend to work to the detriment of Leninism. The dictatorship of the vanguard, the paradoxical strengthening of the state and the conditions governing the transition to a new society are so central to Lenin's theory that it is proper to concentrate attention on them. When we do so, we see that the points of divergence between elite theory and Leninism are not flattering to Leninism. It not only has objectionable features in common with elite theory: it has highly objectionable features peculiarly its own.

This enables an astute elite theorist like Dahl to observe that centralised state bureaucracy leaves the existing hierarchical structure of authority intact, or even strengthens it, and to that extent constitutes a move *away* from 'industrial democracy' (Dahl 1970: 126-8). The point, indeed, can be generalised. In the discussion of participation theory, I expressed misgivings over how far the existing industrial context could be used in isolation for building democratic structures and increasing the efficacy of participants. Nevertheless, the lesson we learnt from participation theory is that, when we do encounter apathy or defective rationality in a political context, we can either merely record the facts and develop a theory to fit around them, or we can try to develop theories designed to enable us to change those facts. And the options confronting us here also apply to the immediate, short-run context. In contrast to the favoured alternative of participation theory — the industrial arena — I have a number of times proposed the political arena itself as the appropriate object of our concerns. The flaw in Leninism is that in its plans for the political transformation and therefore for *more* than the immediate short run, it *acquiesces* in the apathy and defective rationality, rather than embodying strategies to strengthen, foster and develop the contrary tendencies.

In that respect, as I have tried to show, Leninism departs from strictly defined Marxism (and, we might add, from some other strains in broadly defined Marxism). With striking anticipation Engels, for example, implicitly condemns the

Leninist strategy in these remarks:

If conditions have changed in the case of war between nations, this is no less true in the case of the class struggle. The time of surprise attacks, of revolutions carried through by small conscious minorities at the head of unconscious masses, is past. Where it is a question of a complete transformation of the social organisation, the masses themselves must also be in it, must themselves already have grasped what is at stake, what they are going in for, body and soul. The history of the last fifty years has taught us that. But in order that the masses may understand what is to be done, long, persistent work is required . . . (Engels 1895: 134)

The immediate tasks, he suggests, are 'slow propaganda work and parliamentary activity' (*ibid.*). Kautsky is in accord on that point, urging that it is necessary 'to strive to enlighten and convince the masses by intensive propaganda before we can reach the point of bringing Socialism about' (Kautsky 1918: 95).

These sentiments denote adherence to Marx's self-emancipation thesis discussed in chapter 9, and make plain the contrast between Lenin and Marx concerning the order of precedence between revolutionary change and conformity to democratic practices. Propaganda, the attempt to convince, is the paradigm activity in democracy. For strictly defined Marxism, that is precisely what is required now to hasten the move towards revolutionary change. For Leninism, revolutionary change must come first, and independently.

It has been important to understand and see the deficiencies in Leninism, because of the widespread acceptance of a near-identity between Leninism and Marxism, noted at the beginning of this chapter. This has led to the monstrous glorification of the Party in the name of Marxism, as in the claim that it is 'the active incarnation of class consciousness' whose strength is 'fed by the trust of the spontaneously revolutionary masses' and their 'feeling that the party is the objectification of their will (obscure though this may be to themselves)' (Lukacs 1921: 42). And it has enabled one commentator to say 'Democracy, for Marx and Lenin, meant in the first instance, rule by or for the proletariat' (Macpherson 1966: 36) — as if Marx and Lenin, or rule *by* and rule *for* a group, could simply be equated.

For anyone who believes, as I do, that Marx's own theories are both plausible and deeply democratic, this collapsing of Leninism and Marxism has been literally tragic. Hitler is reported to have said that Nazism is what Marxism could have been, had it freed itself from the absurd, artificial link with a democratic system (Dunn 1979: 21 n. 50). On the contrary, Leninism is what it became when its natural link with democratic principles was forcibly severed.

FURTHER READING

Lenin 1969 contains a selection of Lenin's writings. Harding 1977 and 1981 comprises a work of substantial scholarship on the whole of Lenin's writings. A number of contributors in Hampshire 1978 discuss justifications for condoning immorality in politicians. Miliband 1977 and Parkin 1979 both deal with the issue of constitutionalism. Carrillo 1977 lays out the idea of Eurocommunism. Blackburn 1977 Part One contains a number of interpretations of Lenin more sympathetic than I am able to furnish, and Hindess 1980 also expresses a view very different from mine.

Conclusion: Theory, practice and Utopia

'A map of the world that does not include Utopia is not even worth glancing at . . . Progress is the realisation of Utopias.'
Oscar Wilde *The Soul of Man under Socialism*

Conclusion: Theory, practice and utopia

The main argument is now at an end (though far from finished). In Parts One and Two respectively we have investigated pure theories, embodying the abstract principles which underlie conceptions of democracy and bring out its very strong appeal for us, and applied theories, embodying principles of a less abstract character, suitable for conceptions of democracy relating more directly to the world we actually live in.

Beginning from the basic idea of democracy as self-rule, we examined the role of liberty and equality as components in that idea, and I suggested that the grounds for favouring political liberty and equality dictated a concern with arrangements in the broader social context, not just the narrower political one. However, the grounds for favouring liberty and equality (roughly, the idea of individual human beings as rational, autonomous moral agents) also create problems for dealing with dissent in a democratic context. The standard acceptance of majority decision-making as part of democratic procedure is problematic because it compromises the individual's autonomy. Or so it seemed. In the end, I suggested that this was not a compelling argument. Nevertheless, its power is broken only by a recognition that a shift in perspective is required. Social life involves entities other than individuals, and this ought to influence the conception we have of individuals themselves, as well as leading to a greater emphasis on the notion of corporate decisions reached in consensus.

But how can applied theory be built on these notions? In elite theory we encountered a distrust of the masses, a belief that those who make it up depart very radically from the conception of human agents earlier employed. The resulting theory of

233

democracy jettisoned ideas of equal political influence, in favour of opportunities of a more limited kind to select leaders whose prerogative it was to decide issues. This, I suggested, stretched the basic idea of self-rule to its limit, and perhaps beyond.

In contrast to elite theory, which at least *presents* itself as entirely descriptive and explanatory, participation and Marxist theories, in their different ways, constitute theorised proposals for changing the *status quo*. Even if entirely misguided in their substance, they illustrate the possibility of forming theories which do not simply rest on an acceptance of current facts as unalterable data. They do, nevertheless, differ in the extent to which they involve a challenge to existing arrangements, and it is far clearer that Marxist theory includes a proposal for entire social transformation. Participation theory favours the encouragement of greater involvement in decision-making in specific limited contexts, most notably industry, perhaps preparatory to wider change; whereas Marxist theory regards significant change in some of the limited contexts as itself excluded from the agenda without parallel change in the wider context. But I suggested that Marx's theoretical commitments invest his proposals for change with a high degree of conformity to the abstract principles earlier discussed.

Finally, Leninist theory shares with these other two the characteristic of being a theorised proposal for change, but shares with elite theory a deep distrust of the masses, and therefore endorses the exclusion of its members from a substantive influence over the decisions which affect them.

Many questions have gone unanswered in the course of our discussion. I have suggested that there is a great deal of potential help in strictly defined Marxism for the most important of them (though it would take more than another book to establish this). The abstract notion of consensus employed in Part One needs further elaboration, for example, and Marx's class theory provides some. It involves the postulation of an important type of corporate entity, and gives some of the grounds for rational identification with such entities on the part of individuals. This, in its turn, prefigures the possibility of rational identification with the whole community on the part of individuals, though Marx insists that the elimination of class society is a precondition for its actualisation.

The theory also provides a diagnosis of the chief material source of inherent conflict in existing society, and relates this systematically to other areas of conflict, and the resulting need for politics in the form familiar to us. The programme for the abolition of the existing basic, material relation is then also a programme for the abolition of politics in the existing form, as the expression of the interests of a privileged class, with a particular set of institutions geared to that function. Though politics in that form would disappear, social decision-making would remain. What the programme posits there, by implication from Marx's comments on the Paris Commune, is a set of relations which reverse the relation of dominance currently obtaining between public officials and populace, and greatly increase the control exercised by the latter. In those respects the democratic character of the posited new society bears a close resemblance to the character of democratic institutions in the ancient Greek setting. The consequence, consistently with Marx's view of the connexion between material and other relations, is that the break between existing political institutions and their replacements will be as great as the break between existing material relations and *their* replacements.

Consider now a very natural reaction to these suggestions. They may provoke an impatience with both pure and applied theory if they are to be handled in a way which exhibits so little concern with the concrete aspects of already existing social institutions. For example, even amongst those theorists who reject the implicit conservatism of elite theory, because of its resolute confinement to aspects of the *status quo,* there is a belief that theory must not stray too far from concrete social reality if it is to avoid being condemned to a futile utopianism. For this reason it might be thought entirely inappropriate to look to the origins of democracy in ancient Greece for any useful inspiration for a twentieth-century theory of democracy. After all, there were perhaps never more than 45,000 adult male citizens in Athens, spread over only 1,000 square miles; the spoken word was the main medium of communication; and a large proportion of the citizen population would have had direct experience of government (cf. Finley 1973: 17-19). This was, moreover, an all-embracing community, whose members had a *sense* of community and common destiny. Nothing in the modern world, it may be felt, can resemble any of this.

For the same reason, doubts may be expressed over the parallels which I have tried to maintain between democracy in very circumscribed contexts like families and committees, and democracy in the wider social sphere. The two types of context, it may be said, are just too unlike. Whereas participation to a high degree and a striving for consensus may make sense in the circumscribed contexts, we know that in the conditions of modern society many particular decisions must be delegated, thus giving greater power to those making them and excluding from participation those not making them. We know, too, that millions of those so excluded would find it tedious in the extreme to have to bother their heads over such decisions.

In the circumstances, it may be urged, it is not merely utopian but positively irresponsible to attack the institutions which at least afford a measure of control, in an indirect way, for the mass of people. Vague ideas about consensus are of infinitely less than careful, limited proposals for change which begin from existing concrete institutions and which can therefore be measured against experience. In that spirit, Dunn is critical of Marxists for assailing capitalist society without inhibition when they have no experientially related proposals for a superior form of society to replace it (Dunn 1979: 100-1). In a similar spirit, Thompson argues that the model for a perfectly acceptable idea may not be the best guide to practice, since it may urge reforms which make the present system worse (Thompson 1983: 239).

Essentially, two issues arise here. One is the question of the difficulties presented by the conditions of modern life; the other is the question of the gap between theory and reality. On neither score, it seems to me, is there justification for the stigma of utopian theorising to be attached to the developments I have outlined.

First, the fact of a gap — even a wide gap — between theory and reality does not necessarily reflect ill on the theory. Certainly it calls for further explanation, but, as we have seen in the contrast between elite and participation theory, the explanation may be such as to justify the dominance of theory over reality rather than vice versa. I explained at the outset of chapter 1 that a philosophical theory of democracy is a complicated affair, with normative, conceptual and empirical aspects. In formulating it, we may begin from concrete, existing institutions as a clue to the normative principles underlying our conception of democracy. But as we elaborate on those principles and explore their implications — both conceptual and empirical — then we may conclude that the concrete institutions from which we took our clue are a very inadequate embodiment of the principles (cf. Graham 1985: 35-7). If we remain firmly attached to the principles even after thorough investigation, then we may take the failure of our institutions to live up to them as an indication of the inadequacy of the institutions rather than of the principles.

Of course, this result *need* not follow. It would not follow if we had a well-established theory to show that something in the nature of human psychology or human social life made it impossible to create institutions conforming to the principles in question. But we must take care to distinguish what is impossible from what is attainable only at the cost of fundamental disturbance of existing institutions.

Imagine now a rejoinder. Surely, if the principles involve the idea of rational agents governing themselves collectively in conditions of consensus, then the argument about modern conditions of life does precisely imply impossibility? For suppose we conceded that elite theory involved an academic dressing-up of some unsubstantiated popular prejudices about human nature, and that in different conditions people could participate more enthusiastically and more effectively in decisions affecting their lives. Suppose we also allowed the Marxist claim that it is the unnecessary existence of class-divided society which is responsible for conflicts that are, indeed, ineliminable without going beyond the context of class division. Even then, surely, we cannot envisage conditions so different from those surrounding us at present that rational participation by everyone in achieving a consensus is much of an idea to pursue?

Take size, first. It is true that a state containing many

millions of people is at a great distance from a family or a committee in the forms of discussion, deliberation and decision-making which it facilitates. So, for that matter, is a state containing 45,000 people, as in ancient Greece. In both cases, forms of delegation must be employed, and the degree of final control held by the whole population over matters which genuinely affect all of them may vary considerably. Size *of itself* does not dictate a difference of principle here between the ancient and modern context.

A more plausible candidate for dictating such a difference is the difference in degrees of integration, as it were, in the Athenian city-state and a modern centre of population. Macintyre has commented on the way modernity divides an individual's life into a variety of segments: work and leisure, private and public, corporate and personal (Macintyre 1981: 190). In these circumstances it is much easier to regard 'politics' as an optional interest which many may choose not to indulge, and to accept the inevitability of the whole apparatus of professional politicians, experts, bureaucracies and the like, if the rest of us are to have any time left for other pursuits.

This is a compelling description of life as we know it, but not as it must be. To the extent that political issues requiring resolution arise, directly or indirectly, from the conditions of class-based, property society, the sheer volume of political issues is not a constant and can be reduced. Of course, there are issues calling for decision which are not dependent on the existence of a particular social framework, issues to do with the general living arrangements of a society. But the time which people have available for these issues is not a constant either. The point has often been made that modern technology makes possible in principle a greatly reduced burden of work for people, and allows correspondingly more time for participation and the education which would make greater participation worthwhile. Equally, technology makes possible the consultation of populations consisting of millions of people in minute fractions of time.

The prospect of eliminating some types of political issue, of increasing the proportion of people's lives which can be given over to decision-making, and of facilitating their influence over decisions, suggests that a far greater degree of 'rule by the people' is possible than anything currently visible. What is not evident, of course, is any great pressure to create such a state of affairs. But if, after examination of the principles underlying the idea of rule by the people, our commitment to that greater degree is very strong, then the rational course is not merely to record this absence of pressure but to ask what can be done to rectify it. To describe politics in terms of the existing machinery of government and its workings is to describe what is, for millions of people, a big turn-off. But if we describe the same phenomenon as an area where a small number of people make decisions which have a major impact on how each of us is able to live, then it is clearer why switching off from politics carries a very high price with it. And this second description is as applicable as the first. You would have to be extremely rich or have an unusually meagre or eccentric set of aspirations for your life to be unaffected by the decisions taken in politics.

What I am arguing for is a narrowing of the gaps between pure theory, applied theory and political practice, the need for well thought-out principles really to inform our thinking about concrete social arrangements and our acting to create them. What I am arguing against is the idea that those principles should be kept in a cupboard and only brought out on special occasions, for example when intellectualising, or that they are a harmless piece of rhetoric which may serve a purpose in encouraging the troops. At the same time, I am sensible of the problems raised by theorists like Dunn and Thompson, and their counsel of caution in attacking existing institutions. Is it possible, then, to close the gaps in the way I advocate without running the risk of making the present state of affairs appreciably worse? I want to conclude by indicating why the practical and theoretical context in which discussion of democratic theory has largely taken place in this century makes this such a difficult undertaking.

The main, visible alternative to the system of parties periodically competing to accumulate a number of representatives, who thereby secure a period of political power, has been the one-party regimes of Eastern Europe (with intermittent phases of fascist dictatorship offering an even less appetising prospect). The brutal and oppressive nature of these regimes is such that, if they are the implicit standard of comparison, then our own system is able to maintain high credibility. It is because I believe that Marx's theories contain the suggestion of a different alternative, never put into practice, that I was at pains to separate strictly defined Marxism from the varieties of broadly defined Marxism which underpin the present tangible alternative.

However, great though the distance is between Western parliamentary systems and Eastern Europe, they do share the assumption that there is a need for hierarchical political organisations, a bureaucracy and a tiny minority whose job is politics. And the fact of agreement at this level, between systems otherwise so different, has had the effect of making it more difficult to challenge the existence of the institutions they both endorse. It has been easier to regard theoretical literature on democracy as *either* 'realistic', in accepting the need for structures and institutions of the kind currently in operation, *or* as consisting of utopian fantasy if it challenges that need in the context of modern social life.

For related reasons, a challenge to those structures and institutions at the practical level faces particular difficulties. Conventional political life in the West, and the thought of those who participate to any degree in it, is geared to the expectation that any group holding political power does so for a relatively short period before submitting itself to the test of re-confirmation of its position. As I have insisted throughout, this is vastly preferable to circumstances where an organisation monopolises political power by coercion, but it does present a problem for any programme of wide-reaching social change. A political party aspiring to sponsor such a change cannot rely on retaining political power for a long period unless it makes that its first priority. The trap it then sets for itself is that, when the retention of political power is the first priority, then the compromises and deals which this necessitates come to have greater practical importance than the originally conceived social change.

There is that minimal validity in the strand of Leninist theory which is critical of 'parliamentarism'. But what, then, is to be done? Any proposal to abandon the practice of periodic re-election in the interests of a far-reaching programme of change will justifiably be looked on with great suspicion and horror.

After all, that was precisely the action of the Bolsheviks in closing down the Constituent Assembly in 1918 when a majority of anti-Bolsheviks were returned to it. For that matter, vague talk of different institutions, with greater opportunities for participation at some point in the future, will cut little ice in comparison with the tangible civil liberties which already exist and are valued. To that extent ill-judged attacks on the political institutions of capitalism in operation are indeed to be discouraged. Nor would it necessarily make a difference if a majority were in favour of changing existing arrangements. We have seen enough of the difficulties in simply equating democracy with the wishes of the majority in Part One.

What *would* make a difference, I suggest, would be an ability on the part of the populace to demonstrate that existing forms of political decision-making could be replaced with forms evolved in the course of the populace's own development as a movement for change. Demonstration must take over from theoretical justification at this point. The existence of a political movement quite unlike any familiar ones visible today, where individuals formed a collective and influenced corporate decisions in conditions of substantive equality, this would itself furnish some evidence that people in general can take control of their own affairs without handing the matter over to elites and leaderships. And it is reasonable to say that it is a vital piece of evidence, in the absence of which there is no case for attempting to remove existing institutions. In that way, boldness in conception and in internal organisation could be combined with a decent reluctance to endanger the present state of affairs until it could be replaced to advantage. That is the lost message of Marx's theory which I have attempted to reinstate.

The present is an appropriate time for thoughts of this kind. It is no longer so easy to sustain the credibility of our local political institutions by implicit comparison with less appetising ones further afield, in the light of global crises which they have been powerless to forestall and the alienation of large sections of the population from them. Apathy has been one result, but an increasingly commonplace idea in the last twenty years has been 'extra-parliamentary opposition'. And its manifestation in the prevalence of terrorism on the part of minority groups offers an alternative no more acceptable than Eastern bloc tyranny. Now is the time, therefore, to encourage practices and construct theories demonstrating a further alternative: the possibility of political procedures and practical plans for social organisation which respect the various kinds of normative, conceptual and empirical constraint to which the idea of democracy commits us, and which I have tried to make explicit in this book.

This task will not be easy, partly because of the lack of any overall sense of community, so acutely diagnosed by Macintyre. Part of the problem is precisely to produce not just an overall sense of community but an overall community itself. In that regard, though I think Macintyre's diagnosis is acute, I believe nothing could be more dangerous than his own prescription — the construction of local forms of community to see us through the new dark ages (Macintyre 1981: 245). On the contrary, as it becomes daily more apparent that the crises facing us are global, so it is necessary for us to think in terms of *global* community and sense of community, and a correspondingly wide consensus. This does not commit us to the absurdity of hoping for a state of affairs where everyone in the world agrees about everything; but it may well commit us to working for a state of affairs where most of them agree on fundamentals where their lives impinge on one another, and are prepared to exercise forbearance and adopt democratic means of resolving disputes where they do not agree (cf. Graham 1984: 52-3). Not an easy task, but the problems we now face as a species are unique, and we should not be surprised if they call for unique solutions. Moreover, at least those developments which have given our crises a global character and caused us to recognise that we live in a global village — mutual interdependence, a world economic system, mass communications — can be called in aid. Twentieth-century society is far closer to the Athenian city-state than nineteenth-century society was.

In short, at the level of theory and practice the battle of democracy is far from over. In many ways it has only just begun.

FURTHER READING

For the relevance of utopian theorising, see Nozick 1974 Part 3, Goodwin and Taylor 1982, and Alexander and Gill 1984.

Bibliography

Abrams, M. and Rose R., 1960, *Must Labour Lose?*, Harmondsworth, Penguin.

Alexander, P. and Gill R. (eds), 1984, *Utopias,* London, Duckworth.

Almond, G.A. and Verba, S., 1963, *The Civic Culture,* Princeton, Princeton University Press.

Anscombe, G.E.M., 1958, 'Modern moral philosophy', *Philosophy,* vol. 33, reprinted in Hudson 1969, pp. 175-95.

Arrow, K.J., 1963, *Social Choice and Individual Values,* second edition, New York, John Wiley.

Austin, J.L., 1962, *How To Do Things With Words,* second edition 1975, J.O. Urmson and M. Sbisa, eds, Oxford, Clarendon Press.

Avinieri, S., 1976, 'How to save Marx from the alchemists of revolution', *Political Theory,* vol. 4, pp. 35-41.

Ayer, A.J., 1936, *Language, Truth and Logic,* London, Gollancz.

Bachrach, P., 1967, *The Theory of Democratic Elitism,* Boston, Little, Brown & Co.

—— 1975, 'Interest, participation and democracy', in Pennock and Chapman 1975, pp. 39-50.

Barry, B., 1965, *Political Argument,* London, Routledge & Kegan Paul.

—— 1970, *Sociologists, Economists and Democracy,* London, Collier-Macmillan.

Bedau, H.A. (ed.), 1969, *Civil Disobedience,* New York, Pegasus.

Benn, S.I. and Gaus, G.F. (eds), 1983, *Public and Private in Social Life,* London, Croom Helm.

Benn, S.I. and Peters, R., 1959, *Social Principles and the Democratic State,* London, Allen & Unwin.

Bennett, J., 1966, 'Whatever the consequences', *Analysis,* vol. 26, pp. 83-102.

Benton, T., 1982, 'Realism, power and objective interests' in Graham 1982a, pp. 7-33.

Berelson, B.R., 1954 (with P.F. Lazarsfeld and W.N. McPhee), *Voting,* Chicago, University of Chicago Press.

Berlin, I., 1969, *Four Essays on Liberty,* Oxford, Clarendon Press.

Blackburn, R., 1976, 'Marxism: theory of proletarian revolution', *New Left Review,* vol. 97, reprinted in Blackburn 1977.

—— (ed.), 1977, *Revolution and Class Struggle,* London, Fontana.

Blumberg, P., 1968, *Industrial Democracy,* London, Constable.

Bottomore, T., 1966, *Elites and Society,* Harmondsworth, Penguin.

Brandon, E.P., 1979, 'The key of the door', *Educational Philosophy and Theory,* vol. 11, pp. 23-34.

Buchanan, A., 1979, 'Revolutionary motivation and rationality', *Philosophy and Public Affairs,* vol. 9, pp. 59-82.

Buchanan, J.M. and Tullock, G., 1962, *The Calculus of Consent,* Ann Arbor, University of Michigan Press.

Campbell, A., 1960 (with P.E. Converse, W.E. Miller and D.E. Stokes), *The American Voter,* New York, John Wiley.

Carr, E.H., 1950, *The Bolshevik Revolution 1917-1923,* vol. 1, London, Macmillan.

Carrillo, S., 1977, *Eurocommunism and the State,* London, Lawrence and Wishart.

Clegg, H.A., 1960, *A New Approach to Industrial Democracy,* Oxford, Blackwell.

Coates, K. (ed.), 1968, *Can the Workers Run Industry?,* London, Sphere Books.

Cohen, G.A., 1978, *Karl Marx's Theory of History,* Oxford, Clarendon Press.

—— 1983, 'The structure of proletarian unfreedom', *Philosophy and Public Affairs,* vol. 12, pp. 2-33.

Cole, G.D.H., 1920, *Guild Socialism Restated,* London, Leonard Parsons.

—— 1929, *The Next Ten Years in British Social and Economic Policy,* London, Macmillan.

Connolly, W.E., 1983, *The Terms of Political Discourse,* second edition, Oxford, Martin Robertson.

Cook, T.E., and Morgan, P.M. (eds.), 1971, *Participatory Democracy,* San Francisco, Canfield Press.

Corcoran, P.E., 1983, 'The limits of democratic theory', in Duncan 1983, pp. 13-24.

Dahl, R.A., 1956, *A Preface to Democratic Theory,* Chicago, University of Chicago Press.

—— 1970, *After the Revolution?,* New Haven, Yale University Press.

—— 1979, 'Procedural democracy', in Laslett and Fishkin 1979, pp. 97-133.

Devlin, P., 1965, *The Enforcement of Morals,* London, Oxford University Press.

Downs, A., 1957, *An Economic Theory of Democracy,* New York, Harper & Row.

Duncan, G. (ed.), 1983, *Democratic Theory and Practice,* Cambridge, Cambridge University Press.

—— and Lukes, S., 1963, 'The new democracy', *Political Studies,* vol. 11, pp. 156-77.

Dunn, J., 1979, *Western Political Theory in the Face of the Future,* Cambridge, Cambridge University Press.

Dworkin, G., 1971, 'Paternalism' in Wasserstrom, R. (ed.), *Morality and the Law,* Belmont, California, Wadsworth, pp. 107-26.

Dworkin, R., 1978, *Taking Rights Seriously,* London, Duckworth.

—— 1981, 'What is equality?', *Philosophy and Public Affairs,* vol. 10, pp. 185-246 and 283-345.

Eckstein, H., 1966, 'A theory of stable democracy', appendix B in *Division and Cohesion in Democracy,* Princeton, Princeton University Press.

Elster, J., 1985, *Making Sense of Marx,* Cambridge, Cambridge University Press.

Engels, F., 1875, Prefatory Note to *The Peasant War in Germany,* in Marx and Engels 1962, vol. 1, pp. 652-4.

—— 1884, *The Origin of the Family, Private Property and the State,* in Marx and Engels 1962, vol. 2, pp. 170-327.

—— 1888, Preface to the 1888 English translation of *The Communist Manifesto,* in Fernbach 1973a, pp. 62-6.

—— 1891, Introduction to *The Civil War in France,* in Marx and Engels 1962, vol. 1, pp. 473-85.

—— 1895, Introduction to Marx's *The Class Struggles in France: 1848 to 1850,* in Marx and Engels 1962, vol. 1, pp. 118-38.

Evans, M., 1975, *Karl Marx,* London, Allen & Unwin.

Fernbach, D. (ed.), 1973a, *Karl Marx: The Revolutions of 1848, Political Writings,* vol. 1, London, Penguin.

—— (ed.), 1973b, *Karl Marx: Surveys from Exile, Political Writings,* vol. 2, London, Penguin.

—— (ed.), 1974, *Karl Marx: The First International and After, Political Writings,* vol. 3, London, Penguin.

Finley, M.I., 1973, *Democracy Ancient and Modern,* London, Chatto & Windus.

Fishkin, J., 1982, 'More democracy?', *London Review of Books,* vol. 4, p. 6.

Follett, M.P., 1918, *The New State,* New York, Longmans, Green & Co.

Gallie, W.B., 1955, 'Essentially contested concepts', *Proceedings of the Aristotelian Society,* vol. 56, pp. 167-98.

Goodwin, B. and Taylor, K., 1982, *The Politics of Utopia,* London, Hutchinson.

Graham, K., 1975, 'Moral notions and moral misconceptions', *Analysis,* vol. 35, pp. 65-78.

—— 1976, 'Democracy, paradox and the real world', *Proceedings of the Aristotelian Society,* vol. 86, pp. 227-45.

—— 1977, *J.L. Austin: A Critique of Ordinary Language Philosophy,* Brighton, Harvester Press.

—— (ed.), 1982a, *Contemporary Political Philosophy: Radical Studies,* London, Cambridge University Press.

—— 1982b, 'Democracy and the autonomous moral agent', in Graham 1982a, pp. 113-37.

—— 1984, 'Consensus in social decision-making: why is it utopian?', in Alexander and Gill 1984, pp. 49-60.

—— 1985, 'Regulative political theory: language, norms and ideology', *Political Studies,* vol. 33, pp. 19-37.

Gray, J., 1983a, *Mill on Liberty: A Defence,* London, Routledge & Kegan Paul.

—— 1983b, 'Political power, social theory and essential contestability', in Miller, D. and Siedentop, L., (eds.), *The Nature of Political Theory,* Oxford, Clarendon Press, pp. 75-101.

Hampshire, S. (ed.), 1978, *Public and Private Morality,* Cambridge, Cambridge University Press.

Hansard Society Commission, 1976, *Report on Electoral Reform,* London, Hansard Society for Parliamentary Government.

Harding, N., 1977, *Lenin's Political Thought,* vol. 1, London, Macmillan.

—— 1981, *Lenin's Political Thought,* vol. 2, London, Macmillan.

Harris, J., 1982, 'The political status of children' in Graham 1982a, pp. 35-55.

Hart, H.L.A., 1955, 'Are there any natural rights?', *Philosophical Review,* vol. 64, reprinted in Quinton 1967, pp. 53-66.

—— 1963, *Law, Liberty and Morality,* London, Oxford University Press.

Hindess, B., 1980, 'Marxism and parliamentary democracy' in Hunt, A. (ed.), *Marxism and Democracy,* London, Lawrence & Wishart, pp. 21-54.

Hodson, J.D., 1977, 'The principle of paternalism', *American Philosophical Quarterly,* vol. 14, pp. 61-9.

Honderich, T. (ed.), 1973, *Essays on Freedom of Action,* London, Routledge & Kegan Paul.

Hudson, W.D. (ed.), 1969, *The Is–Ought Question,* London, Macmillan.

Hunt, R.N., 1975, *The Political Ideas of Marx and Engels, Vol. 1: Marxism and Totalitarian Democracy 1818-1850,* London, Macmillan.

Kautsky, K., 1918, *The Dictatorship of the Proletariat,* Ann Arbor, University of Michigan Press 1964.

Keat, R., 1982, 'Liberal rights and socialism' in Graham 1982a, pp. 59-82.

Key, V.O., 1966, *The Responsible Electorate,* Cambridge, Mass., Harvard University Press.

Kolakowski, L., 1978, *Main Currents of Marxism,* Oxford, Oxford University Press.

Kripke, S., 1979, *Naming and Necessity,* Oxford, Blackwell.

Lakeman, E., 1982, *Power to Elect,* London, Heinemann.

Laslett, P. and Fishkin, J. (eds.), 1979, *Philosophy, Politics and Society,* vol. 5, Oxford, Blackwell.

Laslett, P. and Runciman W.G. (eds.), 1962, *Philosophy, Politics and Society,* vol. 2, Oxford, Blackwell.

—— (eds.), 1967, *Philosophy, Politics and Society,* vol. 3, Oxford, Blackwell.

—— and Skinner, Q. (eds), 1972, *Philosophy, Politics and Society,* vol. 4, Oxford, Blackwell.

Lenin, V.I., 1902, *What is to be Done?,* Moscow, Progress Publishers.

—— 1905, 'Two tactics of social-democracy in the democratic revolution' in *Collected Works,* vol. 9, Moscow, Foreign Languages Publishing House, 1962, pp. 15-140.

—— 1917a, 'The tasks of the proletariat in our revolution' in *Collected Works,* vol. 24, Moscow, Progress Publishers, 1964, pp. 55-91.

—— 1917b, 'What the counter-revolutionary steps of the provisional government lead to' in *Collected Works,* vol. 24, Moscow, Progress Publishers, 1964, pp. 321-3.

—— 1917c, 'Meeting of the All-Russia Central Executive Committee, Nov. 4, 1917. Reply to a question from the Left Socialist-Revolutionaries' in *Collected Works,* vol. 26, Moscow, Progress Publishers, 1964, pp. 287-8.

—— 1918a, *The State and Revolution,* Peking, Foreign Languages Press, 1976.

—— 1918b, 'The immediate tasks of the Soviet Government' in *Collected Works,* Vol. 27, Moscow, Progress Publishers, 1965, pp. 235-77.

—— 1918c, 'Speech at the Second All-Russia Congress of Commissars for Labour, May 22, 1918' in *Collected Works,* vol. 27, Moscow, Progress Publishers, 1965, pp. 399-403.

—— 1919a, 'Report on the Party Programme, Eighth Congress of the Russian Communist Party, March 19, 1919' in *Collected Works,* vol. 29, London, Lawrence & Wishart, 1965, pp. 165-85.

—— 1919b, 'Closing speech to Plenum of the All-Russia Central Council of Trade Unions, April 11, 1919,' in *Collected Works,* vol. 29, London, Lawrence & Wishart, 1965, pp. 280-301.

—— 1919c, 'Report at the Second All-Russia Trade Union Congress, Jan 20, 1919' in *Collected Works,* vol. 28, Moscow, Progress Publishers, 1965, pp. 412-28.

—— 1920a, *'Left-Wing' Communism, an Infantile Disorder,* Moscow Progress Publishers, 1975.

—— 1920b, 'Speech on economic development, Ninth Congress of Russian Communist Party, March 31, 1920' in *Collected Works,* vol. 30, Moscow, Progress Publishers, 1965, pp. 472-9.

—— 1920c, 'Draft of the Russian Communist Party's reply to the letter of the Independent Social Democratic Party of Germany' in *Collected Works,* vol. 30, Moscow, Progress Publishers, 1965, pp. 337-44.

—1969, *Selected Works of Lenin,* London, Lawrence & Wishart.

Lindley, R., 1986, *Autonomy,* London, Macmillan.

Lipset, S.M., 1960, *Political Man,* New York, Doubleday.

Lively, J., 1975, *Democracy,* Oxford, Blackwell.

Lucas, J.R., 1965, 'Against equality', *Philosophy,* vol. 40, pp. 296-307.

—— 1977, 'Against equality again', *Philosophy,* vol. 52, pp. 255-80.

Lukacs, G., 1921, 'The Marxism of Rosa Luxemburg' in *History and Class Consciousness,* London, Merlin Press, 1971, pp. 27-48.

Lukes, S., 1973, *Individualism,* Oxford, Blackwell.

—— 1974, *Power: A Radical View,* London, Macmillan.

MacCallum, G.C., 1967, 'Negative and positive freedom', *Philosophical Review,* vol. 76, reprinted in Laslett, Runciman and Skinner 1972, pp. 174-93.

Macintyre, A., 1981, *After Virtue,* London, Duckworth.

Mackie, J.L., 1973, *Truth, Probability and Paradox,* Oxford, Clarendon Press.

Macpherson, C.B., 1966, *The Real World of Democracy,* New York, Oxford University Press.

—— 1973, 'Berlin's division of liberty' in *Democratic Theory,* Oxford, Clarendon Press, pp. 95-119.

—— 1977, *The Life and Times of Liberal Democracy,* Oxford, Oxford University Press.

Mannheim, K., 1936, *Ideology and Utopia,* London, Routledge & Kegan Paul, reprinted in 1976.

Mansbridge, J.J., 1980, *Beyond Adversary Democracy,* New York, Basic Books.

Margolis, M., 1979, *Viable Democracy,* Harmondsworth, Penguin.

—— 1983, 'Democracy: American style' in Duncan 1983, pp. 115-32.

Marx, K., 1849, *Wage Labour and Capital,* in Marx and Engels 1962, vol. 1, pp. 70-105.

—— 1852, 'The Chartists' in Fernbach 1973b, pp. 262-70.

—— 1859, *Critique of Political Economy,* London, Lawrence & Wishart, 1971.

—— 1864, 'Address and provisional rules of the International Working Men's Association' in Fernbach 1974, pp. 73-84.

—— 1865, *Wages, Price and Profit* in Marx and Engels 1962, vol. 1, pp. 398-447.

—— 1867, *Capital,* vol. 1, London, Penguin 1976.

—— 1869, *The Eighteenth Brumaire of Louis Bonaparte* in Fernbach 1973b, pp. 143-249.

—— 1871, *The Civil War in France* in Fernbach 1974, pp. 187-236.

—— 1875, *Critique of the Gotha Programme* in Fernbach 1974, pp. 339-59.

—— 1880, 'Introduction to the Programme of the French Workers' Party' in Fernbach 1974, pp. 376-7.

—— and Engels, F., 1846, *The German Ideology,* London, Lawrence & Wishart, 1965.

—— and —— 1848, *The Communist Manifesto* in Fernbach 1973b, pp. 67-98.

—— and —— 1879, 'Circular letter to Bebel, Liebknecht, Bracke, *et al.*' in Fernbach 1974, pp. 360-75.

—— and —— 1962, *Selected Works* in 2 vols, London, Lawrence & Wishart.

Michels, R., 1915, *Political Parties,* New York, Dover Publications, 1959.

Miliband, R., 1977, *Marxism and Politics,* Oxford, Oxford University Press.

Miller, D., 1983, 'The competitive model of democracy' in Duncan 1983, pp. 133-55.

Nagel, T., 1970, *The Possibility of Altruism,* Oxford, Clarendon Press.

—— 1972, 'War and massacre', *Philosophy and Public Affairs,* vol. 1, reprinted in *Mortal Questions,* Cambridge, Cambridge University Press, 1979, pp. 53-74.

—— 1979, 'Equality' in *Mortal Questions,* Cambridge, Cambridge University Press, 1979, pp. 106-127.

Nelson, W.N., 1980, *On Justifying Democracy,* London, Routledge & Kegan Paul.

Norman, R., 1982, 'Does equality destroy liberty?', in Graham 1982a, pp. 83-109.

Nozick, R., 1974, *Anarchy, State, and Utopia,* New York, Basic Books.

Parkin, F., 1979, *Marxism and Class Theory: A Bourgeois Critique,* London, Tavistock.

Parry, G. (ed.), 1972, *Participation in Politics,* Manchester, Manchester University Press.

Pateman, C., 1970, *Participation and Democratic Theory,* Cambridge, Cambridge University Press.

—— 1979, *The Problem of Political Obligation,* New York, John Wiley.

—— 1983, 'Feminism and democracy', in Duncan 1983, pp. 204-17.

Pennock, J.R., 1979, *Democratic Political Theory,* Princeton, Princeton University Press.

—— and Chapman, J.W., 1975, *Participation in Politics,* NOMOS 16, New York, Lieber-Atherton.

Pitkin, H.F., 1967, *The Concept of Representation,* Berkeley, University of California Press.

Pomper, G.M., 1972, 'From confusion to clarity: issues and American voters 1956-68', *American Political Science Review,* vol. 66, pp. 415-28.

Potter, A.M. (with P. Fotheringham and J.G. Kellas), 1981, *American Government and Politics,* revised edition, London and Boston, Faber and Faber.

Quine, W.V.O., 1953, *From a Logical Point of View,* Harvard, Harvard University Press.

Quinton, A. (ed.), 1967, *Political Philosophy,* Oxford, Oxford University Press.

Rawls, J., 1972, *A Theory of Justice,* London, Oxford University Press.

Rees, J.C., 1971, *Equality,* London, Macmillan.

Reiman, J., 1972, *In Defense of Political Philosophy,* New York, Harper & Row.

Ryan, A. (ed.), 1973, *The Philosophy of Social Explanation,* Oxford, Oxford University Press.

Scanlon, T., 1972, 'A theory of freedom of expression, *Philosophy and Public Affairs,* vol. 1, pp. 204-226.

Schumpeter, J., 1943, *Capitalism, Socialism and Democracy,* fourth edition, 1954, London, Unwin.

Searle, J.R., 1964, 'How to derive "ought" from "is"', *Philosophical Review,* vol. 73, reprinted in Hudson 1969, pp. 120-34.

Sen, A.K., 1970, *Collective Choice and Social Welfare,* San Francisco, Holden-Day Inc.

Skillen, A., 1982, 'Freedom of speech' in Graham 1982a, pp. 139-59.

Skinner, Q., 1973, 'The empirical theorists of democracy and their critics', *Political Theory,* Vol. 1, pp. 287-306.

Strawson, P.F., 1961, 'Social morality and individual ideal', *Philosophy,* vol. 36, reprinted in *Freedom and Resentment,* 1974, London, Methuen, pp. 26-44.

Taylor, C., 1967, 'Neutrality in political science', in Laslett and Runciman 1967, pp. 25-57.

Ten, C.L., 1980, *Mill on Liberty,* Oxford, Clarendon Press.

Thompson, D.F., 1983, 'Bureaucracy and democracy', in Duncan 1983, pp. 235-50.

Valinas, B., 1978, 'Democracy and the silicon chip', *Socialist Standard,* vol. 74, pp. 170-1.

Verba, S., Nie, N.H. and Kim, J., 1978, *Participation and Political Equality,* Cambridge, Cambridge University Press.

Walker, J.L., 1965, 'A critique of the elitist theory of democracy' *American Political Science Review,* vol. 60, pp. 285-95.

Watson, G. (ed.), 1982, *Free Will,* Oxford, Oxford University Press.

Williams, B., 1962, 'The idea of equality' in Laslett and Runciman 1962, pp. 110-31.

—— 1972, *Morality,* New York, Harper & Row.

—— (with J.J.C. Smart) 1973, *Utilitarianism: For and Against,* Cambridge, Cambridge University Press.

Wolff, R.P., 1973, *The Autonomy of Reason,* New York, Harper & Row.

—— 1976, *In Defense of Anarchism,* second edition, New York, Harper & Row.

Wollheim, R., 1960, 'How can one person represent another?', *Supplementary Proceedings of the Aristotelian Society,* vol. 34, pp. 209-24.

—— 1962, 'A paradox in the theory of democracy' in Laslett and Runciman 1962, pp. 71-87.

Index of Names

Index of Subjects

Absolutism, 209
Alienation, 152, 166, 241
Aliens, 13
Altruism, 30, 98
Anarchism, 80
Apathy, 130−4, 149, 150, 155, 161, 166, 167, 191, 227, 228, 241
Aristocrats, 13
Athens, 16, 235, 238, 242
Authority, 36, 75, 79, 80, 82, 91, 92, 153, 162, 200, 228
Autonomy, 3, 4, 22, 39−40, 43−9, 51, 53, 75, 80−91, 93, 95, 100, 101−2, 108, 113, 129, 133, 150, 164, 166, 184, 185, 198, 221, 226, 223
  principle of, 79, 86, 87, 88, 91, 92, 101, 107

Bolshevism, 205, 241
Bourgeoisie, 173, 177, 178, 181, 192, 207, 210, 214
Bourgeois society, *see* Capitalism
Britain, 13, 59−60, 131, 153, 214
Bureaucracy, 135, 166, 199, 202, 211, 228, 238, 240

California, 55
Capital, 176, 179, 222
Capitalism, 161, 176, 179, 180, 186−7,192, 193, 194, 196, 197, 199, 208, 210, 211, 214, 215, 216, 217, 219, 220, 222, 224, 225, 236, 241
Capitalists, *see* Bourgeoisie
Central Committee, 210
Chartists, 181
Children, 13, 15, 18, 19
Christianity, 170
Citizens, 12, 13, 16, 25, 37, 55, 70, 72, 128, 133, 137, 145, 191−2, 201, 211, 235−6
Citizenship, 37, 38, 62, 191
Civil disobedience, 78, 93
Civil liberties, 2, 38−40, 41−2, 46, 48, 52, 208, 215, 241
Civil servants, 193

Class, 172, 173, 191, 195, 203, 209, 234−5, 237−8
  conflict, 178
  ruling, 178, 180, 183, 202, 220
  structure, 192
  see also Bourgeoisie, Consciousness, Middle class, Proletariat
  Classless society, 191, 218, 224
  Clubs, 12, 67, 77
  Coercion, 35, 50, 81, 93, 108, 114, 191−1, 240
Collective labourer, 186−7
Collectives, 21, 29, 50−1, 76, 96, 106−7, 108−14, 120, 132, 137, 145, 186−8, 189, 201, 241
  overall, 120
  see also Collectivism
Collectivism, 3
  ontological, 103−8, 109
Committee analogy, 65−7
Committees, 12, 77, 104, 105, 166, 236, 238
Commodities, 176
Common humanity, 69
Common ownership, *see* Ownership
Communes, 183, 211
  see also Paris Commune, National Commune
Communism, 214
  see also Socialism
Communist International, 218
Community, 25, 62, 96, 158, 178, 234, 236
  global, 242
  local, 151
  overall, 242
  sense of, 120, 152, 236, 242
Community Action Programmes, 151
Competence, 15, 139, 152, 157, 159
  subjective, 153, 158
Compromise, 162
Concepts and conceptions, 8

256